From Mythic to Linear

Time in Children's Literature

Maria Nikolajeva

The Children's Literature Association
and
The Scarecrow Press, Inc.
Lanham, Md., & London
2000

SCARECROW PRESS, INC.

Published in the United States of America
by Scarecrow Press, Inc.
4720 Boston Way, Lanham, Maryland 20706
http://www.scarecrowpress.com

4 Pleydell Gardens, Folkestone
Kent CT20 2DN, England

British Library Cataloguing in Publication Information Available

Library of Congress Cataloging-in-Publication Data

Nikolajeva, Maria.
    From mythic to linear : time in children's literature / Maria Nikolajeva.
      p. cm.
    Includes bibliographical references and index.
    ISBN 0-8108-3713-7 (alk. paper)
    1. Children's literature–History and criticism. 2. Time in literature. I. Title.
    PN1009.5.T55 N55   2000
    809'.89282–dc21   99-055126

  The paper used in this publication meets the minimum requirements of
American National Standard for Information Sciences—Permanence of
Paper for Printed Library Materials, ANSI/NISO Z39.48–1992.
Manufactured in the United States of America.

Contents

Acknowledgments

The first reader of the initial draft of the essay which would eventually be developed into this book was Carina Lidström, whose enthusiasm and valuable remarks encouraged me to proceed with this project. The essay was published in the international journal *Compara(i)son*, guest-edited by Bettina Kümmerling-Meibauer. A considerably reworked version of it in Swedish was given as a paper at the conference "The Art of Storytelling" in Stockholm in May 1995.

I have also had the privilege of presenting a version of it to members of the higher seminar on children's literature at the University of Technology, Sydney, thanks to John Stephens and Rosemary Johnston. The discussion at the seminar, among other things, brought to my attention the question of gender in some of my examined patterns.

My very special thanks must go to David Russell, publications editor of the Children's Literature Association, who patiently explained to me the shortcomings of my first proposal and was kind enough to give me a second chance.

Most of the research for the book was carried out during summer 1997 at the International Youth Library in Munich, which was possible thanks to a fellowship from the Library. I am especially grateful to Andreas Bode for his support.

All the investigations concerning the function of food in children's literature have been carried out within a minor research project sponsored by the Centre for the Study of Childhood Culture, Stockholm University. I am indebted to my partner in this project, Ulla Bergstrand, in the first place for proposing it, and also for her enthusiasm and many stimulating discussions. Some ideas from the project have been presented for various audiences in Sweden, Finland, Great Britain and the United States, thanks to Birger Hedén, Roger Sell, Helena Forsås-Scott, and William Moebius.

I am especially indebted to Rod McGillis for his confidence in my work. Long before the book was in progress, Rod stated in a written assessment of my work how important he expected this new book to be. I simply had to do my best to live up to this expectation.

Another generous supporter has been Jack Zipes. I have come to several valuable insights while working on entries for the *Oxford Encyclopedia of Fairy Tales,* which he invited me to contribute to.

Further, I am indebted to Kimberley Reynolds, Tony Watkins, and John Stephens for bringing some important recent texts to my attention, and to Peter Hunt for general encouragement. I had an excellent opportunity to contemplate the essence of the iterative frequency preparing a paper for a conference on Alan Garner's novel *Strandloper* in Paris, organized by Jean Perrot. My ideas on *The Wind in the Willows* were tested at a symposium at the Centre for International Research in Childhood, University of Reading, organized by Tony Watkins.

Last but not least I must mention Carole Scott, who, besides performing skillful plastic surgery on my English, has introduced me to the courageous method of plunging into a literary text and discovering what is there without any expectations or preconceived opinions. This "intuitive" reading has proved invaluable to counterbalance the rigid structuralist I had been before. Thanks to Carole I have made many discoveries as well as re-discoveries which I would have certainly missed otherwise. By all rights, this book should be dedicated to her.

I'd give all wealth that years have piled,
   The slow result of Life's decay,
To be once more a little child
   For one bright summer day.

A Time to Be Born, and a Time to Die...

The present study investigates children's narrative fiction in a continuum from texts involving nonlinear time, typical of archaic or mythical thought, toward linearity, typical of contemporary mainstream literature.

The conventional way of investigating children's fiction is to divide it into "genres" or kinds: fantasy, adventure, family story, school story, animal story, toy story, etc. Unlike John Stephens, who proclaims the distinction between fantasy and realism "the single most important generic distinction in children's fiction" (Stephens 1992, 7), I do not make such a distinction, instead treating all children's fiction as essentially "mythic" or at least nonmimetic. My point of departure is the concept of literature as a symbolic depiction of a maturation process (initiation, rite of passage) rather than a strictly mimetic reflection of a concrete "reality." My text typology is based on the degree of accomplishment of initiation, grading from primary harmony (Arcadia, Paradise, Utopia, idyll) through different stages of departure toward either a successful or a failed mission, from childhood to adulthood.

The view of children's fiction as a depiction of the maturation process is by no means a revolutionary idea; however, it can be used for different purposes. John Stephens remarks: "Arguably the most pervasive theme in children's fiction is the transition within the individual from infantile solipsism to maturing social awareness" (Stephens 1992, 3). In the present study, I am not specifically interested in ideology in the way Stephens presents it in his book, even though I am well aware, as he maintains, that all literary texts, and particularly children's texts, are ideologically manipulated. My attempt to view children's fiction from another perspective is based on an obvious, but still seldom discussed thesis that all literature, art, religion, and philosophy (that is, all human activity of nonmaterial character) reflects a striving to answer some basic existential questions: who are we? why are we here? is there any reason for life? A possible way of analyzing this striving is to view literature and art as a depiction of the different stages in the individual's—and humankind's—identity quest. Various literary theories offer their models for such an analysis, among which two are of special interest. First are various structuralist models such as Vladimir Propp's function model (Propp 1968) or Algirdas Julien Greimas' actant model (Greimas 1966). The central idea of these models is, roughly speaking, the tension between lack and liquidation of lack (Propp), or between "want" and "must" (Greimas). The tension may acquire forms like struggle, quest, and so on. In structuralist models, these themes are treated exclusively on the narrative level.

The other method is the Jungian, where we see an evolution from the initial harmony (the situation before lack or injury in the structural model) through split toward a new, genuine harmony. It is best described in Marie-Louise von Franz's classical essay "The Process of Individuation" (Franz 1964). For a Jungian literary critic, external events described in fiction are merely projections of the individual's inner world.

It is apparent that the two models complement each other; it is amazing that their respective advocates have overlooked this. In fact, Propp's general plot outline ("sequence of functions") corresponds to the process of individuation, and Propp's system of fairy-tale characters corresponds to the Jungian system of archetypes: "princess"—Anima, villain—Shadow, helper—the Wise Old Man. While the structural model unveils the way the narrative is built, the psychological model explains what is concealed behind the structures. Both models describe our conceptions of what human maturation looks like or should look like.

From this point of departure, I would like to consider a number of children's novels, to see how they are related to the protagonist's place in the maturation process. To anticipate possible objections, I would like to point out that my study is in no way an attempt to organize all children's fiction around one topic. On the contrary, I would like to demonstrate the wide diversity of children's texts, which, however, transgresses the usual boundaries between genres. Perhaps the closest theoretical model is Northrop Frye's "displacement" (Frye 1957 and 1963). Like Frye, I locate literary texts in a continuum between pure myth and a total disintegration of mythical structures. The transformation of the nonlinear time into linear plays an overall important part in this continuum. The texts I discuss in the first three chapters, which I classify as utopian, correspond roughly to Frye's mythical mode; the texts treated as carnivalesque are categorized as romance to high mimetic in Frye's taxonomy, and texts which go under the heading of collapse are low mimetic and ironic (Frye 1957, 33-67). In a way, these categories stand close to the three classes of story described by Peter Hunt as "closed," "semi-closed" (= Bildungsroman) and unresolved (with an open ending, more usual in adult fiction; see Hunt 1994a, 27f).

As will be seen, my approach enables me to disregard, among other things, the traditional, and in my view rather obsolete, division of children's novels into realism and fantasy. Instead, some essential features of children's versus mainstream fiction can be unveiled, a problem which many scholars of children's literature have tried to solve in different ways.

The concept of childhood and innocence is often used to distinguish between children's fiction and adult fiction. Humphrey Carpenter suggests: "Adult fiction sets out to portray and explain the world as it really is; books for children present it as it should be" (Carpenter 1985, 1). This seems very doubtful to me. Neither category—children's or adult fiction—is a homogeneous group of texts. What about adult fantasy and science fiction, pulp fiction, or so-called socialist realism? And what about a good number of children's books which are indeed a boring depiction of "the world as it is"?

I must point out that I am not concerned with the history of childhood as such, nor with the relation of children's fiction to the child, real or fictional, of the type Karín Lesnik-Oberstein (1994) is preoccupied with. My approach is purely literary, and I am, for my present purpose, not interested in what social phenomena might lie behind the texts.

I cannot, however, completely ignore the way in which the concept of childhood is reflected in literature, both literature written specifically for children and literature which uses the child as an image and a symbol, notably the symbol of purity and innocence. It is a commonplace to point out that before Romanticism, children were hardly believed to be different from adults; and certainly not thought to be better than adults (see e.g. Coveney 1967, 52–90). Anglo-Saxon criticism tends to focus on Blake and Wordsworth as sources of the new concept of childhood; however, similar ideas have been developed by Romantic writers in other language areas. The most essential issue is that childhood in the Romantic tradition is equal to idyll, while growing up is equal to loss of Paradise. Many classical children's writers make an extensive use of the symbol of the garden, or enchanted place. However, the idea of the child as innocent continues to influence children's fiction long after mainstream literature has abandoned the Romantic views. Traditional children's fiction creates and preserves what may be called a pastoral convention. "It is assumed that the world of childhood is simpler and more natural than that of adults, and that children, though they may have faults, are essentially good or at least capable of becoming so" (Lurie 1990, xiii). As a consequence, children's fiction maintains a myth of a happy and innocent childhood, apparently based on adult writers' nostalgic memories and bitter insights about the impossibility of returning to the childhood idyll. This myth has little to do with the real status of child and childhood, and indeed most contemporary children's novels successfully subvert this myth. Yet the very texts that Alison Lurie calls subversive ("sacred texts of childhood, whose authors had not forgotten what it was like to be a child," Lurie 1990, x), are examples of the most conservative children's fiction, aimed at preserving the young readers' illusion that childhood is a happy, secure and, not least, an eternal state.

Very few studies of children's fiction take the same point of departure as mine. Although Humphrey Carpenter's book is entitled *Secret Gardens*, and would seem to coincide with the subject of my study, Carpenter does not go further than the labelling of his texts. In fact, his essays on particular writers and texts are quite conventional and certainly do not explore any of the questions I am interested in. However, Carpenter treats Louisa May Alcott's and Frances Hodgson Burnett's novels as "fantasy" or at least "mythic" texts alongside *Water Babies, Alice in Wonderland, The Wind in the Willows, Peter Pan*, and *Winnie-the-Pooh*.

The closest parallel to my own concept, which I discovered long after I started on my investigation, is to be found in an essay by Sarah Smedman (1988). First, she speaks about "mythic" novels, identifying no difference between conventional categories of "realism" and "nonrealism." Further, she introduces the notions of linear and nonlinear time, which are the cornerstones of my examination. Smedman's main source, as mine, is the works of the Rumanian-born mythologist Mircea Eliade, especially his concept of sacred or cyclical time (see Eliade 1955 and 1963). For Eliade, myth describes events taking place in this primordial time, and profane acts only have meaning as long as they deliberately repeat earlier sacred acts (Eliade 1955, 3f). In Greek, the eternal, mythic time is called *kairos*, to distinguish from the measurable, linear time, *chronos* (the word kairos is used in the famous passage on time in Ecclesiastes 3:1-8). In Latin, the counterpart is "in illo tempore," and the closest every-day formula is that of the fairy tale: "Once upon a time." Unlike chronos, kairos is reversible. It can be integrated with linear time through rituals, rites and festivals, human repetitions of primordial acts (cf Smedman 1988, 93). In contemporary literature, it can also be used for parodic or carnivalesque purposes. A similar and very illuminating approach to time in children's fiction is presented in John Rowe Townsend's essay "Slippery Time" (1990). Townsend also points out different attitudes to time in Judeo-Christian and, for instance, in Buddhist tradition (although the difference is certainly still more prominent in archaic, pagan cultures). It is quite essential to my study that contemporary Western children's fiction is written from a philosophical viewpoint based on linear time, which has a beginning and an end, and recognizes every event in history as unique. The change from circular to linear narrative in children's fiction appears in a new light against this background.[1]

The scope of Sarah Smedman's essay does not allow for any in-depth investigation of the significance of kairos for children's fiction. Neither does she connect the notion with the child's percep-tion of time. It is generally believed that small children have no sense of linear time. According to child psychology, children until around the age of 5 live entirely in the present. By the age of 7-8 children learn to handle linear time, that is, clocks, days of the week, months and years.[2] Consequently, small children can be compared, in their apprehension of time, to archaic man, while older children and adults have a "modern" view of time. Adult writers who describe childhood as a cyclical, mythic state are thus reconstructing the archaic form of time, perhaps subconsciously associating children with this form.

The insight about the linearity of time invokes the problems of growing up, aging, and death. Since mythic time, kairos, is reversible, death in myth is transitory. The myth of the returning god, the most universal myth in all cultures, presupposes that death is always followed by resurrection. In many fairy tales used in childhood reading, death is reversible as well (Snow White dies and is brought back to life; the dead mother helps her children against the evil step-mother, etc). The final formula of many fairy tales stresses that the linear progress of the plot is rounded into an everlasting, mythic time: English "lived happily ever after," German "und wenn sie nicht gestorben sind, so leben sie noch heute" ("if they haven't died, they are still alive today"; cf Röhrich 1980).

In children's fiction, the idea of everlasting time is perhaps best expressed by two temporal indications in *Winnie-the-Pooh* and sequel: "Once upon a time, a very long time ago, about last Friday" (2) and "... a little boy and his bear will always be playing" (176). Few adult novels evoke the same sense of timelessness, and these few also have a distinct mythic tone, like *The Enchanted Mountain* by Thomas Mann. Significantly, in this novel, the abolishment of time becomes possible in a tuberculosis clinic, under the shadow of death.

According to Eliade, there are three major components in archaic man's initiation: the sacred, death, and sexuality (Eliade 1961a). If we assume that the state of cyclical time, as childhood is described, introduces the protagonist to the sacred, then the following stages of initiation must involve death and procreation, two most essential aspects of human existence. As soon as children's fiction departs from the innocent, idyllic state, the initiation into these two mysteries becomes inevitable. Alison Lurie remarks: "Of the three principal preoccupations of adult fiction—sex, money, and death—the first is absent from classic children's literature and the other two either absent or much muted" (Lurie 1990, xiv). I will throughout my study show how death and sexuality become manifest, and in some cases dominant in children's fiction. Lurie continues: "Although there are some interesting exceptions, even the most subversive of contemporary children's books usually follow these conventions. They portray an ideal world of perfectible beings, free of the necessity for survival and reproduction: not only a pastoral, but a paradisal universe—for without sex and death, humans may become as angels" (Lurie 1990, xiv). I see this statement as an example of the most dangerous fallacy in evaluation of children's fiction: viewing it as a homogeneous, static corpus of texts. What Lurie names cautiously as "some interesting exceptions" is indeed a vast number of texts, which in some way or other take a radical departure from the cyclical time, in many cases, such as in contemporary dystopias, bringing children's fiction to its antithesis. A number of the world's best children's novels are focused on the child's intuitive reluctance to grow up and take the first step toward initiation: *Peter Pan, The Little Prince, Pippi Longstocking,* the Moomin books, and many more. Most probably, these books reflect the adult writers' traumatic memories of growing up. Therefore the writers allow their characters to solve this problem in different manners; Peter Pan by moving to a place where he does not have to grow up; Pippi by taking a magical pill; Moomintroll's childish dependence on his mamma suspended in later sequels, where the everlasting summer idyll is slowly supplanted by autumn and change. The discovery of inevitable growth must be the most traumatic in a child's life, maybe after the baby's discovery that it does not constitute a whole with its mother. Changes and the necessity to take the first step toward initiation, toward adulthood, become a natural central theme of all children's fiction.

The first stage of initiation offers the child a possibility to investigate the world in the form of play, a temporary departure from idyll and kairos, a short disruption of harmony. It can be described in Bakhtinian terms of carnival (Bakhtin 1968), where the lowest in societal hierarchy—in the medieval carnival a fool, in children's books a child—is allowed to change places with the highest: a king, or an adult, and to become strong, rich, and brave, to perform heroic deeds, to have power. However, the very idea of carnival presupposes a temporal limitation. The child, who has been allowed to leave the security of home and experience breath-taking adventures, is taken back, and the established order is restored. This is what we sometimes call a happy ending. As Pat Pinsent demonstrates, excessive "coincidences" in children's fiction, which sometimes irritate mimetically minded critics, should not be considered artistic flaws since they are part of this restoration of the initial order (Pinsent

1989). Although John Stephens only applies the notion of carnival to nonrealistic texts (Stephens 1992, 120-157), I would argue that the carnivalesque can be present in all "genres": fantasy, romance, adventure, everyday story, young adult (YA) novel, and so on (see Nikolajeva 1996, 98f). The time pattern of these carnivalistic texts goes from kairos to chronos and back to kairos, the protagonist is brought back into the cyclical state, and no further progress toward adulthood is allowed.

The next step in initiation takes the character out of circularity and makes the process irreversible. However, as long as the character lingers on the threshold of adulthood, in the marginal state we call adolescence, we can still speak of an unaccomplished initiation: in Propp's model, before the enthronement, in a Jungian model, before the reunion of the conscious and the unconscious, the achievement of the Self.

The transformation of cyclical patterns into linear ones necessarily involves a change in narrative discourse. While an archaic narrative presupposes a single subject in unity with the world, in "contemporary" linear narrative this unity is disturbed, resulting in polyphony (multivoicedness), intersubjectivity, unreliable narrators, multiple plots and endings, etc. As Linda Hutcheon remarks, contemporary literature "refuses the omniscience and omnipresence of the third person and engages instead in a dialogue between a narrative voice ... and a projected reader" (Hutcheon 1988, 10). This narrative mode creates (as well as reflects) a chaotic view of the world, as opposed to the ordered (structured) universe of the archaic mind. Throughout my study I will observe how the narrative structure of children's novels changes in accordance with the grade of the "displacement" of myth.

One of the most interesting narrative devices connected with mythical time is the so-called iterative frequency: telling once about an event that has taken place several times or is taking place regularly. The iterative is opposed to singulative, the most common frequency in literature, when we assume that the described events take place only once. This idea is once again connected to the notion of kairos and chronos, as well as to pagan versus Christian tradition. In the latter, Christ's sacrificial death is a singulative event, which, unlike the death of the archaic returning god, cannot be restaged during regular rites (cf Eliade 1955, 143).

In his theoretical essay on Marcel Proust, *Narrative Discourse,* Gérard Genette maintains that Proust is, if not unique, then at least highly uncommon in using the iterative frequency (Genette 1980, 113–127). What strikes a scholar familiar with both archaic narratives and children's fiction is that the iterative is widely used in both. In archaic languages, there are often special grammatical categories to express the iterative nature of events, approximately "have always been doing."[3] Modern languages, lacking the need to express the mode, have lost this grammatical category; they have retained the iterative meaning partially in some modalities, such as the English "he used to" or "he would," which, however, are firmly fixed in the past, while the iterative includes the present or, in fact, eliminates the actual, chronological sequence of time. Lexical indications of the iterative in modern languages are, for instance, "always," "sometimes," "often," "occasionally," "every day", etc. Often the iterative is implied rather than expressed directly. A good example of the iterative frequency is to be found in the beginning of *Moominvalley in November:*

> Early one morning in Moominvalley Snufkin *woke* up in his tent with the feeling that autumn had come and that it was time to break camp.
> Breaking camp in this way *comes* with a hop, skip and a jump! All of a sudden everything *is* different, and if you're going to move on you're careful to make use of every single minute, you *pull* up your tent pegs and *douse* the fire quickly before anyone can stop you or start asking questions, you *start* running, pulling on your rucksack as you go, and finally you're on your way and suddenly quite calm, like a solitary tree with every single leaf completely still. Your camping-site *is* an empty rectangle of bleached grass. Later in the morning your friends *wake* up and say: he's gone away, autumn is coming.
> Snufkin *padded* along calmly … (11; my emphasis)

The first paragraph in this quotation is described in the singulative frequency: the event is taking place in a specific time, and the past indefinite tense is used. The second paragraph describes something which happens recurrently, every year, a habit, a ritual. The formal token of the iterative is the present tense. In the last sentence, the event is singulative again, taking place on this particular November morning.

The cyclical, repetitive character of events is the very essence of traditional children's fiction which often has a purpose, conscious or subconscious, to create an illusion of a neverending paradise: " … in that enchanted place on the top of the Forest a little boy and his Bear will always be playing." The circular character of narrative time in archaic thought has been reflected in children's novels because the Arcadian time of individual childhood is similar to the mythical time of the childhood of humankind.

To sum up my arguments, and to bring together some of the theories I have discussed, I have arranged them in a very schematic table, related to my own three main categories:

MY CATEGORY	utopia	carnival	collapse
Jung	harmony;	split;	split toward wholeness;
	unconscious	conscious	synthesis of conscious and unconscious
Hunt	closed	semi-closed	unresolved
Frye	myth to romance	romance to high mimetic	low mimetic to ironic
TIME	kairos	kairos-chronos-kairos	chronos
	cyclical	cyclical into linear	linear
FREQUENCY	iterative	iterative/ singulative	singulative
INSIGHT (Eliade)	the sacred	death	sexuality

My choice of texts for discussion is inevitably subjective. It has been my intention to introduce some lesser known texts and to draw my readers' attention to texts unfairly forgotten or ignored. It has, however, proved necessary to deal with some evident "touchstones" in order to establish an appropriate framework. A balance of familiar and less familiar has been my goal.

Throughout my study, I usually do not provide the names of authors whose texts I am discussing, partly because many of them will be familiar, partly to avoid unnecessary repetition. The only exception is texts which I assume are less known. The index of titles at the end of the book provides the name of the author; the bibliography of primary sources provides all further information. I have myself made the translations from texts not available in English.

Last but not least I would like to make an important reservation. Thanks to extensive travel and conference attendance of the recent years, I have become aware of the dangerous ethnocentricity of many studies of children's literature, including my own. While it has been my intention to go as far as possible beyond the English language material, everything that I may say is only valid for Western (European—North American) children's fiction. Literature in other parts of the world has apparently different structures and laws, and its relation to Western children's fiction should be a subject of a separate study.

AN EXCURSUS ON SIGNIFICANT MEALS

Throughout my study, I will constantly return to the function of food in the texts discussed, the aspect that researchers of myth, with the exception of Lévi-Strauss, often omit. It has been pointed out that food in children's literature corresponds to sexuality in the mainstream (Nelson 1991, 168; Nodelman 1992, 196; Kuznets 1994, 64f; McGillis 1996, 80ff); and since sexuality, in Eliade's theory, is such an indispensable element in the rite of passage, it is of special importance to investigate what role food plays in the texts I am discussing. Although many general studies of children's fiction mention the abundance of food in particular texts, such as *The Wind in the Willows* and *The Famous Five* books (Hautala 1977; Hunt 1996a), *Five Children and It* (Stephens 1992, 132), *Pippi Longstocking* and other novels by Astrid Lindgren (Edström 1992; Metcalf 1995); and a few general surveys have been published (Nières 1987; Ongini 1994), there have been few attempts to discuss the narrative function of food in these texts or, still less, its ritual significance (one exception is Katz 1980, which is, however, quite limited in material and does not go deeper into mythical connections).

The function of food in myth proper is outside my interest; however, I must make some general observations before I can draw conclusions about the ritual function of food in children's fiction. Food is an indispensable part of the initiation rite, since it is closely connected to death and resurrection. Death in a rite of passage is often represented by the novice being eaten up by a monster (Jonah and the whale is an example), which during the rite itself is staged by the novice entering a cave or a hut (for instance the famous Russian hut on chicken legs, inhabited by Baba Yaga). Resurrection is represented by the novice being invited to participate in a meal in the Otherworld, the realm of death. By accepting food from the Otherworld, the hero gains passage into it (the Holy Communion is a remnant of this archaic rite, as is the Jewish Sabbath meal). The Russian folktale hero Ivan replies to Baba Yaga's threats of eating him up: "What is the good of eating a tired traveller? Let me first have some food and drink and a bath." He pronounces himself ready to accept witch food and go through a symbolic purification.

Like all mythical elements in literature, rituals around food have their origins in the most basic aspects of human behavior, connected with archaic beliefs of life, death, and rebirth, and hence also sexuality, fertility, and procreation. None of this is directly relevant for children's fiction, for various reasons. First, myths and folktales have changed and partly lost their original esoteric, sacred meaning. Thus the myths and folktales we know today are retellings of more ancient narratives. According to most mythologists, meals in myths and folktales are circumlocutions of sexual intercourse, but we can reconstruct this meaning only partly from the existing texts.

When folktales were incorporated into children's literature, their motifs changed further, to suit pedagogical purposes, so that the original meaning has become still more obscure (see e.g. Zipes 1983). It is therefore essential to understand what food represents in myth and folktale, before we can interpret its meaning in children's fiction.

The most important role of food in myth is to accentuate the contrast between nature and culture. The origin of food is in nature, but it is used within culture, and it is the result of the transition from nature to culture. Thus food neutralizes this basic contrast. In Claude Lévi-Strauss's anthropological study *The Raw and the Cooked*, a typology of cultures is built upon the attitude to food, based on oppositions: human flesh/animal flesh, raw/cooked and animal food/vegetarian food (Lévi-Strauss 1983). Many etiological myths, especially myths about the origins of fire (which makes cooked food possible, see Frazer 1930), are based on these oppositions and regulate rules and prohibitions around food. These oppositions are also related to all other oppositions within a given culture, such as own/alien, male/female, home/away, sacred/profane, etc. In archaic thought, the notion of own and alien is often connected with food habits. One's own food is apprehended as natural and genuine, while all other food is alien, unnatural, unclean, basically "non-food." We see remnants of these notions in the prohibition against certain foods in Islam and Judaism. Christian rules around Lent have the same origin.

The prohibition against eating human flesh is one of the first steps in human civilization. Cannibalism was universally accepted in the archaic world, but later started to be viewed as alien. Cannibalism is often connected with the Fall, that is the loss of immortality (see also Eliade 1955). In a myth, the so-called cultural hero terminates cannibalism by defeating the cannibal enemy. This is reflected in fairy tales, such as Tom Thumb or Hansel and Gretel. The prohibition of cannibalism expels it to the Otherworld, where it is associated with the evil (a dragon, an ogre, a witch, etc).

The meaning of cannibalism is that by eating up your enemy you inherit his powers. There exists a habit of eating up the eldest man in the tribe to inherit his wisdom. Later this changes into ritual meals. To eat a symbolical figure signifies receiving magical power. To eat and be eaten are two interchangeable notions, which is seen in the Christian tradition's most important sacrament, the Holy Communion. Jesus prescribed that His "body" be eaten, symbolizing a union of those who eat and Him who is being eaten, which together signifies a victory over death and a promise of resurrection. There is an archaic rite at the source of this.

Cannibalism can also be a sign of extreme love when a man (more rarely a woman) eats up his beloved, in order to own her completely. Here is once again a parallel between food and intercourse, oral and sexual satisfaction. In some myths, parents devour their children out of great love.

Thus in archaic thought there is a direct connection between food and sexuality, and between certain food restrictions and certain marriage restrictions, such as incest. Incest and cannibalism, two extreme forms of behavior, are in some archaic languages described by the same word. To eat your totemic animal or to marry it (= incest) was viewed as an equally heavy crime.

Many myths and folktales describe a witch who eats human beings, often children. In most cases the children emerge alive; that is the act symbolizes death and resurrection. It is often presented as positive and necessary; the witch is not evil, but on the contrary a wise guide. Behind it we most probably find initiation rites, which included sexual intercourse. The story of the Little Red Riding Hood is a late retelling of this myth.[4]

Not only human flesh, but all "alien" food, "nonfood" is prohibited in archaic thought. Food in the realm of death (and this includes all foreign countries, real or imaginary) was prohibited for ordinary man; if you eat it you will never come back. In the fairy tale, this develops into depictions of various forms of enchanted food with which the hero is tempted in the Otherworld.

Food in myth is connected to the three elements in the chain of death-fertility-life. It is also connected to sacrifice. The mythical sacrificial death means that the sacrifice ensures fertility and affluence, often also eternal life. In many myths food is featured in marginal situations, around the passage from one existence into another, yet unfamiliar. Festive meals appear around certain holidays like New Year (Eliade 1955, 51); food is important in connection with weddings and funerals. The sacrifice itself includes food. The sacrifice, that is a killing of an animal or a human being, was later changed into something more symbolical, an act like breaking the bread. To eat the meat and drink the blood of a sacrificial animal means receiving new forces. Therefore every meal is by definition a ritual act. According to Eliade there are no profane actions in the archaic world (Eliade 1955, 27). There are many parallels between the altar and the table, the altar curtain and a table-cloth, the sacrificial knife and a butcher's knife, and naturally between a priest and a cook. In Christian tradition, the prohibition of cooking meals on the altar came as late as the 7th century.

In archaic thought, both meal and sacrifice emphasize man's belonging to a totem, a family, a tribe (cf idioms such as "my own flesh" about children). Many myths include details such as gods' food, for instance nectar and ambrosia in Greek mythology. The word ambrosia means "the immortal," since it was the source of the gods' eternal youth and immortality. From this belief we have all the habits around everyday food and festive food, ordinary food and ritual food.

A number of etiological myths describe the origins of various type of food. A common plot is the supreme deity punishing his children (or spouse) by cutting them into pieces and throwing them down from heaven to earth (or hiding them underground); from the mutilated bodies, good and nutritious plants grow. An important mythical figure is the Progenitrix, the incarnation of Mother Earth, the origin of everything. In most myths, she teaches humans to sow and to bake bread.

The sacred food is developed into a magical agent in folktales: bread, milk, honey, apple, beans, etc. As compared to myths, folktales have lost their secret sacred meaning. Folktales collected and retold for children have often acquired the opposite meaning. It is therefore necessary to go back to myth to clarify the function of food in fairy tales, often connected with prohibition against incest. Food as a part of trial appears in many fairy tales; the hero takes food from home when departing on his quest. Many folktales reflect the dream of Cornucopia, described as a magical mill, tablecloth or bag. Food can also be a means of enchantment, when the hero is transformed by eating or drinking something.

Most of these motifs are also present in children's books, in transformed and disguised variants. The origin of food, which in myth is ascribed to the totemic animal or the Progenitrix, is in children's novels connected with parents or other adults, most often the mother. Hence we must interpret all scenes in children's fiction where the mother provides food not only and not in the first place as realistic details (as a traditional female role), but as a remnant of the human notion of the Progenitrix, the source of food and thus of procreation. Also the child's early dependence on breast milk is accentuated. A little child does not wonder where food comes from, but views it as an unlimited supply, a Cornucopia—just like mother's breast. As long as the child stays in the security of the childhood paradise no questions about food are raised, but the frequent appearance of food signals the subconscious fear that one day food can wane.

When the character of a children's book departs from home (a necessary part of initiation), food can serve as a link back home. Since food emphasizes affinity, "own" food, food from home is especially important. It is also important that the mother packs the food and, as in folktale, supplies it with her blessing. This security of home, represented by food, is to be found in all types of children's fiction, including adventure books, where home is treated more like a prison.

Since food from home gives security it can also function as a trial. When protagonists meet other characters, they are often invited to a meal or are encouraged to share their food with strangers, who become friends and helpers. In both cases, shared food is a sign of union. Food becomes a token of belonging together in a quest or struggle, or belonging to a particular group, good or evil. It can also be a passkey into the Otherworld, as in *Alice in Wonderland*. Finally, it can enchant, corrupt and even destroy.

Thus like all mythical elements, food is highly ambivalent: it can be good and evil, and it can easily change its meaning. Alien food can be dangerous, like the apple in "Snow White." The forbidden food is, like so many other elements in the folktale, a circumlocution of sexuality.

Summing up, we can say that food in children's fiction can fulfil a variety of ritual purposes. Food can be a magical agent allowing the protagonist to enter the magical world. It can be the central symbol of security, in the first place by its connection with home. Further, it can be a symbol of community, of belonging to a certain group. By accepting or rejecting food, the protagonist is associated with a group of people. This short introduction to the ritual function of food is necessary, since I am going to return to it throughout my study.

NOTES

1. It is not my intention to discuss the concept of time or its general application in literary texts. For a popular introduction to contemporary scholarly theories of time see Whitrow 1980; Hawking 1988. A thorough

introduction to the various aspects of time in the fairy tale is to be found in Heindricks 1989. See also Cooper 1983, 98–108. For a general study of temporality in literature see Ricoeur 1984.

2. See e.g. Tucker 1981, 155. On a child's concept of time in story see Meek 1984. For a thorough psychological background see Piaget 1969.

3. One example with which I have come into contact is the Pitjantjatjara, the language of the Australian Aborigines around Uluru. As far as I understand, Pitjantjatjara stories are told in this special tense. See Goddard 1992.

4. Many genuine versions of Little Red Riding Hood include cannibalism, see e.g. Zipes 1995, 23–35.

Chapter 1

Secret Gardens, Enchanted Places

In this chapter, I will discuss children's fiction which may be very roughly classified as Utopian: fiction which creates a myth of childhood by describing it as a myth of the Golden Age (cf the title of Kenneth Grahame's adult novel of childhood). There are quite a few studies of particular children's texts from this point of view; in the English language criticism, the text most often suggested is *The Wind in the Willows*, to which Peter Hunt has devoted a complete book, featuring Arcadia in the title, (Hunt 1994b). *The Wind in the Willows* has also been treated, in terms of an Arcadian, pastoral, or nostalgic perspective, by Roger Sale (1978), Fred Inglis (1981), Neil Philip (1985), Humphrey Carpenter (1985), Sarah Gilead (1988), and many others.

The interpretation of Grahame's work is, however, far from undivided. While Tony Watkins remarks that "the crucial importance in the novel ... is ... the tension between a longing for travel and 'nostalgia' (homesickness)" (Watkins 1984, 34), Lois Kuznets argues that the notion of nostalgia has a negative tone, whereas what we encounter in *The Wind in the Willows* is a positive sense of affection for a particular place, the love of home. Kuznets prefers to call this feeling *topophilia*, a term borrowed from Gaston Bachilard's study *The Poetics of Space*, together with another notion, the *felicitous space* (Kuznets 1978; *locus amoenus*, originally from Curtius 1954). Roderick McGillis questions the single-tracked evaluation of *The Wind in the Willows* as an image of Arcadia (McGillis 1984). Peter Hunt argues in his book that Grahame's classic is a Bildungsroman rather than a pure Arcadian novel; he shows, however, that while the Arcadian state is temporarily disturbed by Mole and Toad, it is brought back to order by the end of the book (Hunt 1994b, 77).

Margaret Meek is generally skeptical of the traditional appraisal of *The Wind in the Willows,* especially its treatment by Carpenter. She points out that Kenneth Grahame's own ambivalence about childhood makes *The Wind in the Willows* much more a grownup's escape from responsibility than something a child might appreciate: "The excitement of reading ... for children ... is a dialogue with their future. Here they encounter the author's imagined past" (Meek 1991, 25).[1]

Another favorite example of Arcadian literature is *The Secret Garden* which gave a title both to Humphrey Carpenter's study of classical British children's fiction (Carpenter 1985) and to my own chapter. This work is also discussed by Nodelman (1980), Inglis (1981), Bixler (1984 and 1996), Murray (1985), Wilkie (1997), and many other scholars. Walter Pape calls it "a perfect myth" (Pape 1981, 371-394).

Some other texts commonly labeled as utopian are *Little Women* (Carpenter 1985), Beatrix Potter's stories (Inglis 1981), *Anne of Green Gables* (Nodelman 1980), *Swallows and Amazons* (Inglis 1981, Hunt 1985), and *Winnie-the-Pooh* (Carpenter 1985, Hunt 1992, Hunt 1994a). William Empson includes *Alice in Wonderland* in his comprehensive study *Some Versions of Pastoral,* where he maintains that "the Alices differ from other versions of pastoral in lacking the sense of glory" (Empson 1968, 262).

There are also some less self-evident texts discussed as pastoral, which makes the notion broader and more general, for instance as applied to *Julie of the Wolves* (Stott 1974) or the *Green Knowe* books (Stott 1983). In both cases the pastoral elements are identified as truth, tranquillity, contentment, innocence; some adjectives used to describe the idyllic state are natural, pure, calm. In her discussion of two novels by William Steig as pastoral, Anita Moss identifies features such as "innocence of the characters, their affinity with the natural world, their need for the civilized world of art and companionship ... " (Moss 1982, 125).

If we try to summarize the various features described as being typical of utopian, Arcadian or pastoral works, I think most researchers would agree on the following:

1) the importance of a particular setting;
2) autonomy of felicitous space from the rest of the world;
3) a general sense of harmony;
4) a special significance of home;
5) absence of the repressive aspects of civilization such as money, labor, law or government;
6) absence of death and sexuality;
7) and finally, as a result, a general sense of innocence.

I would like to discuss each of these indicators in more detail to see what they may imply.

The setting of most texts identified as idyllic is rural, and the characters' closeness to nature is accentuated. Most of the texts take place in summer, the weather is always fine, unless an occasional storm is used, often to symbolize a character's state of mind (see e.g. Nodelman 1980). The imagery is often focused on nature: trees, gardens, meadows. "Pastoral literature traditionally demonstrates the human need for the healing power of the simple, rural, or rustic, life by contrasting that life with the complex, urban, or urbane one" (Kuznets 1983). It is also significant that this primordial state is described both as spatial (Arcadia) and temporal (the Golden Age).

As Perry Nodelman notes, in *Anne of Green Gables,* the character starts with an almost perfect place and makes it still more perfect (Nodelman 1980, 150). Anne's first morning at Green Gables gives us a splendid picture of an idyllic setting:

> A huge cherry-tree grew outside, so close that its bows tapped against the house, and it was so thickset with blossoms that hardly a leaf was to be seen. On both sides of the house was a big orchard, one of apple-trees and one of cherry-trees, also showered over with blossoms; and their grass was all sprinkled with dandelions. In the garden below were lilac-trees purple with flowers, and their dizzily sweet fragrance drifted up to the window on the morning wind.
>
> Below the garden a green field lush with clover sloped down to the hollow where the brook ran and where scores of white birches grew, upspringing airily out of an undergrowth suggestive of delightful possibilities in ferns and mosses and woodsy things generally. Beyond it was a hill, green and feathery with spruce and fir. ... (31)

Or in *The Wind in the Willows:*

Green turf sloped down to either edge, brown snaky tree-roots gleamed below the surface of the quiet water, while ahead of them the silvery shoulder and foamy tumble of a weir, arm-in-arm with a restless dripping mill-wheel, that held up in its turn a grey-gabled mill-house, filled the air with soothing murmur of sound, dull and smothery, yet with little clear voices speaking up cheerfully out of it at intervals. It was so very beautiful . ... (17)

Further, the setting evoked is often vanished or vanishing, thus reflecting the nostalgia of the adult writer and perhaps creating a sense of nostalgia for an adult coreader. It is, on the other hand, doubtful that young readers will be seized by the same longing for the times gone by, since they have not experienced them, either personally or through literature. This is especially true about a contemporary, chiefly urban young audience. A common belief is that children prefer actions and dialogue to descriptions and often skip them when reading, since they slow down the plot.

The Arcadian world is also completely autonomous. In *The Wind in the Willows*, Rat says to Mole, in a much quoted passage:

"Beyond the Wild Wood comes the Wide World. ... And that's something that doesn't matter, either to you or to me. I've never been there, and I'm never going, nor you either if you've got any sense at all. Don't ever refer to it again, please ...". (17)

The first venture beyond this safe and secluded world, the first cautious exploration of the Wild Wood takes place, significantly, during winter, the season associated with death and threat, while the setting of the Wild Wood is hostile and strange. If the ever happy Riverbank is childhood, is the Wild Wood the dangerous—but luring—adolescence? And consequently, is the faraway Wide World adulthood? The special rules of the Wild Wood, as explained to Mole by Rat, are reminiscent of teenage culture with its rigid regulations and esoteric codes of clothing and behavior:

If we have to come, we come in couples, at least; then we're generally all right. Besides, there are a hundred things one has to know, which we understand all about and you don't, as yet. I mean pass-words, and signs and sayings which have power and effect, and plants you carry in your pocket, and verses you repeat, and dodges and tricks you practice; all simple enough when you know them, but they've got to be known *if you're small,* or you'll find yourself in trouble. (59; my emphasis)

This passage may be interpreted to mean that as long as you keep away from the temptations of adolescence, you are perfectly safe. The Riverbank world is also utterly stable: "People come—they stay for a while, they flourish, they build—and they go. It is their way. But we remain. —And so it will ever be" (82f). This is a young child's firm belief in the stability of the world and his own immortality.

In many texts, the secluded character of the setting is emphasized, which is especially felt in the many books featuring a garden: "... she felt as if she had found a world all her own... she seemed to be hundreds of miles away from anyone" (*The Secret Garden* 65). The garden walls or fences are boundaries to the surrounding—adult— world, boundaries both protecting and restricting. The seclusion enables children to experience the world on their own, since the world is safe. As Juliet Dusinberre point out: "The child unhampered by parents has become a commonplace of twentieth-century children's books" (Dusinberre 1987, 90). The mythic, nonmimetic approach to literature makes parents superfluous. "As the shepherd of traditional pastoral is removed by occupation from participation in urban life, so the child is barred by age, thus making him a natural agent for the modern writer who casts his evaluation of contemporary life in the form of fantasy for children" (Lynn 1986, 20).

The specific harmony of the idyllic can be stressed in many ways. In *The Wind in the Willows* we meet a company of four different animals who nevertheless are perfectly happy with each other. The universe of Beatrix Potter also involves talking and intelligent animals. Another feature in Potter's texts is a combination of nature and civilization: "The imagery of Beatrix Potter's world balances a colonized, accomplished horticulture and agriculture, and the stable but mysterious Nature which lies untamed beyond the garden wall" (Inglis 1981, 109). In *The Wind in the Willows,* the sense of harmony is enhanced by the existence of two parallel plots, Mole's and Toad's, labeled centripetal and centrifugal (Mendelson 1988). Peter Hunt suggests that the first of them appeals more to adults, and the second to children (Hunt 1994b, 26f). I am not sure about this categorical evaluation of readership; I would rather say a balance between character-oriented and action-oriented narrative, both of which may equally appeal to children and to adults.

In the first chapter of *The Wind in the Willows*, the harmony is stressed by the words "joy of living," "the delights of spring" (8), "birds building, flowers budding, leaves thrushing—everything happy" (9). Mole is "intoxicated with the sparkle, the ripple, the scents and the sounds and the sunlight" (14). Everything unpleasant is for ever banished from this world: "The Mole knew well that it was quite against animal-etiquette to dwell on possible trouble ahead; or even to allude to it" (17). The inhabitants of the idyll are all nice and friendly: Toad, for instance, is "[a]lways good-tempered, always glad to see you," "[s]o simple, so good-natured, and so affectionate" (31).

In pastoral fiction, a human child's ability to understand animal language is a usual trait. Alice has no problems communicating with the caterpillar, the White Rabbit or the Cheshire Cat. I do not think the argument here should assume that this is part of the magic world. It is, of course, but not merely that. A child, like Alice, entering Utopia, is bestowed with certain abilities. When the naughty boy in *The Wonderful Adventures of Nils* is transformed into an elf and is obliged to live among wild animals, he gains the ability to understand their language, which he loses upon becoming human again. Just before this happens, Akka the wild goose, who has acted as his guide and instructor during the journey, urges him to continue to live in harmony with nature and animals.

To understand animal language is a privilege given to the most innocent and childlike. Although Dickon, in *The Secret Garden*, does not actually speak animal language, he seems to have a special affinity with them; and Mary's transcendental communication with the robin is also emphasized. In the much-discussed chapter in *Mary Poppins*, "The Story of the Twins," two very young children understand animal language only until the time they get their first tooth. The process of growing up is thus directly associated with the loss of the immediate connection with nature.

The special significance of home may best be illustrated by the famous quotation from the film version of *The Wizard of Oz*. The more profound meaning of home, as of a pastoral setting at large, must be seen in the notion of the sacred place in archaic thought— the center of the universe (cf Eliade 1955, 12ff). The importance of home has been pointed out in texts as different as *Little Women*, *The Wind in the Willows*, and *The Hobbit*. It is also emphasized in a number of contemporary novels, such as *Homecoming* and *Back Home*. Home in idyllic fiction is the foremost security. Home is where the protagonists belong and where they return to after any exploration of the outside world.

> "When home is a privileged place ... when home is where we ought, on the whole, to stay—we are probably dealing with a story for children. When home is the chief place from which we escape, either to grow up or ... to remain innocent, then we are involved in a story for adolescents or adults" (Clausen 143).

Whereas Christopher Clausen here speaks of children's literature at large, I would reserve this statement for the Arcadia-type narratives. As soon as we leave Arcadia, home becomes a problem, not a solution, a place to escape from, not to find sanctuary in. Lucy Waddey proposes three patterns for the description of home in children's fiction: the "Odyssean" pattern, where home is an anchor and a refuge, a place to return to after trials and adventures in the wild world, as in the Prydain Chronicles; the "Oedipal" pattern of domestic stories, such as *Little Women* or *Little House* books; and the "Promethean pattern," where there is no home at the beginning of the story, and the protagonist creates one as a part of his or her maturation, as in *The Secret Garden*. *The Wind in the Willows* is regarded as a mixture of the three patterns (Waddey 1983). While I find this taxonomy fascinating, it is not wholly unproblematic. In my categorization, it would be essential to start with the "Oedipal" pattern, which corresponds to Arcadia. Further, there is a substantial difference between Mary Lennox creating her own private paradise in the garden and thus conserving herself in the state of eternal childhood, and the protagonists of adolescent novels who leave the childhood home in order to find (or more often fail to find) a home of their own. The "Odyssean" pattern corresponds, in my model, to the "There and Back Again" pattern which I am going to discuss later. However, let us bear these patterns in mind.

The significance of home in *The Wind in the Willows* is accentuated in many ways, the most prominent being the chapter "Dulce

Domum," which most critics have noted. In this episode, home has definitely taken on the function of an anchor:

> ... it was good to think that he had this to come back to, this place which was all his own, these things which were so glad to see him again and could always be counted upon for the same simple welcome. (107)

If we do not apprehend fictional events and fictional time literally, Mole's discovery of the wide world probably corresponds to a very young child's exploration of the surroundings during a couple of hours one morning or afternoon, coming in for lunch or dinner (much like, I am tempted to add, Sendak's Max, coming back from the Wild Things after travelling "in and out of weeks and through a day" and finding his supper still hot).

Similarly, Rat's and Badger's homes, each with their own assets, and naturally the grand Toad Hall, lost and recaptured, become significant. Home is the source of food, an inexhaustible source. Few critics of *The Wind in the Willows* have failed to note the lucullian orgies starting with "coldtonguecoldham ... " (14; see e.g. Hunt 1994b, 93-96). The descriptions continue throughout the text: "biscuits, potted lobster, sardines—everything you can possibly want. Soda-water here ... bacon, jam ... (36). Food is generously served at all hours whenever friends meet, as a confirmation of friendship, a general expression of joy and a hedonistic affirmation of the pleasures of life, as a consolation after long and troublesome adventures, or a gesture of generosity toward those who are smaller and weaker. Even in Mole's abandoned home, the ingenious Rat manages to serve what seems a glorious meal: "a tin of sardines—a box of captain's biscuits, nearly full—and a German sausage encased in silver paper" (99).

However, we may ask ourselves, where do all these delicacies come from in the preindustrial world of the Riverbank? This is a question which a young child never asks; home is a cornucopia, and food is there simply because it belongs there. In other texts, like *Little Women*, home and security are also associated with the mother, the Progenitrix who supplies not only food, but love and care.

Similarly, the question of money rarely troubles the child in Arcadia. The March sisters may believe themselves poor, but they are not really. Not being able to buy fancy Christmas presents is not exactly being penniless. In fact they can "buy what we want, and have a little fun" (12). They do not have to work hard for their bread, although they do work of course and even earn some money. Anne Hollander sees money as a source of moral questions in *Little Women*, but she admits that the March girls have little understanding of real poverty (Hollander 1984, 198f).

There is evidently money in *The Wind in the Willows*. Not only is Toad exceedingly rich, but his friends are also in possession of money: they give a porter at the railway station twopence to keep an eye on Toad; Badger gives the two little hedgehogs "sixpence apiece and a pat on the head" (80); and Rat dispatches the carol-singing field-mice to a shop to buy some good food for a feast. The source of wealth is totally beyond the young child's contemplation. Only once does the absence of money present a difficulty—when Toad is escaping from the gaol in female disguise and cannot pay the railway ticket. The scene has a clear humorous tone and has little to do with the "problem" of money.

Labor and laborers are also portrayed—the washerwoman, the barge-woman, the engine-driver—but it does not affect the characters. We may interpret this, as is commonly done, in terms of class: since the four characters are wealthy they do not have to work (cf Hunt 1988). I would, however, rather apply the terms of childhood, a period of human life when the necessity to earn one's daily bread (at least for middle-class children; so I cannot totally ignore the issue of class) is not a concern. Note that Mole abandons *work*—spring cleaning—to lead a carefree life, regressing from adult responsibilities to total freedom. He "meanders *aimlessly*" (9, my emphasis). The discovery of the Riverbank is for Mole the rediscovery of the pleasures of childhood. Toad, in his turn, is a carefree spoiled child who always gets what he wants without bothering where it comes from. His extravagant hobbies, especially the many cars he ruins, are this little spoiled child's toys which he plays with, gets bored with, and throws away.

Finally, two most important aspects of adult literature, death and sexuality, are totally absent from Arcadian fiction. They are closely interconnected. The characters, whether they are humans or animals, are depicted at the prepubescent stage, the stage of innocence, where their sexual identity has not yet been discovered. Moreover, they are for ever conserved in this stage and have neither wish nor possibility of evolving. Therefore, there is no growing up, no maturation, no aging and subsequently no death.

In *The Wind in the Willows*, the author omits "all aspects of the heroic life that might cause strife and pain and eventually death" (Poss 1975, 83). Similarly, the characters "will never have their Arcadia destroyed by the passion or treachery of love" (ibid, 85). The perfect balance of the world has the function of eliminating desire. Few critics have failed to comment on the all-male nature of Grahame's idyll, a "bachelor Arcadia, unencumbered by women" (Carpenter 1985, 156). Amazingly, nobody has drawn direct parallels to the all-female world of *Little Women* and its implications, similar to Grahame's. The absence of desire can only produce harmony if there is no knowledge about lack of desire either.[2]

I have given a few brief examples from some texts to illustrate the most prominent features of the idyll. Naturally, not all texts will have every one of these features; but all texts identified as descriptions of Arcadia will have most of them. Most important is the overall sense of innocence: sexual, intellectual, social, political; and the intention of the text is to keep the child reader in this illusion.

PARADISE LOST AND REGAINED

In terms of intentionality it is especially interesting to discuss *The Secret Garden*, the text which, as we have seen, many scholars include among Arcadian fiction, but which, with a closer look, has a different structure ("Promethean" rather than "Oedipal").

There are several major factors that make *The Secret Garden* different. The first is that Mary Lennox is, to begin with, presented as a deeply repulsive person. Unlike Cedric Errol, a perfect child in every respect, Mary is selfish, ill-tempered and ill-mannered, and on the whole difficult to identify with.

The second deviating characteristic of *The Secret Garden* is that it actually begins with death. Having just described Arcadia as a place from where death is banished, I find it necessary to account for the function of death in this novel. If the protagonist is introduced to death, then at least one essential element of "innocence" is conspicuously missing. In the beginning of the novel, Mary's parents and her Ayah die of cholera; ten years earlier, Colin's mother died, apparently in premature childbirth caused by her falling from a tree. Both cases are the utmost form of parental "absence," the first and absolutely necessary *function,* in Proppian terminology, in the story from which the plot may proceed. A great number of fairy tales begin with the death of one or both parents, which sets in motion all the further events and complications of the plot. The death of Mary's parents causes her to be sent to England. The death of Colin's mother causes, among many other things, the existence of the secret garden. Just as we do not feel sorry for the death of the fairy-tale hero's parents, because it is an indispensable part of the plot, we do not feel sorry for the death of Mary's parents or Colin's mother (especially since we do not feel much empathy with either of the children on the whole). Neither do the children grieve their dead, for different reasons. Colin has never met his mother, and the servants are forbidden to speak of her (ritual taboo!). He has been brought up to believe that his father hates him because of her death, and this makes him resent her. Having never experienced her presence, he does not miss her. Mary has never been close to her parents, she did not love them or even feel fond of them, so their death is not much of a loss emotionally. In other words, while death certainly has a ritual function in the novel, it is not the kind of death that brings about the characters' insight about their own mortality. On the contrary, the most important part of Colin's development implies the change from his firm belief that he will soon die to an equally firm belief that he will not die at all, from "No one believes I shall live to grow up (105) to "I shall live forever and ever and ever!" (176).

The third aspect which makes *The Secret Garden* different from "typical" utopias is that the initial paradise is definitely destroyed and rebuilt in a different place and with different premises. I have not met any discussions of Mary's life in India as prelapsarian, but it is quite obvious: she lives in an exotic country with eternal summer and lavish with flowers, she has everything she can wish for, without ever having to do anything, not even put on her own clothes; she does not know what it means to be hungry, as she tells Martha, the servant at Misselthwaite Manor, "with the indifference of ignorance" (26). She is thus completely ignorant of any desire, material as well as emotional. The latter circumstance is essential in our evaluating her situation as paradise. As readers we may think that Mary's existence in India is miserable because she is unwanted and unloved and does not love anyone herself. This conclusion is based on our knowledge and experience, which Mary lacks, much like Adam and Eve in their paradise. It is not until her situation is radically changed that Mary starts thinking about it at all:

> Since she had been living in other people's houses and had had no Ayah, she had begun to feel lonely and to think queer thoughts which were new to her. She had begun to wonder why she had never seemed to belong to anyone even when her father and mother had been alive. Other children seemed to belong to their fathers and mothers, but she had never seemed to really be anyone's little girl. (10)

At this stage, the static existence of the first ten years of Mary's life is thrust into motion; there occur some essential changes:

> Four good things had happened to her, in fact, since she came to Misselthwaite Manor. She had felt as if she had understood a robin and that he had understood her; she had run in the wind until her blood had grown warm; she as been healthily hungry for the first time in her life; and she had found out what it was to be sorry for someone. She was getting on. (41)

Significantly, Mary's progress is of physical as well as spiritual nature; Heather Murray speaks of "the correlation of landscape to mindscape" (Murray 1985, 35). Besides learning to skip a rope and to enjoy manual labor, she overcomes her pride in thanking Martha for the skipping rope; she gets to like people, even people she has never met, like Martha's and Dickon's mother; in general, she becomes more mature, emerging from her previous conserved (utopian) state:

> Living, as it were, all by herself in a house with a hundred mysteriously closed rooms and having nothing whatever to do to amuse herself, had set her inactive brain to working and was actually awakening her imagination. (56)

The motif of forbidden rooms and gardens may remind us of Bluebeard, but in fact the secret spaces present no danger whatsoever. Mary's, and later Colin's exploration of the hundred locked rooms would suit a Freudian, but the rooms conceal no sacred knowledge.

Once the garden, and subsequently Colin, its human personification (half-dead and hated by his father), are discovered and brought to bloom, the story becomes completely idyllic and cannot develop any further. Its linear progress has rounded into a circle, and its repetitive character is reflected in the ritual which Colin has invented: every morning they chant magic incantations, aimed at eternal life. It is hard to imagine a better expression of archaic thought.

Finally, Colin's father's rediscovery of the garden completes the circle: his dead wife is brought back to him in Mary's image and he himself is rendered immortal through his son. The ritual of the returning god is performed, and Mary's role becomes the reincarnated Progenitrix (Demeter; her bringing the garden to life accentuates this function). Here we encounter the powerful motif of the child restoring paradise for the adult and defeating death. The nostalgia Mr. Craven feels when travelling is both longing for his physical home and for his lost childhood, both of which he regains through the children. While we hardly meet the motif of an adult liberated by a child in *The Wind in the Willows*, it is felt strongly in *Anne of Green Gables*.

THE SACRAL TIME

The idea of the linear movement changing into a circular one brings me to some more profound markers of the idyllic mode, which I would like to add to the ones discussed above—markers which strangely enough are seldom if ever mentioned in critical discussion:

8) the cyclical nature of time;
9) the iterative frequency.

In all idylls, time is cyclical: either there is no linear progress whatsoever, or the linear development rounds back into the circular pattern, as I have shown in *The Secret Garden*. Characteristically, in "realistic" books such as *Little Women* or *Little House in the Big Woods*, where the progress of chronos is inevitable, the duration of profane time is exactly a year. By the end of the book, the cycle is complete: "The attic and the cellar were full of good things once more, and

Laura and Mary had started to make patchwork quilts. Everything was beginning to be snug and cozy again" (230).

The importance of seasonal changes in *The Wind in the Willows* has been pointed out by many scholars (cf Sale 1978, 175); but these changes are cyclical, repetitive, they bring no radical changes; time is circular, mythical, expandable. Since the characters have no age, they are not getting older. Rat's exalted statement about the River stresses the eternity of existence: "Lord! the times we've had together! Whether in winter or summer, spring or autumn ... (15).

Winter is the season of low activity: "No animal, according to the rules of animal etiquette, is ever expected to do anything strenuous, or heroic, or even moderately active during the off-season of winter. All are sleepy—some actually sleep. All are weather-bound ... " (74). This lack of activity during winter will also be found in the *Moomin* books. Apparently, it reflects the selective memory of children's authors—childhood is remembered as a neverending summer.

Seasonal changes in *The Wind in the Willows* are especially amplified in Chapter 9, where Rat almost decides to leave home and set out for adventures. He asks the swallows why they ever come back to England if foreign countries are so attractive.

> "And do you think," said the first swallow, "that the other call is not for us too, in its due season? The call of lush meadow-grass, wet orchards, warm, insect-haunted ponds, of browsing cattle, of hay-making ... "
>
> ...
>
> "In due time," said the third, "we shall be home-sick once more for quiet water-lilies swaying on the surface of an English stream . . . ." (175)

Home-sick is the key-word in this passage. The cyclical time is associated with the notion of home, and the inevitable return home.

Seasonal changes are also essential in *The Secret Garden*, where they symbolize the return to paradise: "There were trees, and flower-beds, and evergreens clipped into strange shapes, and a large pool with an old grey fountain in its midst. But the flower-beds were bare and wintry and the fountain was not playing" (28). The almost page-long description of the garden at the beginning of Chapter 9 produces a sense of mystery, awe and beauty, suggesting pastoral— or rather a promise of pastoral, because so far everything is dead.

Buried alive in his room, as if in a tomb, Colin is unaware of seasons: "Is the spring coming?" he said. "What is it like? You don't see it in rooms if you are ill" (108). But as soon as he comes out in the garden, the changes are emphasized, the most powerful image being birds building nests, which once again is a token of circularity. The changes in nature correspond both to Mary's spiritual progress (which precedes the blooming of the garden) and to Colin's (which follows it).

Cyclical time is often combined in idyllic texts with the iterative frequency. Although some of the episodes of *The Wind in the Willows* can only be apprehended as singulative (such as Mole's first encounter with the River), many are definitely iterative, in the first place the ending of Chapter 1:

> This day was only the *first of many similar ones* for the emancipated Mole, each of them longer and fuller of interest as the ripening summer moved onward. He learnt to swim and to row, and entered into the joy of running water; and with his ear to the reed-stems he caught, *at intervals,* something of what the wind went whispering so *constantly* among them. (28; my emphasis)

Significantly, winter, the period of sleepy, calm existence is described in iterative form: "In the winter time the Rat slept a great deal, retiring early and rising late. During his short day he *sometimes* scribbled poetry ... there was *a good deal* of storytelling ... " (50, my emphasis). Storytelling is a ritual act, a reenacting of recurrent, mythical events. Also the final paragraphs of the book are iterative, with a strong sense of harmony:

> After this climax, the four animals *continued* to lead their lives ... in great joy and contentment, undisturbed ...
> *Sometimes*, in the course of long summer evenings, the friends *would* take a stroll together in the Wild Wood, now successfully tamed so far as they were concerned ... the mother weasels *would* bring their young ones ... *would* quiet them . ... (261f; my emphasis)

The "successfully tamed" Wild Wood has been discussed by many scholars, mostly as restoration of peace and order (see e.g. Hunt 1994b, 77f). I view this ending rather as a regression into childhood, almost infancy, the total reluctance to accept growing up. Signifi-

cantly, the Wild Wood (adolescence in my interpretation) does not
cease to exist, but is reduced to harmless mothers and babies, who
are told stories about the glorious adventures of the four friends. The
Wild Wood can be successfully ignored.

In his discussion of *Anne of Green Gables* as a utopian novel, Perry
Nodelman suggests that "this is a story without a plot. There is no
suspense, no one action that gets more complicated as the novel
progresses and is resolved at the end" (Nodelman 1980, 148). Nodelman is looking for a male, linear plot, and of course there isn't any.
He remarks further: "The same story happens again and again"
(ibid), which he views as a flaw, while it is in fact a description of
the iterative structure of the narrative. This is a good example of a
more subtle expression of the iterative, where there are no explicit
markers, but the narrative structure as such evokes the recurrent
pattern of events.

The Secret Garden also abounds in iterative:

> At first *each day* which passed by for Mary Lennox was exactly like
> the others. *Every morning* she awoke in her tapestried room and found
> Martha kneeling upon the hearth building her fire; *every morning* she
> ate her breakfast in the nursery which had nothing amusing in it, and
> after *each* breakfast she gazed out of the window across the huge
> moor—
> But after a few days ... (36, my emphasis)

The last sentence marks a passage from iterative to singulative.
However, as soon as paradise is restored, the predominant mode is
iterative again, both in Colin's vision of his future: ("... I shall come
back tomorrow, and the day after, and the day after, and the day
after" (177f), and in the narrator's summaries:

> ... the months that followed—the wonderful months—the radiant
> months—the amazing ones.—
> Colin saw it all, watching each change as it took place. *Every
> morning* he was brought out and *every hour of each day*, when it didn't
> rain, he spent in the garden. Even grey days pleased him. He *would*
> lie on the grass ... (192, my emphasis)

Any linear development is obliterated and made impossible and
superfluous as the narrative goes deeper and deeper into mythical

time: "And the secret garden bloomed and bloomed and every morning revealed new miracles" (212). The word "miracles" evokes the sacred nature of cyclical time.

COLLECTIVE EXPERIENCE, ADULT VIEW

With the discussion of time and frequency, I have already passed from the story level of the narrative (setting, themes, motifs) to the discourse level. There are two purely narrative aspects which I find essential for idyllic texts and which have very rarely, if ever, been mentioned by other scholars:

10) the predominantly collective protagonist;
11) the predominantly omniscient narrator.[3]

Idyllic texts, to a much higher extent than other fiction, make use of a collective protagonist. Paradise is a collective experience; it can only be enjoyed together with a group of soulmates. But this is just one aspect. Idyllic narratives very seldom go beyond the superficial rendering of events; no internal life of the characters is portrayed. For such an external narrative, a collective protagonist offers vast possibilities.

Significantly, collective protagonists are a typical feature of children's fiction in general, while they rarely appear in adult fiction, outside the purely experimental novel. There may be several reasons for this. Collective protagonists supply an object of identification to the readers of both genders and of different ages. Collective characters may be used to represent more palpably different aspects of human nature: for instance one child in a group may be presented as greedy and selfish, another as carefree and irresponsible, and so on. Basically, a collective protagonist is an artistic device used for pedagogical purposes.

Let us consider the collective protagonist in *Little Women*, which consist of four entities, each representing specific traits. The thirteen-year-old Beth is pretty, nice and shy, she is the peace-maker of the family, always content with her fate. Meg is complaining, elder-sisterly, envious of other people's wealth. Amy is spoiled, vain, concerned about her looks; she suffers most from being poor, and she longs most for nice clothes. The fifteen-year-old Jo is singled out by the author, being a kind of self-portrait; she also becomes the main character in the sequel. Jo is different, she is the hot-tempered part of the collective protagonist, which must be suppressed. By allowing only one-fourth of the protagonist to make a revolt, the writer can balance the societal demands on girls being well-behaved and her own aspiration to portray a strong and independent girl. Jo's revolt is suppressed, but she may have shown the way to her contemporary readers.

Most studies of *Little Women* emphasize Jo's role as protagonist; indeed some critics have stated that the book is only interesting because of Jo and her struggle for independence and integrity. However, Jo's special traits only become prominent because they are presented against the background of the three other sisters.

Anne Hollander discusses in all detail the various qualities of the four sisters, making a point of their virtues and faults being "more interestingly distributed than is usually remembered" (Hollander 1984, 192). She does not, however, consider them as parts of a collective protagonist. Hollander shows that Amy is the most interesting character of the four, and a contrast to Jo in almost everything, including creative talent and sexuality. Hollander notes that none of the characters is a child, Amy, the youngest, being twelve, which is well beyond the age at which girls read the book. She goes on: "… this novel, like many other great childhood books, must serve as a pattern and a model, a mould for goals and aspirations rather than an accurate mirror of known experience. … The novel shows that as a young girl grows up, she may rely with comfort on being the same person, whatever mysterious and difficult changes must be undergone in order to become an older and wiser one" (Hollander 1984, 191). I find this last statement highly arguable. The collective protagonist's evident reluctance to grow up reflects the adult author's wish to preserve the illusion of the idyll. Says Jo: "I hate to think I've got to grow up, and be Miss March, and wear long gowns, and look as prim as a China-aster! It's bad enough to be a girl …" (13f). Jo does not simply refuse to grow up, she does not want to grow up to be a woman, to have a sexual identity. Naturally, in a book from that time, it would be impossible to mention puberty, but Jo is about the right age to have her first menstruation, and apparently feels very ambivalent about it. Hollander maintains explicitly that Jo is afraid of sex, which she views as one aspect of her general immaturity (Hollander 1984, 194).[4]

At the end of the novel, Meg is about to accept a proposal of marriage, she is on the verge of adulthood. Jo is desperate because she is not ready to be an adult yet. Beth and Amy, on the other hand, are delighted, because, being younger, they are not as much affected. Besides, Meg is being taken away, which means that the collective protagonist is losing wholeness. Jo says explicitly: "I just wish I could marry Meg myself, and keep her safe in the family" (263). The adult world presents a tangible threat, for one part of the four-fold innocent character is to be initiated into adulthood, and carnally too: "It never can be the same again. I've lost my dearest friend" (302). The notion of the collective protagonist enables us to see clearly the complicated scope of emotions portrayed in this novel.

In his study of *The Wind in the Willows*, Peter Hunt, like other critics, discusses the four main characters of the novel separately. They have been mostly examined in terms of class; for instance, Mole is perceived as a lower-middle-class bachelor, that is, middle-aged, but childlike. As Peter Hunt remarks, "although Mole may have childlike characteristics, he is clearly as adult" (Hunt 1994b, 55). Rat is viewed as a more or less self-portrait of Grahame, a poetical, maybe even Bohemian figure. Badger is a representative of the old aristocracy and a superior father figure, while Toad may be a conceited example of the nouveau riche. Thus, all the characters are considered from the point of view of their social status; many critics also discuss possible models from reality. Gender patterns of the novel have provided the focus of some feminist interpretations (e.g. Marshall 1994). None of these aspects is relevant for my purpose. I am instead inclined to share the view of the four figures as "ageless, timeless, genderless" (Gaarden 1994, 43).

Whether *The Wind in the Willows* is regarded as a children's novel or a piece for adults (which in itself is of little interest for me), its mythical, Arcadian nature presupposes that the characters are, functionally, children, that is existing in the innocent frame of mind. Further, the four characters are parts of a collective protagonist, representing different traits, often contradictory and thus enabling the author to describe some form of inner conflict. Rat is practical, intelligent, loyal, affectionate; he is also fully content with his life. Mole is the naive, curious, enthusiastic part of the child, eager to discover the world, but cautious and still very much home-bound. Badger is the most grownup part, on the verge of adolescence (he also lives in the Wild Wood, which I interpret as adolescence). He is sensible, reliable and provides a sense of security. Toad is the adventurous and anarchistic part of the child, a direct counterpart of Jo March. Toad's obsession with cars is one indication of his curiosity about adult life. A car is a token of adult life (cf contemporary American YA novels), tempting but dangerous. In the quadruple protagonist, the four parts are well counterbalanced: Badger's experience by Mole's innocence; Toad's lust for adventure by Rat's contentment, Badger's calmness by Toad's impulsiveness, and so on.

As in *Little Women*, the suppression of the wildest part of the collective protagonist is a matter of inner struggle. Toad is not lectured to by adults, but by the three remaining parts of the collective protagonist who force the revolting quarter into order. Toad's taming is just as humiliating as Jo's: "henceforth, believe me, I will be humble and submissive, and will take no action without your kind advice and full approval!" (229) Is it not a direct parallel to Jo being chastised into a well-behaved little lady? Toad is intimidated, brought back to innocence. The chapter title "The Return of Ulysses" is slightly misleading, unless we view it as ironical. Like all quest heroes, Ulysses comes back from his journey with greater knowledge and experience. Toad is prevented from acquiring experience. As Badger puts it: "Independence is all very well, but we animals never allow our friends to make fools of themselves beyond a certain limit" (113). "We animals" is to be read "we children," or, bearing in mind the collective protagonist, "I the child." "Our friends" is the part of self which revolts against order. "Beyond a certain limit" implies the interdiction to leave childhood. Wild Wood animals overtaking Toad Hall may be interpreted as adolescent problems, or more broadly, as civilization (they have weapons). They are overthrown, because the child is not yet ready to leave the idyll. What we witness is a recovery of innocence.[5]

The case of *The Secret Garden* is more complicated. Several recent feminist rereadings of the novel have illuminated the fact that Mary, her unpleasantness notwithstanding, apprehended as the protagonist up to the two-thirds of the text, is forced aside by Colin (Murray 1985, 39ff; Paul 1990, 159; Foster 1995, 189). The formal reason for this perception is that we are usually trained to identify focalizers with main characters and from Chapter 21 Colin becomes the focalizer, and Mary is abandoned. The changing identification pattern is typical for stories of The Beauty and the Beast-type, which *The Secret Garden* unmistakably belongs to—the sacrificial female is in the end supplanted in her hero-role by the male whom she has successfully restored to power.[6]

With the notion of the collective protagonist, the emergence of Colin is merely a shift *within* the character. Colin is the lazy, dormant, apathetic part of the protagonist, and Mary's eventual discovery of him, after going through the hundreds of forbidden, locked rooms, and, significantly, after discovering the secret garden, is an essential step in the protagonist's self-fulfilment. Dickon is in this interpretation the most liberated part, and he is also pushed aside when no longer needed. What Dickon is to Mary, Mary is to Colin, the triple character evolving from the eternity of death toward the eternity of life. To make it still more complicated, Colin's father, an adult, is added, joining the amalgam to accentuate the healing effect of the garden—childhood. Regressing into perpetual happiness and interchangeable with his son (the book ends, as we remember, with the two marching hand in hand to everybody's amazement), this adult component of the protagonist suggests that the objective of the whole story was to bring about his resurrection rather than any change in child characters.

All this brings us, finally, to the question of authorial (adult) control and thus the problem of the narrator. It seems that the most common type of narrator in idyllic fiction is the omniscient, omnipresent, not seldom didactic narrator. It is only natural that an adult author, portraying paradise lost, feels such a profound distance from the depicted characters and events, that an omniscient narrator, at best focalizing the characters externally, is the only possible narrative form.

NOTES

1. I might add that this evaluation was liberating for me personally since for some reason I have never been able to grasp the greatness of Grahame's classic. It may have to do with my own childhood.

2. See further on asexuality as a Victorian ideal in Nelson 1991, 29–55.

3. Anita Moss is the only critic mentioning "the sophisticated detachment of the narrator" as a characteristic of pastoral (Moss 1982, 125).

4. According to various sources, menstruation was first mentioned in an American children's book in 1965, almost a century after *Little Women,* in *The Long Secret,* and even then caused censorial interference (see e.g. Lurie 1990, 13).

5. I am well aware of the Marxist interpretations of this episode.

6. Significantly, this also happens in the Disney version of *The Little Mermaid,* when the prince, his blindness for the witch's charms exposed, takes over the leading role in the struggle against her. This is totally contrary to Andersen's original text. I am indebted to my student Charlotte Fredlund for this observation.

Chapter 2

The Domestic Story as Utopia

Books such as *Little Women* or *Little House in the Big Woods* may seem radically different from *The Wind in the Willows,* but they have also been discussed in terms of Utopia or Arcadia. The utopian elements we find in domestic stories are once again the isolated setting allowing for an autonomous micro-society (in *Little Women* also a monogender society), the absence of serious threat, and a general sense of security, happiness and harmony.

Charles Strickland shows in his study *Victorian Domesticity* that Alcott always presents family as idyllic, which he relates to the sentimental values of the American society. He enumerates features like the cult of romantic love, of domesticity as expressed in the saying "There is no place like home," the cult of motherhood, and that of childhood. Alcott's novels are based on the contrast between "home, sweet home" and the "cold cruel world" (Strickland 1985, 8)—an opposition we immediately recognize from *The Wind in the Willows.* In Alcott's world, Strickland goes on, "… good parents … seek to protect the innocence of children by shielding them from exposure to the world and its ways, for if children are not precisely saintly, nevertheless they are vulnerable" (Strickland 1985, 135). Again, we recognize the seclusion, isolation, and a reluctance to go beyond the safe, familiar world. In a way, Alcott fulfilled the Utopian ideas of her father within her own writing by accentuating the strong family bonds and loyalty between women (cf Auerbach 1978).

The domestic Utopia of little women is destroyed, first by death, which claims Beth, and then by Laurie, who "proves to be the insidious if charming serpent in the March Garden of Eden" (Strickland 1985, 146). However, this does not happen until later volumes. The first book is a perfect picture of harmony and idyll.

For the United States, a young nation building up its national identity in the 19th century, the idea of home and family must have been especially important (see also Keyser, 1992; Avery 1994, 155-183). For Sweden, a nation of extensive emigration up to the 1930s, this idea, although touched upon in a chapter of *The Wonderful Adventures of Nils*, does not emerge until after Second World War, when rapid urbanization also furnishes it with a strong nostalgic tone.

NOISY VILLAGE—THE SWEDISH ARCADIA

What *The Secret Garden* signifies in English language literature, *Noisy Village* ("Bullerby") does in Swedish—an image of eternal and happy childhood idyll, a "retrospective utopia" (Metcalf 1995, 54). The universe of the three *Noisy Village* books presents a perfect balance: the three houses form a symmetrical horizontal structure, the three generations a vertical one; there are three girls and three boys, all with mothers and fathers within the traditional gender stereotypes. Lisa, the narrator, lives in the Middle Farm—the center of the world. As she gets her own room on her seventh birthday, in the beginning of the first book, her sense of home is solidly rooted.

Lisa is seven years old (although the American translation has for some reason made her nine), and sometimes her mother tells her that she is a big girl now and can help with the washing-up, while her brothers tell her she is too small to play Indians with them. Therefore Lisa has decided that she is just right. She is a totally happy and harmonious child, firmly believing that the world is good and so are its inhabitants. Even the boys are good and nice, and Grandfather the kindest grandfather in the whole world. There may be some nasty people, for instance the shoemaker, ironically enough called Mr. Kind, but he is not dangerous, his wickedness being primarily that he is nasty to his dog. At one point the shoemaker even gives the children shelter during a snowstorm. Although the two other boys sometimes tease Olaf for playing with girls, they like it too. Gender-specific games are happily shared, as are all secrets. The girls can sometimes say that boys are a nuisance, but they are actually all very good friends.

The children's closeness to nature is stressed by the presence of animals: horses, cows, calves, pigs, sheep, and hens. Lisa has rabbits, Olaf has a dog, and each house has a kitten, which the children are allowed to keep without any protests from the parents. To make the pastoral image complete, Lisa also gets a little lambkin as a pet.

The children do not lack anything, and as in all idyllic texts, the abundance of food is prominent. The story starts, after a short presentation of characters, with a birthday party featuring "a large cake with sugar and currants" (16), "raspberry juice ... and two other kinds of cake" (21). Many of the everyday episodes in the books involve food: finding eggs which hens have laid outside, picking berries or thinning out turnips. In the fields, the children always carry a picnic: sandwiches and hot chocolate to drink. The adults in the Noisy Village are generous and always give the children food if they drop in. After they have been in a snowstorm they get "hot beef broth and dumplings for supper, and it was the best food I'd ever tasted" (64). Food is associated with rescue, comfort, and the security of home. Christmas food especially is described in minute detail, as it is in all Astrid Lindgren's books.

The plot is episodic, describing everyday events, games, school, and chores. The children are aware of the existence of work and money: they earn money by helping in the household and in farm work, but they never apprehend work as a burden; it is more like play and can be fun, especially haymaking. All events, notably farm work, strawberry-picking, the Midsummer feast, the annual crayfish party, and of course Christmas preparations, are iteratives, even when they are more or less described as singulative events, that is, without direct indications of iterative. For instance, Father may say that this year he does not want any children on top of the hay, but this is what he says every year and no one believes that he really means it.

One distinct feature of iterative, widely used in the *Noisy Village* books, is the special use of narrative present tense. When used in contrast with the past tense, the narrative present suggests that the events are taking place recurrently:

> Mommy *has said* that I have to keep my room nice and neat. I *do* the best I can. *Sometimes* I *have* general house-cleaning. Then I *throw* all the carpets out through the window .... When I *forget* to clean my room Mommy *calls* me a draggletail. (24, my emphasis)

The narrative present creates an illusion of an infinite, indeed mythical time: "We *always* have lots of fun when we walk home from school" (43, my emphasis). The common markers of the iterative are used extensively, for instance in descriptions of the grandfather, beginning with "Grandfather sits in a rocking chair" (32) and developing into a routine of the children reading newspapers for him and so on, concluded by the usual reward: "Grandfather *always* has a box of apples in his closet ... he gives us an apple *every time* we go to see him" (34, my emphasis). And of course the last sentence of the first book, a confirmation of the stability of the world:

> All we Bullerby children *always* have such a good time [at Christmas]. We have a great deal of fun at other times too, of course, in the summer and in the winter, in the spring and in the autumn. In fact, we have a happy time all year round, but Christmas is best of all. (92; my emphasis)[1]

Everything is predestined, and nothing can disrupt the order. Recurrent routines accentuate the once and for all established order: "We have always...," "We shall always ..." Nothing changes, nothing threatens the idyll, the big world outside is as far away and as unreal as a distant magical realm.

Dreams of what they will be when they grow up are dealt with in passing, and are very abstract, more like games. Lisa wants to be a mother, because she likes babies. "I have six dolls that are my children. Soon I'll be too big to play with dolls. My, it's going to be sad to get that big!" (13). However, this "soon" is a very distant future.

Moreover, the children are fully determined to preserve their perfect balance. They have figured out exactly how they are going to marry each other when they grow up, as well as the house in which each couple is going to live, so that they can keep the symmetry and stay for ever in their happy limited world.

From the viewpoint of child psychology, the children of Noisy Village are much too old to appear at this developmental stage.

However, Astrid Lindgren does not describe a "realistic" existence. From the adult perspective, the book is a nostalgic retrospect; from the child's horizon, it expresses a strong wish to confirm that the conservative, protective world children live in is indeed imperturbable.

The book which probably comes to mind in comparison with the *Noisy Village* is *Little House in the Big Woods*, written fifteen years prior to it, and describing a period some forty years earlier, but similarly depicting the author's own childhood, although presented in a fairy-tale manner: "Once upon a time, sixty years ago ..." (1). From a child's prespective, sixty years equals indeed the mythical "once upon a time".[2]

Like *Noisy Village*, *Little House* describes a secluded place: "As far as a man could go to the north in a day, or a week, or a whole month, there was nothing but woods. There were no houses. There were no roads. There were no people. There were only trees and the wild animals who had their homes among them" (1f). The little house is the center of the world, or rather the only world there is: "A wagon track ran before the house, turning and twisting out of sight in the woods where the wild animals lived, but the little girl did not know where it went, nor what might be at the end of it" (2).

Most of the book describe the adults' everyday work, in which children take part to the best of their ability: hunting, fishing, salting and smoking meat, churning, baking, cooking maple syrup, cheese-making, honey-gathering, harvesting, gathering nuts—all the chores season-bound and centered round food. These activities suggest an interesting parallel between the child's focus on food and the adults' practical concerns. But there is also leisure: storytelling, play, dance, Christmas. Although the events are described as singulative, we can assume that they are repeated every year, like the first day of spring when one is allowed to go barefoot. Every day of the week has its routines, and Sundays are for rest.

There are no dramatic events and no dangers. If there is a bear, Pa will kill it. There are no conflicts, either external or moral. Laura does not feel sorry for deer or bears which her father kills, nor for the pig being butchered, because she likes good food. The idea of death is totally alien.

The ending of the novel is reminiscent of *Noisy Village*, or indeed of any idyllic text: "She was glad that the cosy house, and Pa and

Ma and the firelight and the music, were now. They could not be forgotten, she thought, because now is now. It can never be a long time ago" (238). The child's strong perception of "here and now" is intensified in this passage.

What may strike us as a major difference between *Noisy Village* and *Little House* is the narrative perspective. As I stated in the previous chapter, the omniscient narrator is the most common type of narrator in idyllic texts. However, in *Noisy Village*, a very specific first-person narrator is involved. First-person narratives generally have the advantage of a deeper penetration into thoughts and feelings, but the disadvantage is a restricted access to knowledge. In the case of a child narrator, further disadvantages are limited life experience, limited ability to self-reflection and limited vocabulary. Seven-year-old Lisa in the *Noisy Village* books is such a naive first-person narrator compeling the author to use simple language and an unsophisticated worldview. We should not, however, see this as a fault, but on the contrary, a daring attempt to render a very young child's perspective, a child living and telling her story "here and now." The first person naive narrator is intrinsic to the way the idyllic mood is shaped.

The childish perspective of the narrator is reinforced by the style of the text, with short sentences, very easy and plain language, imitating direct speech: "Do you know what they have done? … It's just like them." (12) As soon as Lisa is confronted with a notion she is too young to be familiar with, she either refers to an adult or simply admits her ignorance: "I am not going to be one of those whirl-around-trundlebolt-engineers. I don't know what that is, but Karl says it's something very fancy … " (12).

Lisa the narrator is homodiegetic, identical with Lisa the character. However she is not the main character of the story, but simply a mouthpiece for the group, thus the narrator is not autodiegetic. Most often Lisa refers to the group as "we." Sometimes the "we" only includes the three girls, but just as often all the six children. Once again this shared perspective emphasizes the general harmony of the text, from which all conflict is absent.

In *Little House* we meet an adult perspective, a limited omniscient adult narrator looking back, which prevents the reader from experiencing the same sense of a neverending paradise as in *Noisy Village*. Although the narrator in *Little House* may try to convey a feeling of eternity, she knows that Laura has eventually grown up. In *Noisy Village*, adult coreaders may know that Lisa will grow up, but child readers, sharing Lisa's naive point of view, will be kept in the illusion that childhood is forever.

It is worth mentioning that in another idyll by Astrid Lindgren, *Emil's Pranks*, also taking place approximately at the time of the author's childhood, the intrusive narrator tells us that the little rascal Emil will grow up to become "the president of the municipal council and the finest man in the whole Lönneberga." The retrospective view creates a distance between the story and the reader, as in *Little House*.

CHILDREN, ANIMALS, AND TOYS

While both *Noisy Village* and *Little House* are unmistakably nostalgic in tone, with their setting in the author's respective childhood, the Norwegian Anne-Cath. Vestly's *Eight Children and a Truck* is idyllic without any sense of nostalgia, mainly because it takes place in an indefinite "present" and in a big city.

Unlike *Noisy Village*, there is no perfect balance in the group of Norwegian siblings: they are three boys and five girls, and they are of different ages, between twelve and two. But they are all excessively nice, well-behaved and good-natured, and although they all live in a small one-room apartment in the center of Oslo, they never complain. The recurrent words are "cosy," "nice," "well and good," "happy," "fun" (8f and passim). The family is always ready to turn any occasion into a celebration, and before the book is over there will be parties and weddings and Christmas. The parents respect their children and never get mad at their small pranks. If somebody is cross, the remedy is to run three times round the block. Since this is a "realistic" story, the father has to work and support the family; and the children know that there are many things they cannot afford. They compensate for the lack of material things with a rich spiritual life, friendship, and loyalty.

The slight disturbances of harmony come from outside, for instance, when "the lady below" complains about noise or when the truck, which makes a living for them all, is stolen. At one point, Grandma comes to visit from the country and has to be accommodated in their tiny apartment; at another point, they find a stray dog and after some complications are allowed to keep it. They help to extinguish a fire in a block of flats across the street. During the course of the story they become happily reconciled both with the Lady Below and with the truck thief, and these two eventually get married. At the end of the book, the family, including Grandma, moves from their city apartment to a little house in the country, thus exchanging their perfect world for one still more perfect.

I have chosen this less known example in order to encourage my readers to supply their own. It is indeed easy to recollect dozens of idyllic domestic stories from different countries and epochs. One of my special favorites when I was a child was *The Adventures of Chunky* by Leila Berg, a book seldom mentioned in studies of children's fiction as an indispensable masterpiece. Anne-Cath. Vestly herself has written several series of nice, tame domestic stories featuring both girls and boys as protagonists, and even, in the mid-70s, introducing a single mother.

Otherwise, reference sources tend to use categories such as "Domestic Adventures" or "Family Stories" for *Heidi, Hans Brinker, What Katy Did, The Treasure Seekers* and *The Railway Children, Milly-Molly-Mandy, Homer Price, Little Old Mrs. Pepperpot, Ballet Shoes, Lottie and Lisa, Just William,* and *Ramona the Pest.* Similarly *Tom Brown's Schooldays, What Katy Did at School, Stalky & Co, The Flying Classroom, Dimsie Goes To School, Harriet the Spy,* and *My Friend Specs McCann* tend to be listed under the heading "School Stories" (see e.g. Fisher 1964; Arbuthnot 1972; Townsend 1983). There are several special studies of school stories (Quigly 1982; Cadogan 1986; Richards 1992; Löfgren 1993).

Naturally, these texts are not totally homogeneous. *The Treasure Seekers* has more formal elements of adventure than *The Railway Children. Homer Price* is reminiscent of tall tales. Streatfeild's "Shoes" series comes dangerously close to formula fiction. I have also provocatively included two titles which normally are treated under either fantasy or humor (or perhaps "humorous fantasy"): *Mrs. Pepperpot* and *My Friend Specs McCann.* The conventional generic distinction will not allow the mixture of fantasy and realism. In my text typology, I am more interested in the intrinsic qualities of the text than the presence or absence of superficial narrative components, in which category I place magical elements. A brief comparison of *Mrs. Pepperpot* and *The Treasure Seekers* reveals more similarities than differences. Each chapter is centered round an event, often with humorous consequences; the setting is limited; and nothing changes in any character's status. Similarly, comparing *My Friend Specs McCann* with any "realistic" school story, we notice that each chapter is focused on a "prank," a funny event, which causes some trouble but is resolved in a satisfactory way. Magical transformations in *Mrs. Pepperpot* and *Specs* are merely narrative devices to initiate the events.

Some common features of all the abovementioned books are, beside the general lack of serious conflicts, a setting in the country or in a small town; a relative freedom from adult control; a strong focus on traditional values (family, loyalty, friendship); and the absence of linear progress, growth and death.

We may wonder about the appeal of domestic and school stories where the only movement, if any at all, is from good to better. Probably, by considering them in terms of idyll and utopia we can find an adequate explanation: they fulfil the child's need to confirm the stability of the childhood world. Incidentally, Anne-Cath. Vestly's stories have never had any notable success in Sweden, obviously because the need for domestic idyll has been fulfilled by Astrid Lindgren.

In the "domestic idyll" I would also include most of the so-called animal and toy stories, two categories that are usually treated separately in critical studies (see Fisher 1964; Arbuthnot 1972; Stewig 1980; Townsend 1983; Nodelman 1992). Toys most likely fall within the fantasy genre, unless they are picture books, while animals appear as a special text group, even a special genre, unless included among "nature stories." There are two special studies of respective motifs, *Animal Land* by Margaret Blount and *When Toys Come Alive* by Lois Kuznets. Kuznets suggests several purposes which animated toys can serve in a children's narrative (Kuznets 1994, 2), all of which are equally applicable to animals. Margaret Blount emphasizes the nostalgic tone of animal stories: "A countryside populated by small, indigenous animals is many people's wish, hope, and memory; but such a place, if it is to give imaginative satisfaction, has to be happy and romanticised" (Blount 1974, 131).

Most critics agree that there are at least three types of animal stories: those portraying animals in their natural environment and only partially allowing them human-like mental abilities (*Black*

Beauty, Tarka the Otter, Watership Down); those portraying anthropomorphic animals—talking, wearing clothes, thinking and behaving
like humans—in separate communities, with or without contact
with humans (*The Wind in the Willows*, Beatrix Potter's stories,
Charlotte's Web, The Hundred and One Dalmatians, and, to go beyond
the English language sphere, *Little Tiger and Little Bear* stories); and
finally those portraying anthropomorphic animals living among
humans, as friends or intelligent pets (*Babar, A Bear Called Paddington, Purrkin the Talking Cat*). Margery Fisher distinguishes between fantasies about animals (primarily cats and mice),
countryside stories (that is, mostly animals in their natural surroundings) and animal satire, where she puts *The Wind in the Willows, Stuart Little, Doctor Dolittle* stories, *The Animals'
Conference*—and *Animal Farm,* which, she argues, also offers young
readers much pleasure (Fisher 1964, 64). Since I am not concerned
with ideology or authorial intention, the satirical element is irrelevant.

As to toys, some recurrently mentioned texts are *The Nutcracker,
Pinocchio, Winnie-the-Pooh, Adventures of a Little Wooden Horse, The
Dolls House, Rufty Tufty the Golliwog, Five Dolls in a House,* and *The
Mouse and His Child.* A recent and original contribution to the type,
as yet not treated in secondary sources, is *The Mennyms* series.

Animal and toy stories are most often presented as genres specific
for children's literature, and indeed there are not many adult books
with these motifs. Obviously, the Romantic belief in the child's unity
with nature has contributed to the vast number of animal and nature
stories for children, while the nostalgic idealization of play accounts
for the abundance of toys. Texts which were probably not addressed
primarily to children, but describe wildlife, have often become part
of children's reading, like *Wild Animals I Have Known* or *The Incredible
Journey.* These texts have an origin and purpose totally different
from the two other categories. *Black Beauty,* for instance, was written
as a plea against cruelty to animals.

Anthropomorphic animals, on the other hand, represent children, while the stories have the same narrative structure as regular
adventure or family stories (of course, *Black Beauty* can also be
interpreted in these terms). "Giving ... animals human qualities is
to put them out of reach of inevitable fear, pain and death which is
their natural lot. But the device also ... makes humans small, giving

them animal qualities and cutting them off from human miseries and frustrations, sexual pangs, jealousy, bitterness or revenge, so that these minute societies have the best of both worlds" (Blount 1974, 131f). The common denominator is, once again, the innocent childhood (see also Rayner 1979).

As we have seen, some critics prefer to view the characters of *The Wind in the Willows* as adults rather than children, which I have questioned; I think that Margaret Blount's argument above confirms mine. Most critics agree, though, that there is not much of the animals' nature in the Riverbankers; they are definitely humans in disguise (see e.g. Sale 1978, 178; Rayner 1979, 83; Hunt 1994b, 48-54). Finally, stories describing a wonderful pet who can communicate with the child protagonist reflect transformations of a magical animal-helper in folktales.

In toy stories, too, we should probably distinguish between toys existing in a world of their own (notably, doll-house stories, and *Winnie-the-Pooh*) and toys in contact with a child protagonist. Toys coming alive together with a lonely child may act as substitutes for missing friends, siblings, or even parents.

For my purpose, there is no point in distinguishing between animal stories and toy stories, since both have the same structure, and toy or animal characters share the same function, primarily representing the child (cf the treatment of the "animal-toy league" in Kuznets 1994, 136–156). Clearly anthropomorphic animals (such as Beatrix Potter's or Janosch's) are especially hard to distinguish from animated toys. Paddington is another good example—the bear is something in-between an animal and a toy (in illustrations, he definitely looks like a teddy-bear) and has the unmistakable function of an "imaginary friend." Margaret Blount includes toy animals in her investigation (as well as a vast number of purely mythical and imaginary creatures, like the Phoenix, unicorns, dragons, Sendak's Wild Things, Wombles, Moomins, and Hobbits).

There are many marginal cases, like *Winnie-the-Pooh*, where some characters seem to be more toys, while others are more animals. It is thus arguable whether *Winnie-the-Pooh* is a toy story or an animal story (at least in Scandinavian sources there are different opinions on this point; and Margaret Blount includes Pooh among her animals), and this may also be a matter of child versus adult perception.

For a child reader, the characters of the book are "real," that is, animals, while adults probably tend to see them as toys.

Let us, therefore, not be deceived by the superficial form. Both toys and animals in children's texts must be seen as representations of children and the texts themselves are, in my text typology, in no way different from domestic stories. When writers present their characters disguised as animals or toys, it is merely a narrative device, which has little to do with genre. There are few similarities between *The Jungle Book, Babar* and *Peter Rabbit*, besides their portraying animals; on the other hand, each of them can be related to other books without animals. For instance, *The Jungle Book* to Robinsonnades, *Babar* to a sentimental story about an orphan who is finally taken care of (*Little Lord Fauntleroy, The Foundling*); *Peter Rabbit* to any didactic naughty-boy book.

Toy and animal stories are even more heterogeneous than "realistic" domestic and school stories; moreover, they very clearly fall into two separate categories, corresponding to my notions of circular and linear time, or, in more conventional terms, idyll and quest. Autonomous societies of toys or animals obviously fall under the category of idyll, as all studies of *The Wind in the Willows* agree. *The Trip to Panama* can illustrate many features I have discussed as idyllic:

> Once upon a time, a little bear and a little tiger lived down by the riverside. ...
> They lived in a nice little house with a chimney.
> "How happy we are!" said Little Tiger. "We have all we could wish for, and we are not afraid of anything ..."
> ...
> Every day, Little Bear took his rod and went fishing and Little Tiger went out in the woods looking for mushrooms.
> Little Bear cooked their dinner every day, because he was a very good cook. (n.p.)

And so the stories go on, page after page, book after book. The two friends may venture on little harmless excursions, much like Mole, but they always return home, which is waiting for them, where they can live "for ever and ever" (n.p.).

Doll houses doubtlessly qualify as idylls, but they equally suggest imprisonment, especially in Scandinavia, where the image of a doll house, going back to Ibsen's drama, has been used in several contemporary YA novels concerned with female liberation (see Edström 1984).

The happy symbiosis of a child and his intelligent talking pet, doll, teddy-bear or steam-shovel,[3] in a neverending stream of nice, safe, harmless domestic adventures, is unmistakably idyllic. "Human is what the child wants his toy or pet to be, the substitute friend or brother, like himself but exempt from all the dreary rules attached to childhood and growing up, the eternal confidant or companion, steadfast and unchangeable" (Blount 1974, 170). Horse and pony novels, commonly regarded as formula fiction rather than animal stories, are a good example. Although horses seldom speak in these, their function is that of a best friend and often of a "transitional object" for a young girl heading toward a real sexual relationship (see Lindstam 1982; Haymonds 1996).

By contrast, quest stories, whether they are dealing with an animal or a toy, belong in a different category. They are stories of growth and maturation. Consider three "mice fantasies," in Margery Fisher's terminology, *Here Comes Thursday, Stuart Little* and *The Mouse and His Child:* two of them portray real animals (although one of a peculiar origin), the third toys; all three are quests rather than idylls. I have in another context tried to contemplate why mice are so popular as characters of children's fiction; I could easily enumerate several dozen from different countries and periods, not to mention a vast number of picture books.[4] Mice are widely represented in folktales, both as protagonists and as helpers. Apparently, there is a subconscious identification on the part of children's writers of a small and helpless child with one of the smallest animals, also known—maybe without reason—for its lack of courage. While rats are in many children's stories presented as ruthless enemies, mice—in reality similarly harmful—are portrayed as harmless and sympathetic. The emblematic meaning of animals in art and literature deserves special attention; there is an enormous diversity between cultures. However, in most ancient mythologies, mice are chthonic animals, worshipped as powerful and benevolent toward humans.

In her study of toy stories, Lois Kuznets is especially preoccupied with the transformation of a toy into a living being and the sexual implication of this transformation, notably in *The Nutcracker, Pinoc-*

chio, and *The Velveteen Rabbit*. There is an Italian text, *The Befana's Toyshop*, included in Lois Kuznets' bibliography, but not discussed in her study, although it fits perfectly into her examination of toys coming alive. In the story, toys run away from the owner of the toyshop, a benevolent, but whimsical witch who plays the role of Santa Claus in Italian folk belief.[5] The purpose of their escape is to find a poor boy, Francesco, whom they have seen at the shop window and who, they know, will not get any Christmas presents this year. Failing to find him, but obtaining a list from the Befana's maid of all children who will not get any presents (not because they have been naughty and not eaten their spinach, but because their parents are too poor to pay the Befana's bills!), the toys perform the noble deed of spreading Christmas joy: they go around and put themselves into Christmas stockings. There is, however, one character in this colorful crowd, a toy puppy, who remains true to Francesco and continues to search for him. Love and loyalty perform a miracle, and the toy becomes a real dog. Although there is hardly any sexual subtext in this transformation, the text obviously goes beyond the simple paradise of animated toys.

Of the texts which Lois Kuznets discusses, I have doubts about *The Nutcracker*. Both Marie and the Nutcracker develop into sexual beings (she by growing up, he by metamorphosing from doll to human), and they get married (cf Kuznets 1994, 64). The metamorphosis is brought about by Marie's love—a variant of Beauty and the Beast, I may add. However, they regress back into childhood (the Land of Dolls) where they are for ever conserved. Do they remain humans at all or do they metamorphose into dolls both of them, for ever young, innocent and—sexless? Thus whereas Pinocchio's transformation is positive and definite, the Nutcracker's is reversible and negative.

From the discussion above it should be clear that while I consider most toy and animal stories, alongside domestic and school stories, as being idyllic, some narratives, commonly treated under these generic labels, definitely belong to another category, which I will examine in detail in later chapters. To idyllic narratives, I would like to add some stories, most often treated as "fantasy," about supernatural creatures who have exactly the same function as an animal or a toy, for instance *The Little Water-Sprite* and *The Little Witch* (see Nikolajeva 1988, 56f). To make the field complete, why not consider the autonomous society in Terry Pratchett's *Truckers* in terms of Utopia?

GASTRONOMIC UTOPIAS

The dream about the Land of Plenty—Cocayne or Schlaraffenland—has haunted humanity for many centuries. One of the earliest literary descriptions of this paradise is to be found in the German Hans Sachs's verse from mid-16th century. 19th-century German picture books especially depicted travels into elaborate lands of sweets and cakes, with the inevitable didactic consequence of stomach ache (see Bergstrand and Nikolajeva 1996).

Twentieth-century children's writers are much more liberal in their Schlaraffenland variations. The most famous contemporary tale of Schlaraffenland is *Charlie and the Chocolate Factory*. The title itself may be seen as an allusion to early children's books about gluttony. As in many such books, the story starts with a description of poverty and hunger:

> There wasn't even enough money to buy proper food for them all. The only meals they could afford were bread and margarine for breakfast, boiled potatoes and cabbage for lunch, and cabbage soup for supper. Sundays were a bit better. They all looked forward to Sundays because then, although they had exactly the same, everyone was allowed a second helping. (14)

The big family does not starve, but "every one of them ... went about from morning till night with a horrible empty feeling in their tummies" (15).

It is a torture for Charlie to have a chocolate factory in the vicinity. Marvelous tales are being told about the factory, well in accordance with the tales of the Schlaraffenland, for instance that Willy Wonka "has ... invented more than two hundred new kinds of chocolate bars, each with a different centre, each sweeter and creamier and more delicious than anything the other chocolate factories can make" (19) and "a way of making chocolate ice cream so it stays cold for hours and hours without being in the refrigerator" (21). The tall-tales accelerate to stimulate the reader's imagination.

Five children are allowed to visit the factory, and we can easily guess that Charlie will be one of them. The description of the Schlaraffenland matches the traditional stories: rivers and waterfalls of hot chocolate, trees and flowers of "soft, minty sugar" (64), a pink boat made of "an enormous boiled sweet" (76), mountains of chocolate and lakes of boiling candy. Mr. Wonka's inventions are marvelous as well: Everlasting Gobstoppers, edible marshmallow pillows, lickable wallpaper for nurseries, hot ice cream for cold days, cows that give chocolate milk, not to mention "luminous lollies for eating in bed at night" (107), "invisible chocolate bars for eating in class" (107) or "fizzy lemonade swimming pools" (108). It is almost inevitable to assume that Roald Dahl read a good deal of Schlaraffenland tales as a child.

There are, however, a few controversial details, for instance something that is presented as a salvation for humanity, a so-called chewing gum meal, which is an obvious satire on Western countries' solution of hunger in the third world. Another detail, which has irritated most of Roald Dahl's critics, is his portrayal of Wonka's slaves, Oompa-Loompas, whose love of cocoa beans Mr. Wonka has been exploiting. There is actually a scene in the book which can be interpreted as a conscious creation of alcohol addiction in the tiny creatures.

The four nasty children are punished, as can be expected, one by one. Augustus Gloop, who cannot resist drinking from the chocolate river, falls into it and is sucked into factory pipes. The chewing-gum lover Violet Beauregard defies the prohibition to taste the unfinished magic gum and swells like a balloon. The spoiled Veruca Salt, who is used to getting whatever she fancies, goes into a prohibited room and is thrown down the garbage chute, as a "bad nut" (101). The TV-fan Mike Teavee shrinks. But Charlie, the real hero, inherits the factory. However, it is never mentioned whether he, thereafter, only eats sweets, or, like Mr. Wonka, prefers "fish and cabbage and potatoes" (102). Anyway, Dahl manages to squeeze in the usual morals about healthy and unhealthy food in his story. Since it is Charlie's passion for chocolate that makes him the master of the factory, the moral is quite ambiguous.

Another well-known story of gluttony, which chronologically precedes Dahl, is to be found in Eric Linklater's *The Wind on the Moon*, where greed is presented, in the old-fashioned manner, as sinful. Dinah's and Dorinda's governess, Miss Serendip, states that knowledge is the most important thing in the world. Dinah is hesitant:

> "I know something that's far more important than knowledge."
> "What is that?" asked Miss Serendip.
> "Food," said Dinah. "Can I have some more pudding, please?"
> "I'm hungry too," said Dorinda.
> "I think I must ask Dr Fosfar to come and see you," said their mother. "You're eating far more than you used to, and you're both getting so fat."
> "We're fond of eating," said Dinah.
> "Very fond," said Dorinda.
> "Because food is the most important thing in the world," said Dinah. "I love food." (9ff)

Sickly interest in food is a natural sign of immaturity. The girls are too young to have control over their bodies, and still less over their emotional needs. Dinah realizes that being shamelessly greedy is the best way to be naughty, which reflects the general attitude toward children and food, as well as the atmosphere in England in 1944, when the book appeared. Mrs. Grimble's love of food causes indignation in adults, while Dinah gets carried away by her imagination: "First of all she had an omelette made out of twelve partridge eggs that she had found. Then she ate the partridge itself, with bread sauce and cauliflower and fried potatoes. Then she had junket and cream, and a piece of birthday cake with almond icing on it" (12). This is the voice of a child who is delighted by food. But behind her we see a writer in a country devastated by war, with meager food rations, whose own memories of hunger in a boys' boarding school are still vivid. Linklater's listeners (as we know, he told his story to some real children first) were also hungry war children.

The great gluttony starts with the following description: "Dinah had two plates of soup, three helpings of tongue, and three helpings of gooseberry tart. Dorinda had three plates of soup, one helping of tongue and four helpings of tart" (16). For a Swedish reader, this description evokes Pippi Longstocking, both in the amount of food, and in the details:

As time went on, Dinah and Dorinda ate more and more. For breakfast they ate porridge and cream, fish and bacon and eggs and sausages and tomatoes, toast and marmalade, and rolls and honey. For dinner they ate roast beef and cold lamb, boiled mutton with caper sauce, Scotch broth and clear soup, hare soup and lentil soup, roast chicken with thyme and parsley stuffing, boiled fowl with oatmeal and onion stuffing, roast duck with apple sauce, apple-tart and cherry pie, Yorkshire pudding and plum pudding, trifle and jelly, potatoes and Brussels sprouts and cauliflower and French beans and green peas, and all sorts of cheese. For tea they had scones and pancakes, crumpets and pikelets, muffins and cream buns, plum cake and seed cake and cream cake and chocolate cake, and often some bread and butter as well. And for supper they had stewed fruit and fresh fruit, oranges and bananas and baked apples, and half a gallon of milk at the very least. (17)

By this time, the story has abandoned all realistic proportions and gone over to the truly grotesque. The girls get fatter and fatter, their clothes explode. Gluttony gives them no satisfaction, since they know that it is naughty to be greedy, but they simply cannot stop. This is a didactic narrator's voice, who does not trust his hungry readers, real and implied, to blame the girls. But since the descriptions themselves are so unmistakably sensual, we must assume that Linklater is trying to deceive the adult coreader with a few moralistic remarks:

So then, between breakfast and dinner, Dinah and Dorinda ate biscuits and strawberry jam, and Devonshire cream with raspberry jam, and sponge cake with damson jam. Between dinner and teatime they usually ate a pound of chocolate and some candied fruit and a few caramels. And about midnight they often woke and went downstairs to the kitchen, where they ate whatever they could find, such as cold chicken and hard-boiled eggs and custard and plum tart and a slice of two of cake. (19)

The girls get fat and round as balloons, until they can no longer walk but must be rolled. Their mother tries to appeal to their female vanity, reminding them how pretty they used to be. Then they get shocked: the woman takes over from the child! In their balloon forms, the girls are humiliated, they cry, they lose their appetites and

become thin as matches—another grotesque scene, which anticipates modern medical and literary descriptions of anorexia-bulimia.

The gluttony episode in *The Wind on the Moon* is, however, just a
prelude to the plot. The food theme is echoed during Dinah's and
Dorinda's transformation into kangaroos. They receive a magical
potion from the witch, and they choose to become kangaroos because they want a pocket to carry their tooth-brushes, clean hand-
kerchiefs, a notebook and—not surprisingly—some chocolate. But
when they are captured and locked in a cage in a zoo, they get food
which is more suitable for animals: "some hay and some turnips, a
few pounds of carrots, a couple of cabbages, and a bucket of
beans"—they discover that "carrots and hay, to their surprise, now
tasted rather like roast chicken and chocolate pudding" (76). The
food emphasizes that the girls belong to the animal world, "the other
world," along with their ability to understand the language of
animals.

NOTES

1. The last three examples are taken from the British edition, entitled *The
Six Bullerby Children*, since the quoted passages are omitted in the American
edition.

2. Sixty years is also the mythical cycle of the universe in some forms of
archaic thought. I doubt that Laura Ingalls Wilder was aware if this.

3. On the function of machines in children's fiction see Schwarcz 1967.

4. John Stephens discusses such an amount of children's books portraying mice that he feels obliged to apologize: Stephens 1992, 190.

5. The name comes from the corrupted "Epifania," Epiphany, since she
is most active during the first week of January. I am indebted to Ann Lawson
Lucas for this information.

Chapter 3

Social Utopias

While England is without doubt the home country of what may be called fantasy utopia (whether or not it has supernatural elements), social utopias, featuring children in power, seem to be a much more popular genre in Germany (see e.g. Frommlet 1978; Mattenklott 1989; Doderer 1992). A special study of the highly appraised German author Gudrun Pausewang is focused on the Utopian motifs of her novels (Tebbutt 1994).

It is not my assignment in the present study to speculate upon possible reasons for this; I would otherwise be obliged to take a variety of historical, social and political reasons into consideration. However, I will venture to say that the particular historical conditions in Germany have most probably affected the role its literature for young readers has acquired in society. Let me simply state that while Arcadian fantasy of the type discussed by Anglo-Saxon critics is practically nonexistent in the German language children's fiction, the socially committed, utopian portrayals of childhood are strikingly prominent. Gundel Mattenklott unhesitatingly includes gang-books among social utopias, since they describe an alternative, autonomous and in many ways harmonious world of children (Mattenklott 1989). Among these, she notes *The Red Zora* by Kurt Held, *The Children on the Island* by Liza Tetzner, and quite a number of other similar novels. Interestingly enough, there is a Swedish social utopia, *The Secret Island* by Sven Wernström, unmistakably inspired by the Socialist ideas of Held and Tetzner.

I will concentrate on social utopias from the Soviet Union, since they are totally unknown in the West. I have no room for even a very short survey of Soviet children's fiction. However, some of its major traits relevant for my arguments can be seen clearly from a brief comparison of Soviet adaptations with the original versions of some world classics. *The Golden Key, or The Adventures of Buratino* (1935) by Alexei Tolstoi is an adaptation of *Pinocchio*. Not only is the Russian book considerably less sophisticated in composition and narrative structure, but its central idea is directly the opposite of Collodi's. The main goal of the wooden puppet Pinocchio is to become a real boy. The goal of Buratino is to find the door opened by a golden key which he receives from a beneficial donor. His main adversary, Karabas the director of a puppet theater (a minor character in the original), is also in search of the same door and the key. Whereas Pinocchio's quest is spiritual, with "moral and ethical implications" (Kuznets 1994, 69), Buratino's is purely material. Tolstoi has taken the first half of the original book, up to the point where Pinocchio is cheated out of his golden coins by the Cat and the Fox. To this, the author adds the story of the golden key, resulting in a primitive, single-tracked plot, in which Buratino is assisted by friends, chiefly the two puppets Pierrot and Malvina (the counterpart of the Blue-Haired Fairy) and hampered by opponents—Karabas, the Fox and the Cat. Behind the secret door, the puppets find, not surprisingly, puppets' paradise, a splendid puppet theater, which they successfully run, ruining the affairs of their rival the cruel puppeteer Karabas. Thus, whereas Pinocchio's quest is individual, a true mythical hero-quest (cf Russell, 1989), Buratino's achievement is collective labor for the benefit of society.

Pinocchio's transformation forms the basis for is a didactic tale. As a puppet, he has proved to be unable and unworthy of love, causing the death of the Blue-Haired Fairy. When he meets her again, she is an adult and thus acting as a mother rather than a beloved, and he is more prepared to go further:

> " ... But how did you manage to grow so fast?"
> "It's a secret."
> "Teach me the secret; I wish I could grow a bit too. Have you noticed? I've always stayed knee-high to a cricket."
> "But you can't grow," replied the Fairy.
> "Why not?"
> "Because puppets don't ever grow. They are born puppets, live as puppets and die puppets."

"Oh! I'm tired of being nothing but a puppet! ".... "It's time I too became a man ..." (90)

This is an important insight. Pinocchio is told that there is a way for him to become human. Didactic as it may be, the objective is crucial. It proves to be easier said than done, and it takes Pinocchio another round of trials to reach his goal. Becoming human, he obviously becomes mortal. Another implication is, as in many other similar transformations, that he obtains a sexual identity (cf Kuznets 1994, 73ff).

The wooden puppet Buratino remains a puppet, since becoming human has never been the purpose of his trials. As a puppet, he may have superficial gender attributes, just as Malvina has her pretty dresses and her blue hair; but he is just as sexless as the piece of wood from which he is made. Malvina in this version is also a puppet, a runaway from the cruel puppeteer Karabas. Sweet, innocent and simple, she lacks the mystery and the nurturing power of the Blue-Haired Fairy, who invites both Freudian and Jungian interpretations (cf Kuznets 1994, 69 and her further reference to Camton 1973 and Heisig 1974). The mythic dimension of the original story is gone from the Russian version.

While death and resurrection are inevitable parts of a spiritual quest (cf Morrissey 1983), death is never a threat to Buratino. A puppet theater appears here to be a perfect symbol of eternal childhood, in which the characters of *The Golden Key* are imprisoned.

Another symptomatic example is a rewriting of *The Wonderful Wizard of Oz*, the all-time greatest favorite of Russian young readers, entitled *The Wizard of the Emerald City* (1939) by Alexander Volkov. Since Oz has been treated by many scholars as an American myth (e.g. Zipes 1994), it is extremely illuminating to see how it is transformed to suit the purposes of Soviet education and propaganda. Since such a comparison has been carried out by Xenia Mitrokhina (1997) I will restrict myself to just a few comments.

A crucial question for me is why Volkov has retained Kansas as the primary world of his fantasy. Volkov wrote his version at the time when the fairy tale was considered improper and even dangerous; to anchor it in Soviet reality was out of the question. The only possibility was to create a more tangible fairy-tale situation. The Magic Country (as Oz is, less imaginatively, called in his series) is thus twice removed from the reality of the readers; indeed, for young Russian readers, Kansas is just as magical as Oz (cf Mitrokhina, 1997, 186).[1] Elly does not come back to "reality," but to another "alternative world," as fascinating and mysterious for the reader as the Secondary world she has left behind. The idyll is amplified by the fact that Elly's father (in this version she is not an orphan, which also has its implications) has built a nice new house to replace the one blown away; and also that soon after her return, Elly is taken to town where she meets James Goodwin, as the Wizard is called, performing in a circus. In her own reality, she is easily compensated for whatever she may have lost in the Magic Country, including new nice shoes.

I will now take a closer view of some of the Soviet children's classics, equally popular with young readers and highly appreciated by critics. They are thus representative of the whole of Soviet fiction for children.

A DESTROYED PARADISE

One of the early Soviet children's novels, still read and admired today, may serve as an illustration of similarities between the utopia of childhood and the utopia of Communism. *Schwambrania* (1928–31) by Lev Kassil, based on autobiographical matter, portrays two brothers, Lev and Osip, growing up in a provincial Russian town immediately prior to and after the revolution of 1917 and the subsequent Bolshevik coup. One day when put into a corner for punishment, they contemplate the injustice of the world:

> The world was very big, our geography books told us, but there was no room for children in it. All the five parts of the world were ruled by grown-ups. They governed history, rode horses, went hunting, led battleships, smoked, made real things, waged wars, fell in love, rescued, kidnapped, played chess … Children were put into corners for punishment.

Bored by dull reality, they invent a land of their own which has everything their real life lacks:

> In Schwambrania, we lived in the capital, on Main Street, in a
> diamond house, 1001 flights up. In Russia, we lived in [a little provin-
> cial town], on Hay Market, ground floor.

Schwambrania is not a Never-Neverland or Narnia; the author
never leaves any doubt of the fact that the two boys are just playing
make-believe. The source of their imagination is their profound
reading. Their realm is inhabited by the Prince and the Pauper, Max
and Moritz, Tom Sawyer and Huck Finn, Oliver Twist, Little Women
and Jo's Boys, Captain Grant's children, Little Lord Fauntleroy, the
Twelve Huntsmen, the Brave Little Tailor, Don Quixote, Nat Pink-
erton and Sherlock Holmes, Robinson Crusoe, the Last Day of
Pompey and Arabian Nights. Schwambrania is the land of complete
justice, balance, and harmony. Even its map is perfectly symmetrical. The brothers see that real life lacks justice, that while they are
privileged by coming from wealthy middle class, there are "lan-
dless" children from poorer families who never get sweets and are
often beaten up. In reality, the boys sometimes face terrible things,
like accidents in factories where people die. They state with a sense
of security that nothing like this can ever happen in Schwambrania.
School especially is the source of much injustice, punishment, and
humiliation. Adults rule the world, therefore Schwambrania is definitely the realm of child power.

> Unlike books where the good triumphed and the evil was pun-
> ished in the last chapters, in Schwambrania heroes were rewarded
> and villains destroyed from the beginning. Schwambrania was the
> country of absolute perfection.

After a while, the brothers notice that there cannot be any development without at least some struggle between good and evil, and
introduce villains, who nonetheless are always bound to surrender.
Schwambrania is a totally male society, and the first attempt to let
females enter it, when the nine-year-old Lev falls in love with a
pretty girl, is a complete failure. For the rest of the book, Lev remains
a misogynist and even refers to virgin lands as "masculine lands."
The adventures in Schwambrania reflect everything the boys
experience in reality. As Russia joins the First World War, so is
Schwambrania involved in many wars, where, however, nobody
can be killed or even injured. As revolution takes place, the Schwam-

branian emperor is overthrown and a republic is established. Eventually, more profound changes take place. As a first step, the children become aware of death. There is a severe epidemic of typhus around them, so they can no longer pretend that there is no death in the world. Significantly, the younger brother demands the introduction of death into their Eden. The older boy tries to compromise by letting some minor character die, but little Osip is adamant:

> —What kind of game is it where nobody dies? ... They live for ever! ... Let somebody die who we'll feel sorry for.

Death must be real and tangible, so they stage a pompous funeral for their most favorite figure.

Further, the events of reality, the first manifestations of a Communist utopia, initiated by grown-ups, start to cast even more dark shadows on their paradise. Step by step, the boys lose all tokens of security in their lives. They are forced to move into new and constantly smaller flats, losing their home, which has been the center of universe for them and a guarantee for the stability of the world: "the greatness of Home (with a capital H) has been exposed." The illusory Schwambrania alone remains a foothold. New homes are cold because there is no fuel. There is no electricity. Hunger haunts them, and they can only escape to the eternal plenty of Schwambrania:

> At that time, our Schwambranian games were mostly imaginary gluttony. Schwambrania was eating. It had dinners and it had suppers. It had feasts. We indulged in wonderful-sounding and long menus taken from old cook books.

In reality, they save tiny lumps of sugar they are given at school, and in their imagination these grow into sugar mountains in Schwambrania.

The utopia in reality also abolishes time:

> I don't know how much time went by. Maybe a year, maybe a month.... There were no calendars. It was impossible to measure time. Its flow had lost its regularity. When we managed to exchange my old school uniform for a piece of lard, the days were gobbled up at one go. Other, dry-bread days felt like weeks—long and hungry. Daily

routines became totally different. Earlier, dinner was the central point
of the day, the usual moment when the whole family got together—a
solemn meal, a sacrament, a ceremony of food, and the day was
measured into "before dinner" and "after dinner." Nowadays, we
never had any proper dinner. We ate when there was food.

The regular life is gone, and their very existence feels temporary.

At one point, the children are obliged to explain to a representative of the new regime what their make-believe is about:

We have a dream, I said, that everything is beautiful. In Schwambrania, we have fun! Paved streets everywhere, and everyone has
strong muscles! Children are free from parents. And there is as much
sugar as you wish. Funerals are rare, but there are movies every day.
And the weather—always sun, but there is shade if you want it. All
poor people are rich. Everybody is happy. And there are no lice.

The man (who is with the secret police, a dangerous person at the
time) is fascinated by children's fancies, but feels obliged to object:

We should not dream, we should do something about it. We'll also
have paved streets, muscles and movies every day. We'll abolish
funerals and conquer lice. Just wait!

Isabelle Jan treats this novel as a counterpart to Philippa Pearce's *A
Dog So Small*—a warning to the child about the dangers of confusing
make-believe with reality (Jan 1973, 70). I am afraid that, by neglect-
ing its historical and political context, she has missed the point
completely. Adults promise the children paradise on earth instead
of their dreams. The author, writing with Soviet censorship in mind,
tries to convince us how enthusiastic the boys, like everybody else
around them, are that they are building a new happy society; but
what he actually shows, using the naive perspective of the first-person narrative, is a total disintegration of society, moral decline,
devastation, and poverty. The newly won freedom, as compared to
the hard discipline and order of the old-regime school, appears to
be uncontrollable chaos and school is turned into complete anarchy.
While some young readers may be deceived by Lev the narrator
stating, at the end of the book, that life in Soviet Russia has become
so wonderful that he and his brother do not need their imaginary

country any more, a more sophisticated look reveals his hypocrisy. The adults have destroyed their magical dream and given them a soap bubble instead. Childhood utopia has been replaced by an adult one, which, as history has unfortunately shown, very soon proved to be a bitter illusion.

However, it is the intention of Soviet children's writers to reinforce the sense of eternal happiness in their readers, which in most cases results in what might be called pseudo-conflicts. By pseudo-conflict I mean a confrontation, or merely an event, which does not present any moral dilemma for the protagonist, and does not change his initial situation. Pseudo-conflicts are a distinct token of the official Soviet literature (see Clark 1981).

The vast majority of Soviet fiction for children can be put into one of the two categories: domestic stories, which I have already discussed in terms of utopia; and gang stories. I will name a number of representative texts, without going into a deeper discussion of them, since they are all written according to the same pattern. *Vitya Maleyev at School and at Home* (1951) by Nikolai Nosov is a typical title, and it is not even a naughty-boy story allowing some moral improvement on the part of the character. His only fault is bad marks in mathematics, but by the end of the book he becomes a model student. *Tall Tales* (1945), a collection of short stories by the same author, may be more reminiscent of *Just William*, with their boys who are slightly naughty but never evil or in need of improvement (see a sample in Morton 1967, 87). *Dennis's Stories* (1966) with a number of sequels, by Victor Dragunsky, are likewise a neverending string of anecdotes, told from a young child's naive point of view, but never reflecting upon any serious matters. Not even when Dennis gets a baby sister does it change his innocent life; and the puritan attitude of Soviet pedagogues toward procreation does not allow the author to let his hero wonder where this baby comes from. He might just as well get a new bicycle or a puppy.

It is no coincidence that the short story is so popular in Soviet literature for young readers: the scope of a short story allows a description of an episode, a funny situation or event, but it can seldom involve any deeper characterization.

All the abovementioned books are explicitly humorous, and their profound innocence and deliberate ignorance about any serious aspects of life makes them enjoyable for younger readers. It could then be expected that novels for older children would demonstrate a clearer tendency toward psychological development, but this is hardly the case. Two classic novels, *Timur and His Gang* (1941) by Arkady Gaidar, and *Vassiok Trubachov and His Comrades* (1947) by Valentina Oseyeva, signal their contents by the titles. The collective characters of both books preclude any individual development. In the first book, a group of children perform "good deeds" in a true scout manner, while they compete with a rival group of hooligans. In the second novel, two-thirds of the book is written as a conventional school story with small everyday conflicts, the race for good marks, and rewards for diligence, while the middle part is a description from the first weeks of the Second World War in the Soviet Union, where a group of children on holiday are forced to stay under Nazi occupation in the Ukraine.

The pseudo-conflicts of these novels have one single function: to demonstrate that Soviet children are perfect in every respect and that any threat can only come from external forces, the "remnants of bourgeois mentality" in *Timur,* and foreign occupants in *Vassiok Trubachov.* Since there is no moral lesson to learn, and no room for any psychological development, the books consist of superficial events; the perfect harmony may be disturbed temporarily, but it is always immediately restored. The characters do not mature, physically or spiritually; the problems of food or money are never touched upon, and naturally there is neither death nor sexuality present in any tangible form. Not even in the portrayal of war in *Vassiok Trubachov,* where several children in the gang get killed, do we meet any reflection on death beside the statement of the fact.

A very important feature of most of Soviet children's fiction is the absence of any conflict between children and parents. Adult authority can never be questioned, and children, characters and readers equally, are reinforced in the conviction that adults are always right and always know best. The conflicts, or rather pseudo-conflicts can only involve classmates, friends or siblings.

The iterative character of these novels follows naturally from their premises. Since the principle of the so-called socialist realism is "typical characters in typical situations," the events described are supposed to be universal, they have happened and are happening all the time, they are not unique. The aim of Soviet children's fiction is to create a sense of stability and permanence, where life is getting better and better every day.

A UTOPIA OF MITES

In *The Adventures of Dunno and His Friends* (1954) by Nikolai Nosov, we meet a seemingly conventional Utopia of miniature people, called Mites, living "in a town in a fairyland" (see text samples in Morton 1967, 104–120). Writing within the context of "socialist realism," the author hurries to state at the beginning of his book:

> Perhaps you don't believe this. Perhaps you think such things don't happen in real life. Well, nobody says they do. Real life is one thing, and fairy-tale life is another. Anything can happen in fairy tales. (Morton 1967, 105)

Apart from this pedagogical reservation, the miniature society is built up quite consistently. The first description of the town is typically Arcadian:

> Their town was very beautiful. Around every house grew daisies, dandelions and honeysuckle, and the streets were all named after flowers: Bluebell Street, Daisy Lane, and Primrose Avenue. That is why the town was called Flower Town. (Morton 1967, 104)

It is a perfectly harmonious world, lacking money and production, or any form of government. The environment is of normal size, so the Mites can pick berries, fruit, mushrooms and nuts. Among the foods mentioned are also a variety of cakes and cookies, so obviously the use of fire is known, and elementary agriculture is practised (the cultivated vegetables are also of normal size, and detailed pictures are given of the toil of harvesting). There is no mention of meat or any domestic animals.

There are some professions mentioned, such as a hunter (named Shot, with a dog named Dot) or a doctor (Dr. Pillman) as well as poets and artists (painter Blobs and musician Trills). These are hobbies rather than occupations. As to doctors, they mostly remind us of children's play, since there are no serious diseases.

There are very few tokens of technology, and no explanation is given as to where things come from. There is an astronomer who has learned to produce magnifying lenses out of broken bottles. However, it is not specified where the bottles come from in the first place. There is a variety of metal tools (saws, hammers, files, screwdrivers) and domestic gadgets (irons) adjusted to the size of Mites. There are musical instruments of quite advanced character (violins, harps, and brasses); there are oil paints for the artists; and there are medicines the doctors administer (mostly iodine and castor oil), but the origins of these things are not accounted for. There are nice clothes, of fabric as well as leather, but it is never mentioned that clothes are being made. The houses are quite modern too, as well as furniture and many luxury items, such as carpets, mirrors, china, soap, and toothpaste. It is mentioned that the Mites know how to make rubber from flower juice. At one point they also collect silkworms to make a net, so presumably they can produce silk for their clothing. However, as in any Utopia, the crucial question of where things come from is never asked.

The only really advanced technological implement is a car which uses soda-water instead of gas. The occurrence of a car in Arcadia may be reminiscent of *The Wind in the Willows*, but here it does not have any implication of disturbing the idyll. It is merely another plaything.

There are gender differences, as the Mites are of two sorts, "he-Mites" and "she-Mites" (in Miriam Morton's sample text, they are called boy-Mites and girl-Mites, but in fact the author carefully and consistently avoids the words "boy" and "girl"). The distinction is totally superficial:

> The boy-Mites wore long trousers or shorts held up by straps, and the girl-Mites wore dresses made out of brightly colored cloth. The boy-Mites couldn't be bothered to comb their hair, so they cut it short; but all the girl-Mites wore their hair long. They loved to comb it in all sorts of pretty ways. Some wore it in long braids with ribbons woven into them. Others wore it hanging about their shoulders with big bows on top. (Morton 1967, 105)

All Mites are of the same age, and they are definitely children (judging from somewhat caricature-like illustrations, aged between five and ten), and they do not grow up. Thus neither death nor reproduction is known in this world. The two species live in separate abodes and avoid each other's company, which is a reflection of very strict gender stereotypes in the Soviet Union. She-Mites are described as vain, gossip-loving, simple-minded and possessing a number of other derogatory qualities associated with women. They are ardent supporters of cleanliness, eager to take care of the sick and injured, and teach good manners. He-Mites are characterized—by she-Mites, not the narrator—as naughty, violent, destructive, and in all ways morally inferior. However, they are indispensable when it comes to car repairs!

The plot rotates around a journey which a group of male Mites make with a balloon, taking them to another town inhabited by female Mites. The journey has the same function as every fictional journey: exploration of the world, and the broadening of horizons. However, the Mites do not discover anything extraordinary beyond their own boundaries. The pseudo-conflict of the plot is that Dunno, the main character, claims to be the inventor of the balloon and coaxes his friends to support him while the real engineer has parachuted from the crashing balloon and arrives after a few days to reveal the impostor.

Dunno (*Neznaika* in Russian, literally "One-who-doesn't-know-anything") is a typical hero of Soviet children's fiction, a lazy good-for-nothing who will necessarily be reformed by the end of the book, not because of his own moral maturation but exclusively thanks to the beneficial influence of society. He also becomes friends with a she-Mite, called significantly Blue-Eyes, whose effect on his moral qualities is astonishing: she makes him wash properly as well as bringing him to realize that it is evil to tell lies. However, their friendship is in no way a transgression of the gender frontiers existing previously in their world. Blue-Eyes is simply a vehicle for the males' moral improvement.

The female society, however, presents a higher degree of civilization, including a water-supply system made of reed, and a clever agriculturist who creates new, more useful brands of fruit and vegetables.

Dunno's and his friends' sojourn brings about the welcome reconciliation with the nearby community of he-Mites, so that the only lack of harmony in this Utopia, that between genders, is repaired and celebrated by a huge feast. Characteristically, the reconciliation is brought about by collective labor, harvesting. The inevitable return home implies a restoration of the initial order with few alterations beyond the immediate and effortless construction of a water system, electricity, telephone, and television. If the first of these improvements may be accounted for (water pipes made of reed), the other three presuppose quite a high level of technology. The two clever engineers build a television set "to watch movies and shows," but no mention of any production or network is given. This new society is already far from the initial rural idyll. Industrial progress is gathering pace, the distribution is exclusively communist, everything is free.

In the sequel, *Dunno in Sun City* (1958), the author apparently feels obliged to introduce some form of contrast in order to take his character further toward moral perfection. Dunno, a she-Mite he has befriended, Button, and a male companion, Dirty, start on a new journey, which takes them to still another miniature town, a ideal technological utopia. Sun City (one cannot help thinking about Tommazo Campanella) has all the wonders of modern civilization, at least those conceivable at the time the novel was written. There are steamboats, railways, aeroplanes, advanced agricultural machines, a variety of fantastic transportation devices as well as communication and automation, and a vast number of domestic gadgets. The description of these commodities takes the largest part of the book. We have, in other words, arrived in a science fiction world within the world of miniature people. This is a Communist Utopia, and the social structure of society is just as devoid of conflict as it is in the first volume: no government, no money. Food is served in communal kitchens. Guest-houses for travellers are free. The source of all well-being is said to be radiomagnetic energy. The moral aspects of the society are equally idyllic: everyone is friendly and well-behaved, and the only crime is traffic violations.

The ideological background for this description is one of the greatest fallacies of the communist doctrine: the belief that as soon as the working class takes power, all economic problems as well as social injustices will take care of themselves. Significantly, one of the best political studies of Communist Russia is called *Utopia in Power* (Heller 1986).

However, mere description of the wonders of technology cannot constitute a plot, so the author supplies a didactic story making Dunno learn another moral lesson before he returns to his home town, fully determined to fulfil the utopia there as well, which he and his friends do by the beginning of the third volume of the trilogy, *Dunno on the Moon* (1964-65). It is stated that two and a half years have passed since Dunno came back from Sun City, but he has not grown any older. The improvements in society are all the more profound—all the wonders Dunno admired in Sun City have been successfully implemented. The author points out that while two and a half years may not seem a very long time for us the readers, for the Mites time goes at a different pace. It is all the more astounding, I might add, that Dunno and his friends have not grown up, but totally consistent with the idea of utopian time.

Like any technological utopia, the story cannot simply develop by amplification of technical achievements. The author is painfully in need of a conflict. However, there is no room for conflicts in the perfect and harmonious society he has created. He is therefore obliged to send his character elsewhere. Like many Soviet books, children's and adult alike, the principal conflict is that between ideologies, the Communist and the Capitalist. The society Dunno arrives in is a caricature of the West, with all its stereotypical traits recognizable from Communist propaganda (most Soviet writers were never allowed to travel abroad).

By now the Mites have started an exploration of space and prepare a trip to the Moon. Dunno and his friend, Doughnut, launch a spaceship by mistake and arrive on the Moon, which appears to be inhabited on the inside by a civilization of Mites. Despite its high technological level, this civilization is the direct opposite of the harmony on Earth: there are private property, severe laws, a police force, prisons, weapons, money, exploitation of labor, unemployment, and other tokens of a Capitalist hell. The moral features of lunar Mites are far from idyllic: there is crime, corruption, hypocrisy, and every possible human fault. Needless to say, our travellers are unprepared for this. Dunno is exploited for mercenary reasons as a sensational visitor from space, and the young readers get a thorough lesson in political economy.

There is one interesting aspect of the story, which the author probably was not aware of. The lunar Mites are adults, at least judging from illustrations (they are also exclusively male). The corrupt, immoral lunar society is thus the society of adults, which at once makes this portrayal more relevant to my study. Although we cannot fully ignore the ideological aspect of the narrative, the implication I suggest is significant. When the rest of the Mites from Earth come over to the rescue, a revolution takes place, and the society is restored—or reformed—into a prelapsarian utopian state. A communist paradise is established, and the Earthling Mites can return home to their own utopia.

The evolution in the trilogy is thus from traditional rural idyll through a technological utopia to political utopia. The implication is that every aspect of civilization, including labor, money, and law is evil and has to be eliminated. The basis of utopia is innocence. We may add political and social innocence, but one of the main premises is obviously the absence of maturation, sexuality and death.

A very brief and superficial comparison with another text describing miniature people and sometimes treated within the context of utopia, *The Borrowers*, illuminates the conservative character of Nosov's novels. The Borrowers, representing children, live in conflict with the world of humans (= adults) and in constant threat from them. At the same time, they are dependent on humans for their survival, "borrowing" everything they need, basic necessities as well as objects of luxury. The balance between dependence and autonomy, the longing for independence and the insight of its impossibility is the essence of the story. The Mites, on the other hand, are completely autonomous. No other civilization is ever mentioned, and there is no threat. Their world is a perfect fulfilment of a very young child's dream: to be totally independent from adults, and at the same time to have no responsibilities. Everything a child may want, both the very basic needs like food and clothes, and the wildest dreams like speedy cars and spaceships, takes care of itself. Unlike *The Borrowers*, and indeed unlike most of children's fiction, Nosov's trilogy gives the readers a sense of stability, conserving them in a state of false security where the necessities of life are not to be reflected upon.

One essential thing lacking from the world of Mites is love or any sort of affection. Dunno may become "friends" with Blue-Eyes or Button; he may even suggest teasingly that Button is in love with him, whereupon she gets deeply offended. But there are no further implications in this. Button is perhaps necessary to provide identification for female readers, but she has no real female function in the story. Blue-Eyes's function is, as I have shown, to instruct the character, that is, she performs the role of an adult, an absent and within this world impossible mother. No marriage or other family ties are ever mentioned. The Mites are either eternal children or, in the lunar world, eternal adults. Nosov's utopia is sexless and emotionless.

In *The Borrowers*, the harmony is disturbed: there is the struggle for survival, there is a strong need to provide food and other necessities, there are dangers, there is death. Since the three remaining Borrowers are parents and a child, sexuality and procreation is implicit, and affection between parents and child is important. The central conflict in the book is Arrietty's curiosity about the wide world, her need to be independent. While Nosov's book confines the reader in the illusionary perfection of childhood, Mary Norton's books subvert the very idea of this perfection.

THE OMNIPOTENT CHILD

Uncle Theodor, the Dog and the Cat (1974) by the Russian author Eduard Uspensky presents another version of childhood utopia, with an almost "realistic" setting. Uncle Theodor, a six-year-old boy (he is called Uncle Theodor because he is very clever, sensible, and independent), runs away from home to live on his own in protest when his mother does not allow him to keep a stray cat. He escapes from the world of authoritative adults, represented by a big city, into a rural paradise, which, however, has a clear realistic undertone: he finds refuge in one of the abandoned villages which became a token of rapid urbanization and catastrophic impoverishment of the countryside under the Communist rule. Nothing of this is explicitly present in the book: the rural setting is a typical commonplace of the pastoral, and Uncle Theodor's ability to communicate with his animal companions, the cat and the dog, contributes to the sense of harmony.

The importance of home is promptly emphasized. When the boy, the cat, and the dog decide which house to choose, they go around to investigate and come back having discovered a perfect house each. The cat has valued a house with a big warm fireplace. The dog has found a house with a big kennel. The boy has chosen a house with big windows, red roof and a big garden. When they go to see each other's choice it appears to be the same house.

A young child living completely on his own may be reminiscent of *Pippi Longstocking*. However, the difference is profound. Apart from the ability to understand animal language (which Pippi incidentally lacks or else hides), Uncle Theodor is an ordinary child. He has neither magical powers nor any special qualities comparable to Pippi's strength which give her moral as well as physical superiority over grownups. Uncle Theodor does not, unlike Pippi, impose his liberated way of life on anyone else; his emancipation is wholly individual.

There are, however, some superficial similarities, in the first place, in the solution of the problem of money and food. Pippi has an unlimited supply of golden coins which allows her to be generous towards other children. Uncle Theodor is an ordinary child and has to eat and provide food for his friends. The first parley over pecuniary problems in the book is a marvelous example of a young child's attitude:

> - Why don't we have any milk [the cat says]? I'll soon die without milk. We ought to buy a cow.
> - Yes, indeed, says Uncle Theodor. But where can we find money?
> - We can borrow, the dog suggests. From the neighbors.
> - How shall we pay back? says the cat. We'll have to pay back.
> - We'll pay back with milk.
> The cat does not agree.
> - If we pay back with milk, what's the use of a cow?
> - Then we can sell something, says the dog.
> - Like what?
> - Something we don't need.
> - In order to sell something we don't need, says the cat angrily, we must first buy something that we don't need. And we have no money.

Uncle Theodor puts an end to this discussion by suggesting that they search for treasure. Since this is Paradise, the treasure is easily found at the first attempt, and Uncle Theodor, like Pippi, becomes the happy owner of a chest of gold coins. His needs are, however, extremely modest: he buys a cow to have milk, a nice little tractor, almost a toy, using food (!) instead of gas, subscribes to a popular children's magazine and offers to buy his two friends whatever they wish. Although Uncle Theodor is now rich, he works diligently in his garden and also takes care of sick and injured animals. Another marvelous utopian invention is an artificial sun which the three friends order from the Research Institute of the Sun (Department of Sunrises and Sunsets) and paste on the ceiling in their house. Not only does the story take place in the eternal paradise of summer, they also have their personal sun indoors when winter comes. Thus we meet all the necessary markers of an idyll: an isolated, perfectly balanced, asexual, eternal and immortal world of plenty, with a child as an omnipotent and solicitous ruler over a variety of humanized animals.

The world of adults is, however, not completely out of reach and presents a threat. It comes in the image of postmaster who is suspicious of Uncle Theodor living all alone:

> - Whose boy are you? How did you come to live in our village?
> Uncle Theodor says:
> - I am not anyone's. I am on my own. I've come from the city.
> …
> - It will never do that children are on their own. Children must belong to someone.

Again, a parallel to *Pippi Longstocking* is obvious, and perhaps conscious:

> All children must have someone to advise them, and all children must go to school to learn the multiplication tables. (*Pippi Longstocking* 38)

The treacherous postmaster manages eventually to contact Uncle Theodor's parents, who immediately come to perform their parental rights and take their child back home, to civilization and adult control. Among other things, they remind Uncle Theodor that he will soon have to go to school. The author is, in other words, aware of the implausibility of his Utopia. The Paradise is temporal, and the child will grow up. However, the children (I include the animals in this category) and the adults arrive at a compromise: Uncle Theodor will spend his summer holidays in his idyllic realm, thus occasionally retreating from civilization into the harmony he has created for himself. The parents instantly recognize the pleasures of countryside life; our familiar pattern of the child restoring Eden to adults is present here.

TROLLS IN THE BALTIC WOODS

My last example, although not Russian, but Estonian, is also part of the Soviet utopian tradition. The four volumes of *Three Jolly Fellows* by Eno Raud, featured on the Andersen Medal Honor List, tell the story of three imaginary troll-like creatures, called Mossbeard, Half-shoe, and Muff, and their crazy, incredible and funny adventures in an otherwise perfectly realistic world. The trolls seem to be unique of their kind, there is no mention of other creatures like them. They live in harmony with most people and animals, although they do not speak animal language. The setting is rural, and there seems to be no problem for them to provide food. They often buy ice cream when they come to town, but it is never mentioned how they pay for it. They do some shopping in department stores. They drive around in a van which is their home.

The only conflicts described in the books are of a humorous and adventurous nature. The three friends have to solve some problems, which they do with their wits, and they are treated everywhere as heroes. The primary task is to keep nature in balance (a chapter in volume two bears the title "Balance of Nature"), and after a few mistakes the three fellows manage. In the third volume, Mossbeard is kidnapped by a lady who wants him for a pet. He is pampered but also humiliated, and thus forced into a "civilized" childhood:

> True enough, it looked as he had no right to complain about anything. The lady took good care of him, he had plenty to eat and could enjoy all the comforts of the lady's home ... And yet ... he loathed this kind of life. He craved passionately for the smells and sounds of nature. (vol 3, 85)

In volume four, Muff is carried away by a wolf and used to train his cubs. After he is rescued, the three friends quarrel, and Halfshoe leaves on his own, but of course they become reconciled and live happily ever after. All these events illustrate perfectly my notion of pseudo-conflict as well as the utopian character of Soviet fiction for children. The three friends have nothing to worry about, and events do not change their initial situation once the problem is eliminated. The chain of events is arbitrary and can be continued indefinitely. The world described is balanced and essentially good, and all villains are soon reformed. The events are only described superficially, through external focalization, and an omniscient and omnipresent narrator is used. No inner life is involved, no emotions or psychological development exist or even are possible. The time is static; or rather there is no time of the chronos-type, the time is, technological tokens notwithstanding, the "once upon a time" of the fairy tale. The characters have no age, they are neither children nor grown-ups, they are formally male, but actually sexless.

A very superficial comparison with a few seemingly similar texts reveals profound differences. There is nothing in these books comparable to the heroic pathos of *The Hobbit*. There is none of the strong emotional charge of the *Moomin* stories, nor their subtle, but profound psychological evolution. If anything, there is a vague similarity to *The Wind in the Willows*, lacking, however, its nostalgic tone. Muff, Halfshoe, and Mossbeard are merely three carefree, independent children, without parental supervision, without money problems, without obligations, immortal and never having to grow up, free to investigate the fascinating and fairly safe world—a perfect Utopia!

CHILDREN IN POWER—KING MATT

One of the famous childhood Utopias, *King Matt the First*, was written in 1923 by the Polish educator Janusz Korczak.[2] It is based on the author's firm belief in children's rights as well as his profound knowledge of their psychological needs (one of his best known books on education is entitled *How to Love a Child*). However, the pessimistic ending of the novel leaves no illusions as to the possibility of the fulfilment of his ideals.

The setting is a fictional, although apparently European, kingdom in the beginning of the twentieth century. Little Matt is six or seven years old when his father the king dies, and he becomes king. He is good and naive and knows very little about the world outside the palace. The Council of Ministers governs the country in his name, and he is at best allowed to participate in parades and celebrations. His naive assumption is that kings have power, that is, unlimited free will, and his execution of power does not go beyond ordering a ten-foot high doll for a little girl he once met in a park.

Matt manages to befriend the son of a guard soldier, Felek, who opens his eyes to the real state of events in the country. He learns that the adults have been deceiving him. He learns that there is a war going on. Together with Felek, little Matt runs away from home and joins the troops. He experiences many hardships, is wounded, taken prisoner, faces death, and really learns about the needs and hopes of his people. When the war is over and he returns in glory, he is fully determined to change his country for the better. Naturally, he starts with children, whom he has understood to be the most oppressed.

He gives his ministers the power to govern over adults, while he decides to be king of the children. He grants his subjects a constitution and establishes two parallel parliaments, one for adults and another for children. It is hard to imagine a closer picture of a child's utopia. But the author knows better.

The narrative structure of the story supports its central idea. The point of view is totally Matt's—naive and innocent. Even the language is explicitly simple. We see the corrupt world of adults through Matt's eyes. At the same time, there is a shift between the character's and the reader's point of view, known in narratology as filter. Because of it, as readers, we often feel that Matt is doing wrong, that his unreserved idealism is leading him into a trap. The author obviously wishes to show his readers that children can never gain power. When Matt has all his ministers arrested as the first act of his rule, he suddenly realizes that he has no idea how to govern a country. He understands that he is dependent on the adults' experience.

Matt's utopian fancies clash with boring reality. His first decree is to give every child a pound of chocolate the very next day. This is a very typical childhood dream, expressed in a vast number of gastronomic utopias. In a conventional utopia, the orders would be carried out immediately, since the child does not stop to think where food comes from. Not so in this book. The Ministers point out for Matt that since there are five million children in the country, it will take the factories ten days to produce the chocolate and another week to deliver it.

How good it is [Matt thinks] that I have such experienced assistants. Without them, I wouldn't even have known how much choco-

late was needed and who would make it. And I forgot that it would
have to be delivered throughout the whole country. (104)

Matt's kingdom is not an operetta-like realm where everybody is
rich, healthy, and happy. It is a realistic picture of a central European
country after the First World War, with much poverty, disease, and
social injustice. Matt sets out to see to the happiness of his people.
He wants to build summer camps for poor children and open a zoo
with exotic animals. He prioritizes the way a child does. Once again,
his dreams meet with hard reality, since the state budget must cover
factories, bridges, and railroads—grown-up things, which a child
normally does not conceive of as the first necessity.

The problem with Matt's attempts at reforms is that he is a child
and can only fulfil a child's dreams:

> ... every child is to be given two balls to play with in the summer
> and skis for the winter. Every day after school, all children are to be
> given a piece of candy and a nice piece of cake. Each year, the girls
> will be given dolls, and the boys will get jackknives. Every school
> should have a seesaw and a merry-go-round. Also, pretty color
> pictures are to be added to all schoolbooks. (154)

Matt discovers that his secretary is constantly disposing of the letters
that children write to him. As he reads the letters, he realizes that
some children have other needs than sweets and toys. A girl's
mother is sick and has no money to buy medicine. A boy has no boots
to go to school.

Matt's somewhat unexpected wealth, once again of utopian proportions, like boatloads of gold, comes from his friendship with
African kings. For a contemporary reader, this aspect may appear
imperialistic and racist; however, the book must be read within its
cultural context. Bruno Bettelheim accounts for it in his "Introduction" to the American edition. Matt's attitude to black Africans is no
more racist than Pippi Longstocking's, who has also been accused
of racism. Besides, Africa in the book, like the Cannibal island in the
Pippi stories, must be interpreted metaphorically. Had it not been
called Africa but Narnia or Eldorado, nobody would have protested
against it. The savage, uncivilized, but also in its way innocent
Africa/Eldorado is a contrast to the cultural, civilized Europe, of
which Matt's kingdom is a part. It represents the unspoiled child-

hood that Europe has left behind. While the three fictitious European kings, as well as Matt's own ministers, are deceitful and insincere, the black African king Bum Drum is Matt's true friend. He might just as well be a nice magician.

It is hard to detect exactly when things start to go wrong and whose fault it might be. Matt is advised to create a children's parliament by a journalist, an adult. Is this person responsible for the failure of the childhood utopia? Is it the cunning adults' careful design? As it appears by the end of the book, the journalist is indeed a foreign spy—that is, a spy and saboteur from the world of adults. Matt's old friend Felek, who has become the Children's Prime Minister, seems to be another traitor. Significantly, Felek is much older than Matt, he has started to smoke cigars—a token of his adult status, so he is no longer on Matt's side. He, too, has been serving foreign—adult—purposes.

At the opening of Children's Parliament, Matt comes with a passionate speech:

> Until now, I was all alone. I wanted to make life good for everyone. But it's very hard for one person to know what everybody needs. It'll be easier for you. Some of you know what the cities need, and some of you know what the countryside needs. The little children know what little children need, and the big children know what big children need. I hope that someday children from all over the world will meet together ... and present their own special needs. (246f)

The first session of the children's parliament is a complete disaster. Children complain about poor treatment in the summer camps which Matt has built for them. They have enormous demands of the kind Matt himself started with—they want pets, watches, telephones, bicycles, trumpets, weapons. They want to be taken to school by car, go to the circus every day, and be allowed to break a window once a month. They want to own cars, ships, houses, and railroads. Some wish for totally impossible things, like Halloween every day. Some of the propositions, like having as many pockets as adults, or writing in red ink like teachers, because it is prettier, may seem crazy, and they are in no way top priority for adults. However, among a flood of crazy demands, the author's weak voice is heard, speaking for the true rights of children.

Further, there is a proposal to abolish girls. The arguments are: "Girls are crybabies. Girls are gossipy. Girls are tattle-tales. Girls are fakers. And so dainty. Girls have butterfingers. Girls are stuck-up. Girls are touchy. Girls have secrets. Girls scratch" (254). From the point of view of contemporary feminist ideology there is much to discuss in this scene. Again, we must remember that the book is written in the '20s in a very conservative social context. However, for my purpose it is interesting to reflect upon the idea as such. No matter how crazy and infeasible the proposal, King Matt's Children' Parliament envisions a children's paradise free from girls, which means, eventually, free from sexuality and procreation.

Very soon things start getting out of hand. Children do not want to go to school any more, and they do not respect their teachers or their parents. The parliament decides that adults should go to school to see how unfairly children are treated. The adult parliament then decides that children should try to work: "When the children realize how much knowledge work requires, they'll have more respect for us" (270). So adults go to school, and children go to work. There are lots of problems, "because most of the boys only wanted to be firemen or drive a truck and the girls wanted to work in toy stores and pastry shops" (271). They do not listen to reason: "I just want to do what I want" (ibid). The adults get childish, start playing games, chase each other and fight. Most often they enjoy being allowed to behave like children. It goes worse for the children, who lack experience. Girls who are supposed to be housewives do not know how to cook. Shop assistants cannot add the prices. Policemen cannot maintain order. Telephones are working badly, letters are not being sorted properly. There are railroad accidents, and hundreds of people get killed. In a week's time, the country is in complete chaos. All cars and public transportation are ruined. Factories are at a standstill because children refuse to work. Stores are closed, because everything has been stolen. Children who are supposed to be soldiers have used up all ammunition for fireworks, and ruined cannons and airplanes. Children who work in hospitals are scared and helpless, and patients are dying.

Matt tries to put things right by sending the children back to school and adults to work. He tries to regulate the work of the Children's Parliament so that it only comes with proposals, while the adult parliament will carry the decisions. For a while, everything seems to have gone back to normal. The short period of child power has been a carnival; now it is time to restore the initial order.

However, it is too late. The final blow comes when the journalist-spy publishes a forged letter from Matt to the children of the world, urging them to revolt against grown-ups and claiming to be the king of all the world's children. The neighboring country declares war, and since all industry is destroyed, Matt is defeated. He is sentenced to be exiled to a desert island.

This ending may be considered in terms of a personal return to a childhood paradise, but given the overall social context of the novel, it is doubtful. For Matt, for the author, and for The Child, it is the ultimate defeat. The Child has been betrayed by adults; however, the children have also proved to be unable to build up a world of their own. There is no solution to the problem.[3]

NOTES

1. When I was a child, I had no notion whatsoever of "the great Kansas prairies," but I had spent several summers in the great Kazach prairies, and in my ignorance I was sure it was the same thing. So for me personally, the story had a firm link to reality.

2. Korczak, who was the director of an orphanage in Warsaw ghetto, voluntarily followed the children into the gas chambers of the concentration camp Treblinka. See Bruno Bettelheim's "Introduction" in Korczak 1986.

3. There is a sequel to the novel, "Matt on the Desert Island" (not available in English), which in my opinion is derivative and weak in structure and does not take the character any further. It merely repeats the central idea of the first book, that a child's hope of improving the world is futile. It is almost painful to read, and I am not going to discuss it here.

Chapter 4

The Haunting of Time

PUER AETERNUS

We have now come closer to one of the most painful themes in children's fiction: the child who is reluctant to grow up. I have already mentioned the twins in *Mary Poppins* who discover that growing up means losing some of their natural abilities. I have also mentioned the hints of change in *The Noisy Village*.

Peter Pan is the first text illustrating this theme that comes to mind. Jacqueline Rose's much-debated study of this figure is a good starting point. According to Rose, Peter Pan fails to grow up not because he does not want to, but because someone is preventing him (Rose 1984, 3). It is tempting—and not very challenging—to see the sexual sub-text of *Peter Pan* originating in the author's pedophilia; however, the fallacy of biographical connection is much too obvious for me. The only incident in Barrie's biography which might be of interest for the discussion of *Peter Pan* is that his older brother died in an accident at the age of thirteen, which to a certain extent explains his obsession with the idea that dead children do not have to grow up (cf Lurie 1990, 119f). Still, I do not wish to speculate on any biographical reasons for Barrie's choice of theme or character, least of all his sexual problems. I will throughout my study give a number of examples of connection between death and eternal childhood without the authors' necessarily having lost a relative.[1]

It is also very easy to slide into purely psychoanalytical interpretation of Peter Pan, as does Jacqueline Rose or Michael Egan (1982), and still more Kathleen Kelley-Lainé with her Freudian, author-oriented approach (1997). I find it much more stimulating to discuss the reluctance to grow up as such. Alison Lurie comments that "Victorians preferred children who have not yet reached puberty, forever pure and happy" (Lurie 1990, 118). True, but not all Victorian children's writers have created a figure who not only has conserved himself in eternal childhood, but also seduces other children to follow his example. Rose discusses at some length the opening line of the novel; she notes the amplification in the first passage: "grow up," "will grow up," "must grow up" (Rose 1984, 68). According to Rose, this is a clear adult voice, belonging essentially to the *one child* who does not grow up. In making this observation, Rose equals narrator and character. This is again something that I will try to avoid.

While Freudian interpretations inevitably focus on Peter's Oedipal confrontation with Hook, for my purpose the conflict between Peter and his mother is much more interesting. The subject of mothers is apparently very sensitive for Peter: "Not only had he no mother, but he had not the slightest desire to have one. He thought them very over-rated persons" (32). This is rather a puzzling statement, since Peter's desire is to have Wendy as his mother. But the desire is extremely ambivalent, and the Lost Boys can only speak of mothers in Peter's absence, "the subject being forbidden by him as silly" (63). "Now, if Peter had ever quite had a mother, he no longer missed her. He could do very well without one. He had thought them out, and remembered only their bad points" (127). We know that Peter ran away the day he was born, because he heard his parents talk about what he was to be when he became a man, which was not his intention: "I don't want ever to be a man ... I want always to be a little boy and have fun" (35). We do not know until almost the end of the novel that Peter did go back after a while and found his window shut and a new baby in his cradle (this episode is emphasized in *Peter Pan in Kensington Gardens*).

The reluctance to grow up is natural for a child, and it is also natural that it passes. Like Peter, Wendy and her brothers escape from their parents to have fun in the Neverland. In Wendy's bedtime story, "they stayed away for years and had a lovely time" (122). But the story also contains a vision of them all grown up, as well as a firm belief that the window will always stay open for them. Here is the difference between Peter and the other children. He has been betrayed. His existence in the Neverland is an exile. They have come of their own free will, and subsequently, "[s]o great indeed was their faith in a mother's love that they felt they could afford to be callous for a bit longer" (123). But after the storytelling, both John and Michael, as well as the Lost Boys, are prepared to go home (cf Tucker 1982, 45f).

The following chapters are seemingly unnecessary for the part of the plot that I am concerned with, although they surely add suspense before the closure; but the psychological aspect of the plot has already been decided—the children are going home. Possibly, the final battle with the pirates is *Peter's* frantic attempt to keep Wendy and the boys on the island. The interchangeability of Peter and Hook has been noted by many critics (Egan 1982, 53f; Lurie 1990, 131). For a Freudian, it might be a little boy wishing to castrate and kill his father. For me, the crucial point is that the conflict with Hook is merely a part of Peter's many adventures in the Neverland (I am aware of the Freudian identification of Hook and Mr. Darling). To evaluate them properly, we must decide what the Neverland represents, besides the landscape of the mind: "Never-Never Land is … a refuge from the shut universe of rules and duties" (Lurie 1990, 128). Indeed, as the Lost Boys return to real life they soon discover the contrast: "Before they had attended school a week they saw what goats they had been not to remain on the island; but it was too late now" (183). Like every paradise, the Neverland lacks everyday—adult—concerns and responsibilities; it is fully possible to have make-believe meals and survive.

On the other hand, the Neverland is identified by Lurie as the land of the dead. She even reflects on the euphemism "someone has lost a relative," especially "she has lost her child," to illustrate the true status of the Lost Boys (Lurie 1990, 130). At first sight, these two statements are a contradiction. A refuge from rules and duties is an Arcadia, a happy mythic realm, as contrasted to the linear, ordered, structured world of "reality," or adulthood. An escape to this paradise must be viewed as positive. Can an escape to the land of the dead be viewed as positive? Hardly. By the beginning of the Twentieth century, the idea of death in children's fiction has shifted far away from *Water Babies* or *At the Back of the North Wind* (cf Butler 1984a; Plotz 1995).

However, the Neverland is unmistakably the land of the dead, with all its implications. In Mrs. Darling's vague childhood memories of Peter, "when children died he went part of the way with them, so that they shouldn't be frightened" (15). Peter's famous statement: "To die will be an awfully big adventure," is based on the idea of reversibility of death. This is not a Christian, but a pagan (archaic) notion. To die in the Neverland means to return to the natural cycle and be reborn in due course; that is why Peter can challenge death so easily. Indeed, death in the Neverland is an everyday matter, and the author deals with it quite casually: "Let us now kill a pirate, to show Hook's method" (62). This is only possible, because it is not real death, but make-believe. Wendy is shot down by the not-so-bright Tootles and lies dead for a while, mourned by the boys, emerging from the little house in a perfect "returning-goddess" ritual. Even Tinker Bell, having taken poison, can easily be resurrected, because her life and death are merely a question of belief. If all the inhabitants of the Neverland are already dead, then of course they are not afraid to die.[2]

In this mythical land of immortality, time is definitely circular, archaic. I find Alison Lurie's comment on the crocodile who has swallowed the clock illuminating (Lurie 1990, 130). The adult, measurable time is abolished in the Neverland: "it is quite impossible to say how time does wear on in the Neverland, where it is calculated by moons and suns, and there are ever so many more of them than on the mainland" (85). In fact, Peter Pan is an unusual text in its treatment of time. The most common temporal pattern in fantasy, introduced and vastly commented on by Edith Nesbit, and adopted by most of her successors, from C. S. Lewis to Ruth Park, is that the primary time, the adult, chronological time, stands still while the child protagonists are away in a magical realm or in another historical period (cf Nikolajeva 1988, 65ff). One of many practical reasons is that the adults do not notice the children's absence. Not so in Peter Pan, where the children are missed and grieved. There is, however, no way of saying exactly how long the children have been absent: just one night, a week, a month, or many years. Their adventures in the Neverland may have taken "many moons" of the Never-time, but the children have not grown any older. Peter, as the permanent inhabitant of the Neverland, "had no sense of time" (183). At the end of the novel, "Wendy was pained to find that the past year was but a yesterday to Peter; it had seemed such a long year of waiting to her" (184). But it is quite natural, since in the land of the dead, time does not exist, or rather, time is totally mythical. At the moment of Wendy's arrival, there are six Lost Boys on the island, but there have been other numbers, "according as they get killed and so on," states the narrator calmly, and "when they seem to be growing up, which is against the rules, Peter thins them out" (58). Life on the island is described in iterative:

> In his absence things *are* usually quiet on the island. The fairies *take* a hour longer in the morning, the beasts *attend* to their young, the redskins *feed* heavily for six days and nights, and when the pirates and the lost boys *meet* they merely bite their thumbs at each other. But with the coming of Peter, who *hates* lethargy, they *are* all under way again …. (58, my emphasis)

The emphasized narrative present, a sure marker of the iterative frequency, expresses the recurrent nature of the events; it has always been like this and will always be like this, before Wendy's visit and after. The events during Wendy's stay are equally iterative: "To describe them all would require a book as large as an English-Latin, Latin-English Dictionary, and the most we can do is to give one as a specimen of an average hour on the island" (89). Then the author "tosses" to choose one adventure to tell, the rescue of Tiger Lily; that is, even though described as a singulative event, it is merely one of many constantly replayed games. Bearing this in mind, I am inclined to treat the imprisonment with the pirates and Peter's combat with Hook just as another of these many adventures. Since we know it is all play and make-believe, it does not change anything. As I have pointed out, Wendy is already prepared to go home.

It should be clear from my argument that I do not view Peter as the protagonist of the novel. The most important criterion for deciding on the protagonist should be the question of who develops, who changes, who is affected. Obviously, a boy who does not grow up does not change or develop. Although omniscient and extremely intrusive, the narrator never enters Peter's mind. In fact, it is impossible to identify with Peter. Admire him in a way—yes, pity him—yes, but not identify. He is the evil power of the story (with or without identification with Hook), the seducer, the revenger—betrayed by his mother, he wants to deprive other children of what he himself is missing most of all: "he was looking through the window at the one joy from which he must be for ever barred" (178).

Michael Egan makes a point of Peter's and Wendy's "marriage" (Egan 1982, 45); however, it is clearly seen in the text that the marriage, just like the many make-believe meals, is mere play—much to Wendy's despair, we may add—but still nothing but play, since Peter regards Wendy exclusively as his mother and to her straightforward question about his feelings answers: "Those of a devoted son" (117). Unlike Egan, I cannot even see any incestuous implication in this reply, because of Peter's total innocence: "You are so queer," he said, frankly puzzled, "and Tiger Lily is just the same. There is something she wants to be to me, but she says it is not my mother" (117). Both Wendy's, Tiger Lily's, and Tinker Bell's feelings are totally beyond Peter's comprehension. If we exchange Freudian tools for Lacanian, Peter is so obviously stuck in the pre-Oedipal, mother-obsessed stage, that Hook's role becomes indeed superfluous. Peter's abode in a narrow underground cave is a sufficient indication. If Peter has no fear of death, he has all the more fear of sexuality, a natural part of growing up. Peter's reply to Mrs. Darling's offer to adopt him, "Keep back, lady, no one is going to catch me and make me a man" (181), although echoing his earlier statement, is highly ambiguous.

Wendy, on the other hand, apparently understands that Peter will never want her to be anything but his mother, and this is partly, or maybe primarily the reason for her decision to go home. It is also the reason why she declines going back to the Neverland when Peter invites her. Obviously, she resents having to bear the burdens of a mother without the pleasures of being a sweetheart. Peter has a chance to stay with her, and grow up together with her, and she even promises to love him in a beard, but he is not interested. It is rather fruitless to speculate, but if Peter had asked Wendy to return to the Neverland as his beloved and not his mother, she might have consented. As it is, she realizes that she and Peter have different paths to go. The narrator's comment is: "You need not be sorry for her. She was one of the kind that likes to grow up" (185). Had I been inclined to lean on biographical links, I would have said that Barrie is here envious of his heroine. She has successfully escaped the temptations of eternal childhood. "She was not a little girl heart-broken about him; she was a grown woman smiling at it all" (190). She has also escaped the worst curse of the Neverland—loss of memory. Let us not forget that the main reason for Peter's return to "the mainland" is that in the Neverland there are no stories. Lots of adventures, but no memories of them, not even of the arch-enemy Hook! And without memory, there is no real life—an idea most strongly expressed in Lois Lowry's *The Giver*.

Being a married woman and having a baby, Wendy has been introduced to sexuality. She has lost the innocence which gains her entrance into the Neverland: "When people grow up they forget [how to fly]—Because they are no longer gay and innocent and heartless. It is only the gay and innocent and heartless who can fly" (186). The privilege of growing up has its price.

Humphrey Carpenter suggests that Barrie subverts his own myth, relying on children to see the Neverland as untrue (Carpenter 1985, 185). I find it doubtful, an adult rationalization. On the contrary, the ending of the novel attempts to confirm the eternity of the Neverland, not surprisingly expressed in the iterative:

> Jane is now a common grown-up, with a daughter called Margaret; and every spring-cleaning time, except when he forgets, Peter comes for Margaret and takes her to the Neverland ... When Margaret grows up she will have a daughter, who is to be Peter's mother in turn; and thus it will go on, so long as children are gay and innocent and heartless. (192)

LAND OF (CONDENSED) MILK AND HONEY

I will now join some critical voices who have accepted the challenge of Frederick Crews (1979) by discussing the *Pooh* books. These have been treated in terms of Arcadia, but I am inclined to agree with Roger Sale who suggests that the books "are essentially about the fact that Christopher Robin is now too old to play with toy bears" (Sale 1978, 17). The books present a subtle balance between the creation of Arcadia and the subversion of it, so that our final interpretation of them can easily topple over to either side, which we also see clearly in many studies of *Pooh*. I would argue that Milne is trying very hard to create an illusion—for himself, for child readers, or for the adult coreaders—that Paradise is indeed eternal, while the text subverts the author's intention. A significant part of the build-up of this particular paradise is food—maybe more significant than in most other "idyllic" stories, and definitely more significant than in *The Wind in the Willows*, where it has received so much attention.

It is for me essential to see how Milne's books diverge, often in minute details, from every trait of Arcadia which I set up in Chapter 1. The result is a highly ambivalent text, which continues to puzzle and fascinate its adult audience. The appeal to children is probably less problematic.

The setting of this Arcadia is undoubtedly safe, autonomous, "limited in time and space," ... [which] emphasize security and control, fighting against flux and change" (Kuznets 1994, 48). Also Paula Connolly highlights the Arcadian setting (Connolly 1995, 58–70). Alison Lurie sees *Pooh* books as an intact idyll, with their strong "reversal of parental authority" (Lurie 1990, 145). Like so many other Arcadias, the Forest is a "self-contained universe without economic competition or professional ambition" (Lurie 1990, 147). Any danger that can threaten always comes from natural causes (much, I would add, like the *Moomin* stories, which *Pooh* books have been compared to, e.g. Jones 1984). Apart from occasional bad weather, it is a perfectly safe world. It is also basically stable. Tigger's and Roo's arrival in the Forest is like the appearance of a sibling in early childhood, "inexplicable and unexpected" (Lurie 1990, 149), reminding one of the baby sister in *Noisy Village*. Both characters soon become an integrated part of the idyllic world.

In contrast to Lurie, Humphrey Carpenter sees in the *Pooh* books the British Golden Age's farewell to enchanted places. He is dissatisfied with the ending, saying that it is "out of place when applied to the Pooh stories themselves" (Carpenter 1985, 209). I think this essentially wrong. The ending and the final statement, expressed in the iterative ("will always be playing"), is the very essence of the *Pooh* stories; from Milne's side it is a confirmation of his own position. I am, however, as in Barrie's case, reluctant to discuss children's texts as therapeutic vehicles for their authors, as Peter Hunt proposes for *Pooh* (Hunt 1992, 122). If Milne spent his childhood estranged from his parents, as Hunt remarks, Tove Jansson or Astrid Lindgren did not. While Carpenter suggests that Milne is saying goodbye to the stories and the characters, I view it the other way round, as the confirmation of the stability of Milne's universe.

Indeed, for many generations of readers, the little boy and his bear *have* always been playing in the Forest, reenacting the ritual of eternal childhood.

Some of my arguments derive from and coincide with Lois Kuznets' interpretation, based in the first place on the pastoral and nostalgic quality of the story (see Kuznets 1994, 51). Unlike the characters of *The Wind in the Willows*, Kuznets argues, Pooh characters have no need to leave their paradise, partly because they do not know about the existence of an outer world, partly because they do not long for it. But in this case we may ask: what happens when they do learn about it, that is when Christopher Robin is about to go away? Do they long to follow him? It seems that one of the fallacies in many interpretations of the *Pooh* stories lies in treating them as static, similar to *The Wind in the Willows*. The difference is, however, profound. Unlike Mole and Toad, Christopher Robin has to leave Arcadia, and the tragedy of his toys (that is, the childish, or rather childlike parts of him) is that they cannot follow him into the Wide World. Actually they are not even allowed—and neither are the readers—to enter Christopher Robin's house, this sacred, tabooed place, apparently leading into the Wide World, the world of adulthood. All scenes involving Christopher Robin's house take place outdoors, including the party he gives at the end of the first book.

Apart from this, homes and houses play a significant role in the books, especially in the sequel, where "house" is featured in the title. When Pooh and Piglet decide to build a house for Eeyore they observe that "even Rabbit's friends and relations have houses or somethings" (7). However, the basic security of home is undermined in the sequel by Owl's house being blown down, and Piglet being unceremoniously removed from his beloved home. This undermining of the traditional security of home anticipates Christopher Robin's departure.

The Forest is a natural world, where civilization has not yet entered, at least not in the beginning. "*Winnie-the-Pooh* is essentially a modern version of an archetypal legend … the story of a peaceful animal kingdom ruled by a single benevolent human being" (Lurie 1990, 154). However, Lurie as well as Kuznets and other critics cannot but observe that the final threat to the Forest comes from knowledge and education (Lurie 1990, 154f; Kuznets 1994, 52f). Pooh's poems represent oral, mythical culture, while the education that Christopher Robin receives in the outside (read: civilized) world is written and therefore linear. In Lacanian-Kristevian terms, Pooh's poetry is semiotic (cf Stanger 1987, 42ff), while Christopher Robin is trained in symbolic language. In the chapter "What Christopher Robin does in the mornings" Piglet believes that the letter A is a Heffalump trap, that is he sees the "imaginary," "iconic," not the symbolic (conventional, male, adult) value of the sign. When Christopher Robin writes his first correct message, he has taken a definite step away from the innocence of childhood.

This naturally even includes sexual innocence, and I am rather skeptical of attempts by feminist critics to ascribe Pooh and other characters any gender qualities (see e.g. Stanger 1987; Nelson 1990). If anything, the Forest is a "pregender" universe, the world of a sexless child, and is therefore appealing to readers of both genders. The transformation of the cyclical pattern (childhood) into a linear one (male) is the basic movement of the books, and though it may trouble adult readers, it is most probably ignored by the young.

Many of the dilemmas encountered by critics can be eliminated if we consider the characters of the *Pooh* books as a collective protagonist. Alison Lurie views the characters as representing faults and virtues particular to some adults and some children, while "Pooh, the hero, has the virtues and faults common to all children" (Lurie 1990, 150). Peter Hunt's description of the characters is also focused on their specific traits: Pooh is the bland, the confident, the mystic child; Piglet the small, nervous, but very brave child; Tigger the wild child; Roo the baby (nobody can find anything of interest to say about Roo!). Rabbit is the egocentric, sarcastic adult; Owl the pretentious and insecure egocentric adult; Kanga the loving, but firm mother. While these characteristics are certainly true, I do not find them sufficient.

Lois Kuznets investigates what she calls the child-toy relationship (Kuznets 1994, 34). She regards the events of the *Pooh* stories as child's play. She also tends to see toys as "transitional objects" and the Forest as a "transitional country" in a Klein-Winnicott spirit (Kuznets 1994, 47ff), while I rather prefer to apply the Jungian model: all characters are parts of the collective character—Christopher Robin—and projections of his various features. Thus I view the Forest as a child's inner landscape.

Rabbit is the most conservative part of this collective protagonist; he is against change; he wants to get rid first of Kanga and Roo, later of Tigger. Hunt interprets this as an adult feature (Hunt 1992, 119), while I see it the other way round: he is the most childish, the most reluctant part of the child. "Rabbit's clever … that's why he never understands things" (*House* 126), says Pooh. This is a stubborn child who has made up his mind never to accept changes.

It is also Rabbit who attempts to "unbounce" Tigger, much like the three animals in *The Wind in the Willows* trying to intimidate Toad, or the three March sisters trying to intimidate Jo. The superficial events are in fact reflections of the child's thorny road to self-knowledge, with many questions on the way. Does Pooh's and Piglet's moving together at the end of the second book signify a fusion of character? Or is it an intrusion into Pooh's integrity?

It is also noteworthy that the characters are introduced successively, one or two at a time in every chapter, as in a cumulative narrative. This may be viewed as the child's successive discovery of his own traits.

The dual nature of Christopher Robin supports my interpretation. In the outer frame, Christopher Robin is small, powerless, and oppressed. In the Forest, he is the God (cf Kuznets 1994, 51). Although the boy's *deus ex machina* function is often emphasized by critics, it is seldom observed that he is never focalized, while all other characters are, if only briefly (including Rabbit's tiny relative Alexander Beetle). It is essential that in the traumatic depiction of the boy's departure from his enchanted place, the point of view lies not with the boy, but with the other characters—his grief is subdued by their misunderstanding, naivete, or simply indifference.

In her thorough analysis of the narrative perspective of the *Pooh* books, Barbara Wall discusses the disappearance of the metadiegetic, didactic narrator in the sequel (Wall 1991, 182f). It is, paradoxically, inevitable, as the story progresses toward an increasingly adult, detached view of the events. Contrary to Wall, Peter Hunt apprehends the didactic narrator as a disturbing narrative form: "… the element that *most* threatens that enchantment of the world of the *Pooh* books is the intrusive voice of the adult narrator" (Hunt 1992, 114). The attraction of Pooh's world, Alison Lurie comments, lies in the fact that adults see it as "both the lost past and the ideal future—at once the golden rural childhood they probably never knew, and the perfect commune they are always seeking" (Lurie 1990, 155). Peter Hunt echoes: "For adult readers, there is one extra dimension in the books, that of nostalgia" (Hunt 1992, 122). But if the didactic narrator can be a nuisance, this is, as I have previously shown, typical of idyllic fiction. Moreover, the narrative situation is unmistakably iterative, as also Lois Kuznets notes, without using the term: "the narrator intimates that this is a repeated scene, sometimes followed by a game and sometimes by a quiet sit in front of the fire" (Kuznets 1994, 48). Each episode may have been told by the metafictive father (narrator) to the metafictive son (narratee) many times. The cyclical, mythical time: "Once upon a time, a very long time ago, about last Friday" (2) is brought back in "will always be playing." The *Pooh* books are full of Introductions and Contradictions, which do not always allow us to see them in clearcut categories.

I will now take a more detailed view of food in the *Pooh* books in order to demonstrate how the delicate balance between creation and destruction of idyll is organized round this theme. If anything, the stories are obsessed with food:

> "When you wake up in the morning, Pooh," said Piglet ..., "what's the first thing you say to yourself?"
> "What's for breakfast," said Pooh. "What do *you* say, Piglet?"
> "I say, I wonder what's going to happen exciting *to-day*?" said Piglet.
> Pooh nodded thoughtfully.
> "It's the same thing," he said. (144f; author's emphasis)

Pooh, the kernel of the collective protagonist, is presented to us through his passion for honey. This is naturally the food we remember best from the *Pooh* stories. Pooh is punished for being greedy, although rather mildly as compared to traditional gluttony stories. He realizes for instance that he is dealing with "wrong sort of bees" who make "the wrong sort of honey," which is an excellent way for a little child to admit his mistakes (or rather a way the adult narrator puts forward the moral indirectly, without insulting the child).

The same pattern is repeated when Pooh is stuck in the rabbit hole. Rabbit, the sensible part of the collective protagonist, plays the role of the adult educator: "It all comes," said Rabbit sternly, "of eating too much ..." (25). While Pooh is stuck in the hole waiting to lose weight, Christopher Robin reads a "sustaining" book for him, alluding of course to "sustaining food." In the picture, we see Christopher Robin (who, as we know from other chapters, is not very skillful in reading and writing) reading an ABC-book opened at the letter J for JAM—sustaining indeed! This is a good example of the ironic interaction of text and illustration in a children's book—not only Milne, but also Shepard is making fun of the child.

Food elements in *Pooh* books are many and quite conspicuous. They are always joyful, even though Pooh must occasionally take some exercise. Most adventures are finished off by Pooh going home for lunch; and after the expedition to the North Pole Pooh is off to have "a little something to revive himself" (116). Pooh's meals are always described in a concise and ironic manner: "a simple meal of marmalade spread lightly over a honeycomb or two" (99), a rather extravagant breakfast.

Occasionally Pooh has a picnic breakfast together with Christopher Robin. He always goes home around eleven o'clock, because he has "One or Two Things to Do" (82) or "I've got to go home for something, and so has Piglet, because we haven't had it yet" (*House* 123). Besides he likes to visit his friends in order to hear: "Hallo, Pooh, you're just in time for a little smackerel of something" (*House* 126). When Pooh and Piglet go round to visit everybody, they have lunch with Kanga, stay "until very nearly tea-time" with Christopher Robin and have "a Very Nearly tea, which is one you forget about afterwards" (*House* 128), and then hurry to "a Proper Tea" with Owl.

Trying to understand Owl's difficult words, Pooh always imagines some nice food:

> "Well," said Owl, "the customary procedure in such cases is as follows."
> "What does Crustimoney Proseedcake mean?" said Pooh. (45)

Pooh immediately interprets unfamiliar words as food. Further, when Owl mentions "a large something" as a reward for finding Eeyore's tail, Pooh's association is "a small something" like "just a mouthful of condensed milk or what not, with perhaps a lick of honey—" (46). Pooh is very happy when "Provisions" appear to be "things to eat" (101f). Besides, he judges his friends according to their attitude to food: "[Rabbit] talks about sensible things. He does not use long, difficult words, like Owl. He uses short, easy words, like 'What about lunch?' and 'Help yourself, Pooh'" (55). Hunting the Heffalump, Pooh and Piglet have a long discussion about what Heffalumps may like most, honey or acorns. The idea that *everybody* has the same tastes as oneself is natural for a young child.

The lust for food and the joy of eating is apparent in *Pooh* books, even though the author brings in morals at the beginning. Pooh is supposed to represent a very young child, so young that he has no control of his body yet, but follows the desire to eat when hunger comes, without considering the consequences. In my interpretation of the collective character, we are dealing with Christopher Robin's transferred problems. This is confirmed by the fact that food elements become scarce in the sequel: the child has become slightly older.

To interpret the text as a depiction of an idyllic state it is essential to ask the question about where food comes from in the Forest. Peter Hunt considers the question more or less irrelevant: "The absence of any mundane considerations such as where the jars of honey come from may be a function of the middle-classness of the text— but it is also a function of fantasy, where such matters are generally unimportant" (Hunt 1992, 114). Hunt is wrong in the statement that food in fantasy is generally not an issue, since it depends on the degree of the displacement of myth: while mythical heroes do not need food, the hero of fantasy may feel hunger acutely, as do both the Pevensie children and the protagonists of *Mio, My Son* or *The Brothers Lionheart*. Hunt also oversimplifies the complex attitude to food in *Pooh* books. In fact, all food does not appear from nowhere. Piglet collects acorns, while Eeyore eats thistles (although he has nothing against cake when he gets it). Rabbit, on the other hand, seems to have a larder full of preserves (honey and condensed milk), and he has bread for Pooh. It is never mentioned that Rabbit should eat grass. Kanga also has a larder with jars in it. As mentioned earlier, Christopher Robin is the only character whose house we are not allowed to enter. Apparently, he goes home to his nursery for meals.

Even though Pooh makes an unsuccessful attempt to get honey from the bees, his endless supply of "hunny" seems to be there as if by magic. The characters, or more specifically the actual character,

Christopher Robin, are at the stage when the young child does not ask the question where food comes from, but views home as a neverending supply—the mother's breast. Pooh's recurrent need to go home and take "a little something" or "a little smackerel of something" is the young child's wish to get a confirmation that the food will always be there, as soon as the child needs it; the infant's longing to find his way back to his mother's breast.

The story of the Heffalump is illuminating. Pooh wakes up early in the morning because he is hungry. He is not just in the mood of wanting a little something, but really hungry; the problem is that he has placed his last jar of honey in the Heffalump pit. Here we see the child's first suspicion that food supplies can come to an end. No wonder that hunger takes the form of a terrible monster who eats up his food. The fact that Pooh is punished for his greed by getting his head stuck in the jar is rather a didactic narrator's sense of duty than a psychologically true portrait. As soon as Pooh has got rid of the jar, he and Christopher Robin go home to have breakfast, and Pooh does not suffer from a stomach-ache, unlike the character of a didactic story. When Pooh in the next chapter eats up Eeyore's present he is not punished at all, on the contrary he thinks of an excellent solution. It seems as though the author's sympathy is on Pooh's side. Note that in this chapter there is a new jar of honey in Pooh's cupboard, without any explanation of where it comes from.

In the chapter about the flood, there are ten honey jars to begin with, but they are consumed one after another, and no new ones appear—a new reminder to the child that Cornucopia is not there for ever. Typically, Piglet is never worried about food. If we interpret the characters as representing the different parts of the child's psyche, then Pooh represents lust for food, while Piglet represents fear, and his food problems are not relevant for the story.

Another interesting contemplation on food is prompted by the expedition to the Pole. As in many children's books, a picnic is the important part of any outing. Eeyore's food is a comical detail here: he eats thistles, which is not perceived by others as food, but as a nuisance; Pooh happens to be sitting on a thistle. Eeyore complains, as usual, that he has no picnic with him, while he is the only one who does not need a picnic, since he can always find his food in nature. Together with Owl, Eeyore is closest to the world of adults, which is "the other world" as compared to the Forest. If "ordinary food," children's food, especially sweets, belongs to their "own" world, then Eeyore's belonging to "the other world" is accentuated by his eating "nonfood." The nutritional needs in the Forest are satisfied by a combination of natural food (honey for bears, acorns for pigs) and "cultural" food. It is amazing how easily these notions change places.

Why is Tigger so fussy about his food? At the beginning, Tigger's attempts to find suitable food for himself is a search for identity. He must find his place in the hierarchy of the Forest (=childhood). The characters are associated in this chapter with the food they eat: Pooh eats honey, Piglet eats acorns, Eeyore eats thistles. Nothing suits Tigger; he cannot identify with any of the other inhabitants of the forest. Note that they are all eager to share their food with a complete stranger as soon as they hear that he is Christopher Robin's friend. Even the grumpy Eeyore offers him his most precious birthday thistle.

When Tigger has searched through Kanga's larder without finding anything suitable, it appears that he likes Roo's medicine. Children's hatred of extract of malt is a recurrent motif in children's literature (*Peter Pan, Mary Poppins*). In an earlier chapter, Kanga pours it into Piglet's mouth (when Piglets pretends to be Roo), saying, as all mothers say in similar situations: "it was really quite a nice taste when you got used to it" (97). The purpose of the medicine is: "To make you grow big and strong" (96).

By letting Tigger eagerly eat the hateful medicine "for breakfast, dinner and tea" Milne turns the didactic message from the first book upside down, making fun of the only female character in it. Besides: "when Kanga thought he wanted strengthening, he had a spoonful or two of Roobreakfast after meals as medicine" (*House* 34), another *mundus inversus* device.

It is, however, of profound symbolical significance that the big and strong Tigger's only suitable food is strengthening medicine. Tigger is the first dangerous animal in the idyllic nursery world. Tigers are carnivorous, so both Piglet, Rabbit, Kanga and Roo are in danger. The "harmless food" makes Tigger appear harmless. Since *Pooh* stories were at first told orally to the real Christopher Robin, and many characters in them were the boy's real toys, I can imagine that on getting Tigger, his first question was: "What do Tiggers eat?

Can he eat up Piglet?", so that the father felt obliged to make up a plausible excuse.

Tigger is the only animal who does not have a house of his own and stays with Kanga, which emphasizes his being small (notwith-standing his physical dimensions, strength, and "bounciness") as well as immature; he is not ready to live by himself and provide his own food. It is not accidental that he is adopted by an animal whom he normally would have eagerly gobbled up. He is thus further reduced and disarmed. Tigger is a child who is still at the pre-"mirror stage," which is demonstrated when he does not recognize his own reflection. He may be a baby who has just been weaned and is tasting a number of strange adult foodstuffs.

As already stated, food plays a less significant role in the sequel when the mythical time has started to turn into linear, when changes occur, and when Christopher Robin's imminent departure from the nursery first haunts and finally becomes a fact. The child's emotional development is more prominent in this book, so the food is moved into the background. Even Pooh admits: "Although Eating Honey *was* a very good thing to do, there was a moment just before you began to eat it which was better than when you were" (*House* 168; author's emphasis), an emotional sensation that precedes the physical one.

MIDNIGHT GARDENS, MAGIC WELLS

Still another common denominator in discussions of the Puer Aeter-nus-motif is *Tom's Midnight Garden,* examined, among others, by David Rees (1980), Neil Philip (1982), Humphrey Carpenter (1985), Margaret and Michael Rustin (1987), and Raymond Jones (1985), the last study being perhaps the most exhaustive and the most relevant for my line of argument.

Like the Neverland, the magical *enclosed* garden (a *locus communus* of pastoral) is a paradise, where there is always summer and fine weather, since it is evoked by Hatty's nostalgic memories. Most of the description are iteratives:

> Every night now Tom slipped downstairs to the garden. At first he
> used to be afraid that it might not be there.—

> He saw the garden at many times of day, and at different seasons—
> its favourite season was summer, with perfect weather. (49)

There is only one winter scene, which is also the last encounter between Hatty and Tom, thus suggesting departure and the inevitable movement toward growth, aging, and death. The garden symbolizes lost childhood, and like the Neverland, it offers the child a temporal retreat. Thus, as in all utopian fiction, we note a transformation of a spatial concept—garden—into a temporal state—childhood (cf Jones 1985, 213ff). In Mikhail Bakhtin's terms, we see here an illustration of the *idyllic chronotope*, an entity of space and time, secluded space—mythic time (see Bakhtin 1981). Compare the following passage to any earlier quoted description of Paradise:

> ... a great lawn where flower-beds bloomed; a towering fir-tree, and thick, beetle-browed yews that humped their shapes down two sides of the lawn; on the third side, to the right, a greenhouse almost the size of a real house; from each corner of the lawn, a path that twisted away to some other depths of garden, with other trees. (24)

Or Tom's inner vision of his endless happiness in the garden:

> He would run full tilt over the grass, leaping the flower-beds; he would peer through the glittering panes of the greenhouse—perhaps open the door and go in; he would visit each alcove and archway clipped in the yew-trees—he would climb the trees and make his way from one to another through thickly interlacing branches. When they came calling him, he would hide, silent and safe as a bird, among this richness of leaf and bough and tree-trunk. (25)

But if the spatial aspect of Paradise is clear and unequivocal, the temporal aspect is all the more complicated, built up by the subtle balance of chronos and kairos. The clock, a magical object, which has naturally been observed by all scholars, has an ambivalent function: in chronos, it takes Tom closer to his departure, in kairos, it is his password to the garden: "It would tick on to bedtime, and in that way Time was Tom's friend; but, after that, it would tick on to Saturday, and in that way Time was Tom's enemy" (153). The double nature of Time is emphasized. In general, there is more preoccupation with the notion and nature of Time in *Tom's Midnight*

Garden than in most so-called time-shift fantasies. In Chapter 21, Uncle Alan tries to explain modern scientific theories of time to Tom (modern, of course, for the 1950s, when the book was written). The much-discussed inscription on the face of the clock: "Time No Longer" (Rev. 10:1-6) is a Christian notion, definitely perceiving time as linear, as having a beginning and an end. Neil Philip views the river as a symbol of linear time (Philip 1982, 23). However, the presence of both chronos and kairos in the novel is apparent:

> In the Kitsons' flat Time was not allowed to dodge about in the unreliable, confusing way it did in the garden—forward to a tree's falling, and then back to before the fall; and then still farther back again, to a little girl's first arrival; and then forward again. No, in the flat, Time was marching steadily onwards in the way it is supposed to go: from minute to minute, from hour to hour, from day to day. (98)

Kairos is in this case equal to what may be called "memory-time," which is naturally nonlinear: everything that happens in the garden is evoked by Hatty's memories of her childhood.

> Yet perhaps Mrs Bartholomew was not solely responsible for the garden's being there ... never before this summer had she dreamed of the garden so often, and never before this summer has she been able to remember so vividly what it has *felt* like to be the little Hatty—to be longing for someone to play with and for somewhere to play. (214; author's emphasis)

So what are Hatty's memories evoked by? Tom's longing? His reluctance to grow up? A plausible explanation is that Hatty and Tom are cocreators, while the creative source itself is their innocent, prelapsarian, presexual (cf Philip 1985, 23) love.

The question of who is the ghost, which has occupied many a scholar, including myself (Nikolajeva 1988, 101ff), can be viewed in a new light here. Actually, the question is irrelevant if we consider it in terms of mythical time. In the garden, both protagonists step out of their chronos into kairos: Mrs. Bartholomew by returning to her childhood and becoming a little girl again, Tom by going into the past. They are both ghosts—or rather guests—in this paradise. When Tom says that Hatty is a ghost, she at first protests (because she thinks him a ghost), but her second reaction is much more interesting: she begins to weep saying: "I'm not dead—oh, please, Tom, I'm not dead!" (106). Are we dealing with the aging Mrs. Bartholomew's fear of death, transferred into her memories of childhood?

In his essay on *Tom's Midnight Garden*, Raymond Jones considers the twofold consequences of the child entering Eden, which we have already seen in all the previously discussed texts: restoration and entrapment. Of the two protagonists, Hatty is the one who is reluctant to grow up, most probably because she has not much to look forward to. She is a poor orphaned relative, and her prospects are limited. Tom overhears a discussion by James and his mother of what is to become of Hatty when she grows up. James suggests that they must encourage Hatty to go out, meet other people and make friends, to which his mother retorts: "She doesn't want to grow up; she wants only her garden" (138). Since Hatty is never focalized, we cannot be sure of her true feelings, but supposedly her aunt expresses her reluctance. Significantly, it is James, a male, who wishes to see Hatty grow up and join the ordered, linear world.

In contrast to Hatty, Tom is initially well aware of his own growth, for instance, when he reacts vehemently to his new room, a passage quoted in many studies: "… there are bars across the bottom of the window! … This is a nursery! I'm not a baby!" (12). But as his visits to the garden continue, he feels more and more trapped in its enchantment (the connection between the garden and Hatty's female power is something I will leave for a Freudian to speculate on). The garden offers a nearly *deadly* temptation for Tom (cf Jones 1985, 214), to stay there forever, a temptation, I may add, that almost all time travellers in children's fantasy are exposed to and more or less successfully reject—for instance, Penelope in *A Traveller in Time*, Abigail in *Playing Beatie Bow*, or Rose in *The Root Cellar* (see Nikolajeva 1991; Nikolajeva 1993; Scott 1996a).[3] This is also the temptation Wendy is subject to in the Neverland and which she withstands. This is the temptation to which C. S. Lewis makes his characters succumb in *The Last Battle*. This is the temptation Winnie struggles with in *Tuck Everlasting*.

Tom's attitude toward the newly recovered Eden is highly ambivalent. At one point, he thinks that he is stuck in Hatty's time: he goes to sleep on the floor in her bedroom, and wakes up in his own, feeling happy and relieved about it. He does not seem to be tempted to stay. However, as the novel progresses, his dilemma becomes stronger: "... suddenly he found that he did not want to go home. He wanted above all to stay here—here where he could visit the garden" (63). Home in this case means order, linearity, growing up. The garden symbolizes childhood where, as Tom suddenly realizes, he would like to stay for ever. And even measured by chronos, he stays much longer than he is originally supposed to. However, his desire of the garden is not unproblematic: "He wanted two different sets of things so badly: he wanted his mother and father and Peter and home—he really did want them, badly; and, on the other hand, he wanted the garden" (150). Observe how the meaning of home changes, just as it did in *Peter Pan*. Home is not part of the idyll here, but the obstacle, the prison. On the other hand, Tom's and Hatty's secret meetings in the garden do not imply big adventures, just nice, simple games, harmless pranks, in other words, a complete idyll, which is radically different from many time-shift stories, involving adventures, quest, and safe homecoming. In their Arcadia, the children build a tree-house—a symbolic home of their own.

It is when Tom realizes that primary time stands still while he is in the garden (quite unlike *Peter Pan*) that he feels the temptation:

> He could, after all, have both things—the garden and his family—because he could stay for ever in the garden, and yet for ever his family would be expecting him next Saturday afternoon.
>
> ...
>
> "I could stay in the garden for ever," Tom told the kitchen clock, and laughed for joy, and then shivered a little, because "for ever" sounded long and lonely. (174)

But actually he cannot stay for ever, as each time he falls asleep in Hatty's time he wakes up in his own (which also happens to Alison Uttley's character). On the last night, the garden is not there, and the loss makes Tom desperate. It is never said explicitly that Tom is in love with Hatty. She is just part of the garden, its "princess" and—although he does not know it—its creator. When she leaves the garden, he cannot enter it any more either.

Another clue to the significance of Tom's dilemma is given in the inscription on a memorial tablet at Ely Cathedral: "exchanged Time for Eternity" (184). As Raymond Jones points out (Jones 1985, 216), this indicates death; Tom's staying in the garden would be the same as dying.

Paradoxically, in the novel Hatty grows up while Tom does not, which is possible because of its peculiar temporal structure. Hatty's time goes faster than Tom's, which is illustrated by many time twists, as when Tom says, "I shall see you tomorrow," and Hatty remarks: "You always say that, and then it's often months and months before you come again" (146). In Tom's time, he comes to the garden every night. Therefore the discovery of Hatty's change is such a shock. "Hatty had been growing up, just like the other Melbournes, and Tom had never noticed it, partly because they had been together so much and partly because he was not observant of such things" (141). He is not observant because so far he has not been aware of his own growing up and the "dangers" of it. Hatty's growing up brings to his attention this dilemma. He is jealous of her life outside the garden and without him, and when she says that he is always welcome, he "noticed that she spoke to him as if he were a child and she were not" (141).

What many scholars have overlooked is Peter's role in Tom's returning home. Peter is summoned into kairos when Tom and Hatty are on top of the tower in Ely, and as Tom points out Hatty for him, Peter says "indignantly—'that's not Hatty: that's a grown-up woman!'" (189). It is thus Peter, a brother—blood relative and male—who makes Tom aware of the necessity to leave the garden. And indeed, after having spoken to Mrs. Bartholomew, Tom longs to go home. He has escaped from the temptation of the garden. If Neil Philip reads *Tom's Midnight Garden* as the story of Eden and the Fall, the pattern is somewhat distorted: Eve is not a seducer, but a Savior.

What about Hatty then? Neil Philip insists that the book is not nostalgic (Philip 1982, 24), but I have strong doubts in this matter. On the night before her wedding, Hatty thinks "of all I would be leaving behind me: my childhood and all the times I had spent in the garden—in the garden with you, Tom" (211). In the old Mrs. Bartholomew's account of the events we suddenly see the whole story from another perspective. It is not only (and maybe not primarily) the story of a young boy who is tempted to exchange time for eternity. It is the tragic story of an old woman who knows from experience that time is irreversible. So, a feminist critic might inquire, why is it *Tom's* midnight garden?

The three texts I have so far discussed show a clearly ambivalent attitude toward growing up. The implication becomes still more transparent, if we consider as an intertext the folktale about the realm or island of immortality. It is known in its more archaic mythic form, for instance in the epic of Gilgamesh, and the Irish myth of Tir Nan Og. The legend of Rip van Winkle, mentioned in *Tom's Midnight Garden*, is a variant of it, and the land of Shangri-La in *Lost Horison* is a famous literary interpretation. In the folktale, the hero sets out to seek the land of immortality and seems to find it successively in three places, only to discover that, however slowly, time does pass there too. He eventually comes to the land of fairies where he stays for three (alternatively seven) days, and going back to his own country, often to visit his old mother, discovers that many centuries have passed, and all his family and friends have died long ago (see also Bak 1987).

The fear of growing up in children's fiction goes back to the search for immortality, caused by fear of death, in the folktale. Fear of death and fear of growing up are closely interconnected, since the awareness of growing up and growing old unavoidably leads to the insight of your own inevitable mortality.

In *Tuck Everlasting*, the dream of immortality, expressed in the fairy tale, is transformed into a nightmare. The possible origins of the magical well are explained in passing: "Pa thinks it's something left over from—well, from some other plan for the way the world should be ... Some plan that didn't work out too good" (41). While the Tuck family may between themselves discuss whether their situation is a blessing or a curse, the author is quite explicit, and the critics note the same: "The Tucks are trapped in their immortality: trapped physically, because they cannot die, and also trapped mentally, unable to grow or change or adapt" (Aippersbach 1990, 86).

The very first sentence of the novel introduces the image of the eternal wheel in which the Tucks are for ever caught: "The first week of August hangs at the very top of summer, the top of the live-long year, like the highest seat of a Ferris wheel when it pauses in its turning" (3). The family reunions every tenth year, at the same place, at the same time of year, amplify the sense of their going in circles. Mae's music box is another fascinating image of eternity, always going round, always playing the same melody. Winnie's grand-mother believes it to be elfs' music, and in a way it is, music connected with the enchantment and its temptations.

Although the Tucks have decided that the magical water is evil and must be kept a secret, the attitude of the four family members is different. Tuck says explicitly: "I want to grow again ... and change. And if that means I got to move on at the end of it, then I want that, too. ... it's something you don't find out how you feel until afterwards" (64). Tuck is the only one who somehow has the hope that the curse can be lifted. He has what he calls a good dream "where we're all in heaven and never heard of Treegap." His wife discourages him: "It's no use having that dream ... Nothing's going to change" (10). Mae's opinion is never expressed, but on the other hand it is she who acts when real threat comes.

One of the most difficult aspects of their situations is that they cannot stay long at the same place, which also means that they can never acquire friends or develop affections. While Tuck and Mae have each other, which they state with a sense of reconciliation, Jesse, being for ever stuck at the age of seventeen, has never had a chance to experience love. However, Jesse, with the optimism of the youth, is the most positive of the family: "Just think of all the things we've seen in the world! All the things we're going to see!" (43). Miles is probably the one affected the hardest, having seen his children grow up and his wife leave him in aversion. Miles is also the one who suggests trying to do something useful instead of hiding away. This suggestion, however, does not seem to imply anything like the plans that the man in the yellow suit has for the utilization of the magical water, selling it "to certain people, people who deserve it" (97). When he accuses the Tucks of being selfish he is right in a way, and only his overtly commercial goals prevent the reader from taking his standpoint.

While the Tucks's destiny has been decided by fatal circum-stances eighty-seven years earlier and is irreversible, Winnie is free to make a choice. When we first meet her, Winnie is unhappy with what she is:

> ... I want to be by myself for a change ... I'm not exactly sure what
> I'd do, you know, but something interesting—something that's all
> mine. Something that would make some kind of difference in the

world. It'd be nice to have a new name, to start with, one that's not
all worn out from being called so much. (14f)

Winnie wants to run away, but is scared. She is too young to start on
a quest:

> The characters in the stories she read always seemed to go off
> without a thought of care, but in real life—well, the world was a
> dangerous place. People were always telling her so. And she would
> not be able to manage without protection. They were always telling
> her that, too. (22f)

Winnie's attitude toward her adventure is very ambivalent, and she
changes her mind about the Tucks all the time. She feels safe when
they give her food, but she is terribly homesick when she goes to
bed: "Her joy on the road that morning had completely disappeared;
the wide world shrank and the oldest fears rolled freely in her
consciousness" (68). Significantly, the decisive factor in her trust in
the Tucks is Jesse, who turns out to be a cunning seducer, suggesting
that she wait until she is seventeen and then drink the water. He says
that his parents and Miles don't know how to enjoy it: "... we could
have a good time that never, never stopped" (72). This passage
shows clearly that Jesse is very young and immature; but he will
never be able to learn the lesson which Winnie is about to learn.

Tuck explains to Winnie about the Wheel of life, the great cycle
of life in which everyone has a part. In this, he makes Winnie aware
of her own mortality, and her reaction is normal for a child of her
age: "I don't want to die" (63). Tuck's further comment is addressed
to the reader as much as to Winnie: "... dying's part of the wheel,
right there next to being born. You can't pick out the pieces you like
and leave the rest. ... You can't have living without dying. You can't
call it living, what we got" (63f). Tuck tries to make Winnie realize
the dangers of the magical water, since he believes—or knows for
sure—that most people will not be able to resist the temptation. His
concerns are global, while he seems to leave Winnie to contemplate
her personal dilemma on her own. Miles is more intent on her
realizing the consequences and, in the first place, reconciling with
the idea of death. When he takes her fishing, and she suddenly
cannot stand the idea of killing fish, Miles comments: "People have

to be meat-eaters sometimes .... It's the natural way. And that means killing things" (88).[4]

It is interesting to see how Babbitt has built up her narrative with the repetition of the key-word "forever." When the man in the yellow suit first comes and asks Winnie how long her family has lived in this place, she says "forever." Her reaction reflects a child's perception of time, since anything that goes beyond her grand-mother, whom she knows, is indeed "forever." When the Tucks have kidnapped her and promise to take her home the next day, it feels like eternity: "Tomorrow! It was like being told she would be kept away *forever*. She wanted to go home now, at once, rush back to the safety of the fence and her mother's voice from the window" (34, my emphasis). In the Tucks' cottage, Winnie becomes aware of the contrast between the order of her home (linear) and the chaos of the Tucks' home (circular): "Maybe it's because they think they have *forever* to clean it up" (53; my emphasis). After she has helped Mae escape from the prison and the Tucks are gone, Winnie uses the water from the bottle Jesse has given her to make her pet toad immortal. She does this on an impulse, because she feels a prisoner in her home; besides, she knows there is more water in the woods, and she can find it. To the toad she says: "You're safe. Forever." (133). In Epilogue, the Tucks come back after seventy years, to find the rural idyll changed into urban civilization, and to find Winnie's grave in the cemetery, thus confirming the choice she has made. What they encounter is a toad who does not care about the traffic around him: "Durn fool thing must think it's going to live forever." The leitmotif of the book is marvelously and subtly replayed.

A WISE PROGENITRIX OR A SEDUCTIVE WITCH?

I would not like to create an illusion that Puer Aeternus is a totally Anglo-Saxon invention. Hans-Heino Ewers sets the theme of a child not growing up in a wider context, comparing Peter Pan with child characters in the works of German Romantic authors as well as contemporary German language children's writers such as Michael Ende and Christine Nöstlinger (Ewers 1985). In her comprehensive study of contemporary children's fiction, Gundel Mattenklott also discusses *Moomin* stories, *Pippi Longstocking*, and *King Matt*. The Childlike Empress in *The Neverending Story* is a superb image of a child never growing up, however, she is not a protagonist but a guide/Anima in an otherwise typical quest narrative. Mattenklott also dwells upon the difference between the idea of child power in *King Matt* and *Pippi Longstocking*, demonstrating that while Korczak's conclusion is its impossibility, *Pippi* is totally based on the idea of carnival. But, she continues, a carnival that does not end is not carnival any more (Mattenklott 1989, 184). Mattenklott sees the interruption of carnival in the everyday, work and death. I would like to take this a little further.

Pippi Longstocking, the favorite character of Swedish children's literature, Pippi the rebel, the norm-breaker, has been subjected to serious critical scrutiny in the English-speaking world. Even one of the more subtle evaluations of Pippi uses her to illustrate the essence of children's literature as escape (Moebius 1985). *Pippi* books are often described in the English language reference works as "comic fantasy." Pippi herself has been compared to two American characters, the Cat in the Hat (Metcalf 1995, 78f) and Curious George (Moebius 1985); in both cases the antiauthoritarian spirit of Pippi has been recognized, even though the emphasis has been rather on mischief, escape and compensation. Quite a typical statement about *Pippi* books is "a mock-heroic affirmation of children's autonomy in the face of their powerlessness in the adult world" (Saltman 1987, 83). This is undoubtedly a correct description; indeed, empowering the child is the essence of *Pippi* stories (see also Nikolajeva 1997b).

In *Pippi* books, adults are presented as ridiculous and hypocritical. Pippi is told that children should be seen and not heard—a standard formula of traditional Swedish child-rearing—whereupon she happily retorts: "it's nice if people are happy just to look at me! I must see how it feels to be used just for decoration" (*Pippi in the South Seas* 24).

Pippi's extraordinary strength may seem to be her weapon against adults, however, her challenge of adult order is expressed mainly through language, through interrogation of arbitrary linguistic practices presented as unconditional laws. In fact, Pippi uses her strength only against vile, unfair (and exclusively male) adversaries, like Mighty Adolf, or the burglars Bloom and Thunder-Karlsson. In all other situations, Pippi uses her wits, as in the much-quoted interlocution with the school teacher. Adults in *Pippi* can never acknowledge the linguistic genius of a child. Pippi's "deconstruction" of language through her inadequate spelling skills gives the child readers a confirmation of their own language proficiency. The arbitrariness of the spelling rules imposed by adults is interrogated. At the question-and-answer bee in *Pippi in the South Seas*, Pippi says: "S-e-e-s-i-k is the way I have always spelled it, and it seems to have worked out just fine" (45). Astrid Lindgren allows her character to defy the dictatorship of norms and conventions, of dull reality, of authority, of structure, and order.

Like Peter Pan, Pippi does not want to grow up. However, her reasons are different from Peter's. She does not want to grow into a respectable lady "with a veil and three double chins." She does not want to become what the authorities want her to become: ordinary, obedient, and dull. Pippi defies the capriciously prescribed order by doing as she pleases, which includes walking backwards, or sleeping with her feet on her pillow, or watering flowers in the pouring rain. Pippi refuses to accept that children "must have someone to advise them, and ... go to school to learn the multiplication tables" (40). Pippi's attitude to authorities is marvelously illustrated by the phrase: "Policemen are the very best things I know. Next to rhubarb pudding" (41).

In the orphanage, Pippi learns, she will not be allowed to keep her horse and her monkey, two attributes which reinforce the child's closeness to nature, maybe even her savagery, "monkeyhood" as Moebius chooses to call it (Moebius 1985, 44). Pippi promptly refuses to go to an orphanage, thus rejecting the order imposed by adults. She refuses to be socialized. She is what every child dreams of being, strong, independent and free in confrontation with the world of adults. Unlike the typical underdog character of many children's books, Pippi is secure, self-assured, strong, and rich from the beginning. Everybody wants to be friends with her, and by the end of the first book, when Pippi rescues two small boys from the fire, even adults have to accept her.

The plot of the *Pippi* books is the reverse of the most traditional pattern of children's literature: home (boring, but secure)—adventure (exciting, but dangerous)—home, which may also be described as order-chaos-order. Pippi comes from chaos to disturb order, from adventure to home which is boring and therefore must be turned into adventure. Pippi's function in the story is to stir and wake up the old, stale, conservative, slumbering Swedish society, represented by the philistines of the tiny little town. But she herself does not develop, since she is, like Mary Poppins, perfect from the beginning. Instead, she acts as a catalyst.

Pippi's excess in food marks her defiance of any form of limitation. Pippi's role in the stories is to provide food for others, while with her own joyful eating Pippi sets an example for other children. Her tall-tales, often concerning food and eating, have the same purpose. Eva-Maria Metcalf views the function of food in Lindgren's book chiefly as adaptation to the needs of young readers (Metcalf 1995, 40). However, to reduce the function of food in *Pippi* books to satisfying the readers' desires is to underestimate her totally. Pippi has gigantic proportions both in her cooking ("at least five hundred cookies," 25), in her shopping ("thirty-six pounds of candy … sixty lollipops and seventy-two packages of caramels," *Pippi Goes on Board* 23) and in her consuming ("She heaped as many cakes as she could onto a plate, threw five lumps of sugar into a coffee cup, emptied half the cream pitcher into her cup" 121), and she also eats up a whole cake as if it is nothing (122).

But she is just as generous when she invites her friends for a meal, asking Tommy and Annika to have breakfast with her as soon as they meet, serving coffee and cookies both on the porch and up in a tree, or taking them out on a picnic and on a planned shipwreck, not to mention the wonderful travel to the exotic paradise of the South Seas. When shopping, Pippi behaves like a little Robin Hood, taking from the rich (adults) and giving to the poor (children), especially in the magnificently carnivalesque scene in *Pippi Goes on Board* when she extravagantly pours sweets and toys over the town's children.

Pippi can be generous with food because she has a neverending supply of it. While children in traditional stories seek and find the source of their individual well-being, Pippi is herself the source of wealth. In Pippi, the primary sense is, her wildness notwithstanding, that of security, home, peace, and harmony. Her role in the story is not that of a desirous child, but of a giving, nurturing Progenitrix, the fertility goddess, a figure which also appears in other Astrid Lindgren works. Let us not be deceived by Pippi's childlike appearance; it is merely a disguise.

Pippi has no magic powers and no magic objects to assist her. In the system of characters, whether we prefer Propp's folktale model,

Greimas's actant-model, or Campbell's "hero with a thousand faces," Pippi is not a hero, but rather a helper. In fact, she is not even the main character of the story, in the same way that Peter Pan is not, if we accept as the criterion for the main character some form of development or at least a clear focalization (this interpretation of Pippi is not a common assumption, cf Metcalf 1995, 68). We never share Pippi's point of view. Her role is to set the plot in motion, not to be a primary part of it. Thus, rather than finding herself a helpless victim of evil forces, she stages a shipwreck. She can even turn a fire into a big celebration. In other words, she neither seeks trouble nor shuns it, she is trouble herself.

Of course, Pippi is also the archetypal orphan child, or pretends to be. Her parents, her mother in Heaven "watching her little girl through a peephole in the sky" (14), and her father, "formerly the Terror of the Sea, now a cannibal king" (54), may just as well be imaginary. Both the physical appearance of the father and Pippi's wild adventures in the South Seas in the sequels may be just another tall-tale (a daring, but not impossible interpretation). Who is Pippi? Where does she come from?

As already mentioned, apart from her unusual strength, Pippi does not possess any magical powers. But at least one habit betrays Pippi's supernatural origin. She can eat toadstools. Any dictionary of myth will tell us that this ability signals belonging to "the other world." Pippi is a witch. She is nice, generous, and beneficial, but she is still a witch. Just as the absence of shadow or mirror reflection reveals a vampire, the witch's eating habits reveal her true nature.

> "What have you got in your basket?" asked Annika. "Is it something good?"
> "I wouldn't tell you for a thousand dollars," said Pippi. (79f)

Since Pippi has just eaten a toadstool, Annika's question is not as stupid as it may seem. Pippi has never given them food that has not been good. Annika wonders—subconsciously—whether Pippi is about to initiate them into her witch food, or whether she will once again adjust her witch habits to humans.

Pippi packs the basket while Tommy and Annika run home to ask their mother's permission to go on a picnic with Pippi. The contents of the basket is a surprise for them, as for the reader. Pippi makes them shut their eyes while she sets out the picnic:

There were good sandwiches with meatballs and ham, a whole pile of sugared pancakes, several little brown sausages, and three pineapple puddings. For, you see, Pippi had learned cooking from the cook on her father's ship. (81)

We may think that we are just dealing with another of Astrid Lindgren's many lavish enumerations of food. However, we see the nice picnic as Tommy and Annika see it when they have opened their eyes. The last statement in the quote above comes from Pippi. Pippi's background with her life on her father's ship may be just another tall-tale, so she may have had her cooking lessons anywhere. And why should Tommy and Annika shut their eyes? Maybe Pippi makes the food appear from an empty basket. Maybe she sets the picnic table with witch food—toads, snakes and toadstools—and casts a spell on it to make it look like delicacies?

On another occasion Pippi betrays herself still more, when she says that she used to shoot an antelope or a llama and eat the meat raw. "Raw or Cooked" is the basic opposition in human culture (as well as the title of Claude Lévi-Strauss's famous study in myth and anthropology), and Pippi's eating raw meat confirms once again that she belongs to nature, that she is "an alien child," a "nonhuman."

The very last episode in the Pippi trilogy depicts Pippi tempting her friends with a magical device which will prevent them from growing up. The ritual around the chillilug pill recalls the Holy Communion in its solemnity:

They turned the Christmas tree lights out. ... They sat down in silence in a circle in the middle of the floor, holding one another by the hands. Pippi gave Tommy and Annika each a chillilug pill. Chills ran up the down their spines. Just think, in a second the powerfull pill would be down in their stomachs and then they would never have to grow up. How marvelous that would be! (*Pippi in the South Seas* 123)

The Holy Communion, too, promises eternal life. What does Pippi promise Tommy and Annika? Is she in fact a little Mephistopheles inviting the children into her demonic realm? It is quite easy to interpret the chillilug pill in many various ways, including drugs or

Prozac. Anyway, it is witch food. According to Pippi, she has been given the pills by an old Indian chieftain (that is, a witch-doctor, a shaman), and we can only hope that their power has worn off. It is time for the children to leave the Nurturing Mother and start coping on their own.

Pippi, on the other hand, chooses—or rather has already chosen before—to conserve herself for ever. Liberating the child in the "charming, ... good, well brought up, and obedient" (16) Tommy and Annika and making at least their mother realize the necessity of this liberation reflects the writer's nostalgic longing for everlasting childhood.

A GROWN-UP'S NOSTALGIA

Still another example outside the English-language sphere is *The Little Prince*.[5] Unlike *Peter Pan*, it is perhaps not a self-evident example of reluctance to grow up. However, the little prince is clearly an eternal child and a very extraordinary child. He can speak with animals and with plants. His little realm, a planet no larger than a house, is safe and nice. He "has never been either hungry or thirsty" (88). He does, however, cook breakfast over one of his two active volcanoes. He has tools when he needs them: a spade, a watering can, a screen and a glass globe for the flower. It is never explained where they come from; as in any true idyll they appear merely because of the child's wish to have them. There is one thing lacking which would make the picture of a pastoral complete, and that is a little lamb, which the little prince asks the pilot to give him. The world is so small that the lamb will not go astray—there are, in other words, no restrictions. The little prince is the ruler of his realm, but he has to maintain order, for instance, by weeding baobabs and cleaning volcanoes. His reward is, among other things, the fulfilment of a child's most Romantic wishes, like sunsets. At one point the prince says: "I am very fond of sunsets. Come, let us go look at a sunset now" (29). His planet is a paradise where this wish is possible.

What then is there to disturb the idyll? Paradoxically, the very symbol of paradise, the rose. The rose is a female, and her relationship with the little prince is tangibly erotic. The little prince does not know how to handle it. He runs away, because he instinctively recognizes the nature of this relationship and is scared to accept it. "I was too young to know how to love her ...," he confesses with regret (39). We may of course regard the little prince's journey as a usual fairy-tale quest, but that would be to oversimplify it. He is trying to escape from his own sexuality, which reminds him of the necessity to grow up. When the snake asks: "What has brought you here?" he says: "I have been having some trouble with a flower" (70)—a beautiful euphemism.

The little prince's voyage is without doubt a quest for his own identity. But he only discovers grown-ups who disappoint him. He has left his childhood behind, but he cannot accept that fact. He learns about adult ambitions: to rule, to be admired, to be rich, to have knowledge. His recurrent statement is: "The grown-ups are very strange."

His most important insights come from the fox: "One only understands the things that one tamed ... men have no more time to understand anything. They buy things all ready at the shops. But there is no shop anywhere where one can buy friendship ..." (81). The fox explains the philosophy of childhood to the little prince and the reader. The keyword here is "time." Time on the tiny planet, childhood time, regulated by recurrent sunsets, was circular, mythic, eternal, sacred. Time on Earth, the profane time, measured by clocks and timetables, the grown-up time, is linear. The little prince understands it still better after having met the merchant with the thirst-quenching pills which save you fifty-three minutes in every week.

> "And what do I do with these fifty-three minutes?"
> "Anything you like...."
> "As for me," said the little prince to himself, "if I had fifty-three minutes to spend as I liked, I should walk at my leisure towards a spring of fresh water." (86f)

The fox also reminds the little prince about the ritual and iterative time, by asking him to come at the same time every day:

> "... If, for example, you come at four o'clock in the afternoon, then at three o'clock I shall begin to be happy. I shall feel happier and happier as the hour advances. At four o'clock, I shall already be worrying and jumping about. I shall show you how happy I am! But

if you come at just any time, I shall never know at what hour my heart
is to be ready to greet you ... One must observe the proper rites. ..."
    "What is a rite?" asked the little prince.
    "Those also are actions too often neglected," said the fox. "They
are what make one day different from other days, one hour from other
hours." (81f)

The following has always been for me one of the most mysterious
and fascinating passages in children's fiction: "So the little prince
tamed the fox. And when the hour of his departure drew near—"
(83). Why is it necessary for the little prince to depart when he has
just acquired a longed-for friend? What a strange notion of a happy
ending. However, in terms of a mythic narrative, it is perfectly
consistent. The fox is not a friend in the ordinary sense of the word,
he is a guide, a guru, The Wise Old Man in Jungian terminology (cf
Franz 1981, 89–95. See also James Higgins's interpretation of the fox
in Higgins 1996, 58ff, and 73ff). When he has passed his wisdom to
the hero, his role is played out.
    The lesson the little prince learns from the fox is that his rose is
unique, that "it is only with the heart that one can see rightly; what
is essential is invisible to the eye" (84)—all the most important
secrets of childhood. He realizes that he wants to go back to his
paradise, and there is only one way to do it. The snake, the first
creature he has met on Earth, has promised: "I can help you, some
day, if you grow too homesick for your own planet" (72). As in so
many other books, death is the only sure way to stop growing up.
A snake, who once was the reason Man lost his paradise, is here a
vehicle to regain it (von Franz interprets the snake as the little
prince's Anima: Franz 1981, 76-85).
    So far, I have been speaking about the little prince, keeping to the
child level of the narrative. What, then, about the narrator? For a
young reader, he is most probably just another storyteller, one of
those many didactic adults who say: "Now, dear children, I will tell
you a story." Obviously, the text is significantly more complex. The
narrator is also the character in his own story (homodiegetic), but it
can be argued whether the protagonist of the story is the narrator
himself (autodiegetic) or the little prince. Further, the narrator is
telling the story six years after the event, that is, from another
fictional level (extradiegetic). In her evaluation of the novel, Isabelle

Jan is generally negative toward it on the grounds that it detaches children from adults and makes children feel they are unique (Jan 1973, 76f). According to this judgment, Jan ignores the important difference between the author and the narrator. Who is this character-narrator (I will henceforth call him the pilot) and what is his true relation to the little prince? Observe once again that while Marie-Louise von Franz is discussing the man Exupery and his relation to his own creation, my concern is exclusively the fictitious textual figure.

In his dedication, apologizing to young readers for dedicating his book to a grown-up, the author says: "All grown-ups were once children—although few of them remember it "(5). Apparently, the pilot is one of these few privileged adults who have not forgotten, who actually have remained partly children when they have grown up. At least he seems to be wholly on the child's side—or pretends to be, when he says: "Grown-ups never understand anything by themselves, and it is tiresome for children to be always and forever explaining things to them" (8f). This is a voice trying to share secrets with his young readers.

The contrast between children and adults constitutes an essential part of the book (cf Higgins 1996, 25f). Children's topics of conversation are boa constrictors, primeval forests, and stars. Adult topics are bridge, golf, politics, and neckties. Children and adults evaluate friends in different ways:

> They never say to you, "What does his voice sound like? What games does he love best? Does he collect butterflies?" Instead, they demand: "How old is he? How many brothers has he? How much does he weigh? How much money does his father make?" (20f)

The same goes for houses. If you say to an adult:

> "I saw a beautiful house made of rosy brick, with geraniums in the windows and doves on the roof," they would not be able to get any idea of that house at all. You would have to say to them: "I saw a house that cost £4,000." Then they would exclaim: "Oh, what a pretty house that is!" (21)

So the pilot is a childlike grown-up who has retained his innocence of heart, but has given up hope ever to find a soulmate among adults. One day, stranded with his crashed plane in the Sahara desert, he meets the little prince. A desert is as far away as it can be from a childhood Arcadia, and the pilot is facing death: "It was a question of life or death for me: I had scarcely enough drinking water to last a week" (10). Reading the text on an adult level, we cannot help interpreting the little prince as a nostalgic adult's reveries and reminiscences of his own childhood.

> If I try to describe him here, it is to make sure that I shall not forget him. To forget a friend is sad. Not everyone has had a friend. And if I forget him, I may become like the grown-ups who are no longer interested in anything but figures. ...(22)

Here, by his "friend" the narrator means himself as a child (although I would avoid using the overused term "inner child"). Facing death, he feels an urge to return to the paradise of his childhood, because he suddenly realizes that, his attempts to remain childlike notwithstanding, he is no longer a child:

> My friend never explained anything to me. He thought, perhaps, that I was like himself. But I, alas, do not know how to see sheep through the walls of boxes. Perhaps I am a little like the grown-ups. I *have had* to grow up. (22f, my emphasis)

As an adult the pilot has lost his innocence, which he states with deep regret.

The well which the pilot together with the little prince finds in the desert may suggest many symbolic interpretations (see e.g. Higgins 1996, 48ff). "The well that we had come to was not like the wells of the Sahara. The wells of the Sahara are more like holes dug in the sand. This one was like a well in a village" (90). The village reminds us once again of Arcadia.

However, the pilot is all the time aware of his approaching death. "I felt myself frozen by the sense of something irreparable" (98). He is dying of thirst in the desert, but he translates his misery into the little prince's. In his vision (hallucinations? death agony?), the little prince does not want him to come and watch: "I shall look as if I were suffering. I shall look as if I were dying" (101) "I shall look as if I were dead; and that will not be true ..." (102). This is a rite of passage, a promise of resurrection. It may be tempting to see the little prince as a Christ figure (cf Gagnon 1984, 68f).

The instant before death, the pilot has come to an insight and a reconciliation. Not surprisingly, the insight takes the iterative form:

> In one of the stars *I shall be living*. In one of them I shall be laughing ... You will *always* be my friend. You will want to laugh with me. And you will *sometimes* open your window ... And your friends will be properly astonished to see you laughing as you look up at the sky! Then you will say to them, 'Yes, the stars *always* make me laugh!' (100, my emphasis)

The pilot returns to the eternity of childhood through the only possible gate.

NOTES

1. Another example of an author who lost a brother in early age is Antoine de Saint-Exupéry, whose *The Little Prince* also depicts an eternal child. I am discussing this text later in the present chapter.

2. On the strong sense of make-believe in *Peter Pan*, see Tucker 1982, 47f.

3. There are two well-known cases of time travellers who prefer to stay in the past, mainly because it offers more than their own time: the little orphan Imogen in *The Story of the Amulet,* and Dickie in *Harding's Luck.*

4. This idea was probably not as controversial in 1975, when the novel was written, as it is today, when especially young people often become vegetarians for ethical reasons. The novel takes place in 1880, when vegetarianism was an alien notion in the Western world. As I have pointed out earlier, the difference between meat and vegetarian food is just as essential in human culture as that between raw and cooked food; significantly, the consuming of meat is more archaic and therefore more connected with the cyclical time, of which the Tucks are a part. Therefore killing for food is indeed natural for Miles.

5. Marie-Louise von Franz uses this novel as a master text in her psycho-analytical lectures *Puer Aeternus;* she has a biographical bias, analyzing the author rather than the text. However, many observations in her book are relevant for my argument. See Franz, 1981.

Chapter 5

Picnic in the Unknown, or There and Back Again

"There and back again" is the subtitle of J. R. R. Tolkien's *The Hobbit*, as well as the central pattern of movement in many children's novels. These take their protagonists into unfamiliar worlds and let them undergo trials or perform heroic deeds, but bring them back safely into the familiar world.

In this chapter, I will examine some texts where the circular, mythical pattern of time is temporarily broken, and the characters take their first steps away from the idyllic security of home, meet dangers, and are subject to trials.

It is probably necessary to explain why I have chosen to describe what is usually rather solemnly named "quest" by a much more prosaic term "picnic." The fact is that in most quest stories for children, as I will show, the protagonists, unlike the hero in myth (or a novice during initiation), are liberated from the necessity to suffer the consequences of their actions. What is described is not the real rite of passage, but merely play or, to follow Bakhtin's notion, carnival. The question of consequences and the characters' responsibility will be central in my discussion, since taking responsibility for their actions and gaining experience from their adventures is also the most important deviation from the innocence which was the predominant tone of the texts discussed in previous chapters.

YOU ARE DEAD. PRESS ESCAPE TO PLAY AGAIN

The so-called Secondary World fantasy is probably the best illustration of the picnic pattern. The story starts in the everyday, in a recognizable, realistic world. Then the protagonist—most often a collective protagonist, a group of children, siblings, or friends—is by magical means transported into another magical or mythical realm, where there is a task to perform, for instance, an evil creature to get rid of. The innocent child is transformed into a hero, and furnished not only with material attributes (sword, horse) but wisdom, courage, and spiritual strength. When the task is completed, the character returns to the primary world. The reader identification with the character is stronger than in a fairy tale, since the frame story is related to the reader's own reality.

The pattern leaves room for many interpretations, including psychoanalytical, in which the evil forces of the Secondary World are understood as projections of the dark side of the hero—his Shadow (see e.g. Veglahn 1987; Sigman 1992). The transportation into the Otherworld is most often the result of some form of "lack" (Propp) or "split" (Jung) in the protagonist while he is still in the real world.

Among texts used in discussions of Secondary World fantasy we find *Alice in Wonderland*, the Narnia Chronicles, *Elidor, Mio, My Son*, and *The Neverending Story* (see e.g. Toijer-Nilsson 1981; Swinfen 1984; Nikolajeva 1988). A recent addition, as yet not featured in criticism, is Philip Pullman's *Northern Lights/The Golden Compass* and sequel *The Subtle Knife*. I have chosen the Narnia Chronicles as the most representative text, and will concentrate on the first novel, *The Lion, the Witch and the Wardrobe*. Since the Narnia novels have been examined many times from many different perspectives (see Sammonds 1979; Schakel 1979; Rustin 1987, 40–58; Edwards 1988; Manlove 1993), I will only focus here on what is really relevant for my discussion.

A brief plot summary illustrates the very essence of "there and back again:" from real England during the Second World War, the four Pevensie children find themselves going through a wardrobe into another world, a mythical land, ruled by a wicked White Witch who has imposed an eternal winter on the once happy kingdom. The children take part in a battle against the Witch, led by Aslan the

Lion, Narnia's protector. They then become kings and queens of Narnia, until they one day go back through the wardrobe into their own world. In the sequels, the children enter Narnia in different ways and perform various tasks there.

One important aspect of the secondary world in Narnia novels has been discussed by all critics: the relation between primary and secondary time. When Lucy first enters Narnia she stays there for a few hours and returns in dismay, thinking her brothers and sister are worried about her. However they do not even notice her absence. The Professor explains the nature of fantasy time to the children:

> If she [Lucy] had got into another world, I should not at all be surprised that the other world had a separate time of its own; so that however long you stayed there it would never take up any of *our* time. (48; author's emphasis)

So far, this phenomenon has been interpreted by critics, including myself, as a way of separating worlds and accentuating their independent existence. It is also a convenient narrative device, since the characters can be absent from their own world as long as they please without their relatives getting worried. The principle was introduced in Edith Nesbit's time-travel novels (see e.g. Nikolajeva 1988, 63–74; Nikolajeva 1996, 168f). There is, however, a direct connection to archaic thought in its suspension of profane time during a ritual (cf Eliade 1955, 36), just as the idea of primary and secondary worlds goes back to the division of archaic universe into sacred and profane space. In narratology, a side story which does not take up any of the primary narrative time is called *paralepsis*. Since narratologists seldom have knowledge of children's or popular fiction, I have never met paralepsis exemplified by fantasy in their works, but the temporal structure of Narnia books is an excellent example of this device.

Let us consider Narnian time in terms of chronos and kairos. The real, primary time is linear, and the story is firmly fixed at a specific chronological moment: "during the war" (9). In *The Magician's Nephew*, which is the flashback of the suite, primary time is switched back, but is still quite definable: "when your grandfather was a child … Mr. Sherlock Holmes was still living in Baker Street and the Bastables were looking for treasure in the Lewisham Road" (9).

Entering Narnia, the children leave the linear time behind and enter not only another world, but the mythical, cyclical time. In this time, death is reversible: Aslan is killed and resurrected, and he can also bring the enchanted stone figures to life again. One of the evil schemes of the White Witch is to stop the flow of time altogether, imposing the eternal winter (= period of nonbeing, death) in Narnia. Aslan's death and resurrection—a performance of the ritual of the returning god, with its pagan rather than Christian meaning—restores the cyclical time. Spring comes, as it always has come after winter, as it always will come. The idyllic setting is recovered, Narnia is brought back into its prelapsarian state, as created by Aslan at the dawn of time (described in *The Magician's Nephew*).

The restoration of time implies that the children will now be able to grow up (turned into stone statues, as has been the White Witch's intention, they would have remained children for ever). Indeed, they grow up, but the linearity of time is treated casually, and basically in iterative: "long and happy was their reign," "much of their time was spent," "for a long time there would be," "they … grew and changed as the years passed over them" (166). This is not the linearity of a "realistic" story, but the "lived happily ever after" of a fairy tale. However, the circularity and the iterative are brought abruptly to an end by a singulative event: the appearance of the wish-granting White Stag (amazingly little has been said by critics about this marginal, but powerful symbol). The grown-up Kings and Queens of Narnia are brought safely back to their own world and become children again. The wonderful adventure has been merely a "time-out," a picnic. As in modern computer games, when things become too scary or complicated, you are allowed to press the Escape button and play again. This is exactly what the children do in the sequels, starting over and over again from the same point, until they are too old to be involved.

Although it may seem a side argument, I would like to demonstrate how the trials in the Secondary World are supported by the ritual function of food. A less conspicuous detail in the Narnia Chronicles, food is used to emphasize some basic relations between the visitors to the Otherworld and its inhabitants.

During her first stay in Narnia, Lucy is invited to tea with Mr. Tumnus the faun. He promises her "toast—and sardines—and cake" (17). Indeed, on the table there is "a nice brown egg, lightly boiled, for *each of them*" (my emphasis; this must be inspired by Lewis's memories of the war time in England, when eggs were rationed to one every other week; the story takes place during the war, so the wonderful food is supposed to be a miracle for the evacuated child Lucy), "and then buttered toast, and then toast with honey, and then a sugar-topped cake" (19f).

In his well-known essay "On three ways of writing for children" C. S. Lewis mentions the reaction of a father to this scene: "Ah, I see how you got to that. If you want to please grown-up readers you give them sex, so you thought to yourself, 'That won't go for children, what shall I give them instead? I know! The little blighters like plenty of good eating'" (Lewis 1980, 207). Lewis proceeds to admit that he likes good food himself. More important, he rejects the way of "giving the audience what it wants." Unfortunately he thus fails to acknowledge the parallel between food and sexuality, either being insincere or naive, or both. As I have repeatedly shown, meals in myths and fairy tales are circumlocutions of sexual intercourse, which, in its turn, is the necessary stage in a rite of passage. I doubt that Lewis was unaware of the symbolic and ritual significance of food, but since he pretended to be writing for children he had to observe the proprieties.

Apart from the trivial explanation that Lewis himself liked good food, there is naturally a symbolic, or ritual, significance to the shared tea. A shared meal—which we all know in its refined form as the Holy Communion—is the foremost symbol for affinity. Lewis was well-acquainted with mythology. The faun is the first person Lucy meets in Narnia. Our previous experience of stories prompts us that food comes from the good. Thus we immediately assume that the faun is a good creature. As it is, it is not totally true, since the faun is running the White Witch's errand and tries to deceive Lucy. At the same time, the shared meal prevents the faun from turning in Lucy to his ruler. When you have broken bread with someone, you are committed. A shared meal is a covenant.

When Edmund comes to Narnia after Lucy, he meets another person, the White Witch that the faun has told Lucy about. At this stage, our reading experience prompts us again that we are now dealing with the evil side. Edmund receives enchanted food which ties him to the Witch, in the same manner that the shared tea has tied the faun and Lucy, but this happens against Edmund's wish or knowledge. He may himself choose the food he desires, and he chooses Turkish Delight, a very extravagant wish from a wartime child. "Edmund had never tasted anything more delicious" (37). Why are then we, the readers, alerted and do not trust the Witch? We only have the faun's word about her being evil. However, she talks and acts in a way that betrays her. Among other things, we learn that she knows "that this was enchanted Turkish Delight and that anyone who had once tasted it would want more and more of it, and would even, if they were allowed, go on eating it till they killed themselves" (38). This is something as unusual in children's literature as a description of drug addiction, but in the first place it is a ritual act: Edmund has accepted the food from the evil forces, therefore he is in alliance with them. Even though he realizes that the Witch may be dangerous, he has no control over his desires: "But he still wanted to taste that Turkish Delight again more than he wanted anything else" (42). At the same time he feels sick, an echo from old didactic stories for children. Lucy and the faun eat healthy food—probably with the exception of the cake—while Edmund revels in sweets, eating up a whole box and craving more. The evil food makes him sick.

The children in the story (and the readers with them) are forced to choose sides. They are on their own in an alien world, and they begin to get hungry: "we've brought nothing to eat" (57), "I'm worried about having no food with us" (58). Therefore the food the Beavers provide acquires once again a symbolic significance. The meal with the Beavers confirms the affinity, and it shows that the Beavers are friends. Mr. Beaver says actually: "I must bring you where we can have a real talk and also dinner ... everyone ... was very glad to hear the word 'dinner'" (65). Food and security are closely associated, and beside that the food is a trial. For Edmund, the food does not taste at all: "He had eaten his share of the dinner, but he hadn't really enjoyed it because he was thinking all the time about Turkish Delight—and there's nothing that spoils the taste of good ordinary food so much as the memory of bad magic food" (82). From this supper, Edmund goes to the White Witch to become a traitor (the Biblical allusion is obvious). Characteristically—and in accordance with myth and folktale—Mr. Beaver knows at once that Edmund has become a traitor: "He had the look of one who has been with the Witch and eaten her food. You can always tell them if you've lived long in Narnia; something about their eyes" (80). The ritual significance of food is emphasized again. Edmund can be partly excused for his treachery because the food has enchanted him, and the author accentuates this fact.

In Hans Christian Andersen's *The Snow Queen*, which has many similarities with Lewis's book and may have influenced it, the boy is not enchanted by food, but by a kiss. Food and sexuality are interchangeable in myth. Edmund has been seduced—the treacherous character of the Witch as both Eve and Lilith is unveiled in *The Magician's Nephew*. There are many superficial similarities in the two evil female creatures, apparently projections of the two male authors' fear of women (Veglahn 1987). Andersen's story is more explicitly erotic than Lewis's, especially in the pact between Kai and his enchantress. Also the rest of the story, including the relation between Kai and Gerda, is erotically charged, although quite innocent at the beginning: "They weren't brother and sister but loved each other as much as if they had been" (235f). The fact that they are not siblings opens the possibility, not present in the first Narnia book, that this presexual love will develop into sexual desire. Interestingly enough, in both *The Silver Chair* and *The Magician's Nephew*, the two protagonists are not siblings, thus incorporating the fairy-tale hero-princess relationship.

The Snow Queen opens, after the grotesque prelude about the devil and his mirror, with a picture of idyll in its essence, a rose garden "a little bit larger than a flowerpot" (235). "The peas climbed over the sides and hung down; and the little rose trees grew as tall as the windows and joined together" (236). The boy and the girl sit together in their garden, under the rose-bushes, in complete harmony and innocence: "The two *little* children held each other's hands, kissed the flowers, and looked up into the blessed sunshine (237; my emphasis). The idyll is interrupted by Kai getting a piece of the devil's mirror in his eye and heart. While there are many possible interpretations, the main implication is that he abandons his previous innocence: "He did not play as he used to; now his games were more *grown up*" (238; my emphasis). Significantly, his first action is to desecrate the rose garden.

The Snow Queen's kiss makes Kai forget Gerda, his Grandmother, and his home—a rejection of his own childhood, which may be equal to death. His key to freedom, the magical pass-word, is the word "eternity" which he has to build from the ice jigsaw puzzle. Remarkably, the witch in the Garden, seemingly associated with summer and thus with life rather than death, makes another attempt to keep the child forever a child. The parallel between the Snow Queen and the Garden witch has been noted by Roger Sale (1978, 71). Loss of memory implies imprisonment in a state beyond time, in another eternity equal to death. It is again the roses, symbols of childhood, that make Gerda remember. As she gets out of the garden, where there is eternal summer:

> She looked at the landscape; summer was long since over, it was late fall. Back in the old lady's garden, you could not notice the change in seasons, for it was always summer and the flowers of every season were in bloom. (246)

While Edmund is rescued from the grasp of the White Witch by the sacrificial death of the mighty Aslan (that is, an adult takes over when a child fails), Kai's fate lies in the hands of a little girl. The Finnish woman explains to the reindeer who asks her to give Gerda the power of twelve men to struggle against the Snow Queen:

> "I can't give her more power than she already has! Don't you understand how great it is? Don't you see how men and animals must serve her; how else could she have come so far, walking on her bare feet? But she must never learn of her power; it is in her heart, for she is a sweet and innocent child." (257)

The question is whether Gerda is indeed an innocent child, as Andersen pretends she is. The psalm she sings in the beginning of the story and later on return home ends with the words: "May we ... ever little children be." But as Gerda and Kai are on their way home from the ice-cold realm of death, everything reminds them of the flow of time: the reindeer, who waits for them at the border, has brought a mate, whose udder is full of milk. The robber girl they meet has grown up, and the old crow has died—three important phases of life cycle are evoked. As they come home: "Nothing inside has changed. The clock said: 'Tick-tack ...', and the wheels moved. But as they stepped through the doorway they realized that they had grown: they were no longer children" (261f). Since, as I have mentioned, they are comfortably not siblings, the implications are far-reaching, especially if we regard the story as a variant of the Beauty and the Beast or, maybe more relevant, a gender-reversed Orpheus-motif.

Of course, Andersen wants to emphasize the ever-children-theme: "There they sat, the two of them, grownups; and yet in their hearts children, and it was summer: a warm glorious summer day!" (262). However, a comparison to the complete regression of the four Pevensie children shows Andersen's story in a much more favorable light: he seems to know how to grow up and yet remain a child at heart.

Most scholars who have investigated fantasy novels for children make a clear distinction between what they assume are the two principal motifs: secondary worlds and time displacement (see e.g. Swinfen 1984). Among texts most often described as time-shift fantasy we find *The Story of the Amulet, The House of Arden, A Traveller in Time,* the *Green Knowe* series, *Tom's Midnight Garden, Jessamy, Charlotte Sometimes, Playing Beatie Bow* and *The Root Cellar* (see Cameron 1969; Aers 1970; Nodelman 1985; Townsend 1990; Scott 1996a).

There is undoubtedly more obsession with time as such in the so-called time fantasy: the very notion of time, its philosophical implications, its metaphysical character. But as to the construction of a magical universe and, as a direct consequence, the shape of the narrative, there are surely more similarities than differences in novels involving time shift or secondary worlds as the dominant pattern. A close investigation of the narrative structure of various texts reveals that the principal feature of time fantasy, time distortion, most often expressed narratively by paralepsis (primary time standing still), is also present in the secondary world fantasy, as we have seen in the Narnia novels. On the other hand, what is believed to be the principal pattern of the secondary world fantasy, the passage between worlds, is most tangible in time fantasy. The passage is often connected with patterns such as the door, the magic object and the magic helper. In my study of fantasy, I prefer to speak about the primary and secondary *chronotope* (timespace), thus completely ignoring the difference between secondary world fantasy and time fantasy and instead examining the common patterns, including the impact of the encounter with another time or space (Nikolajeva 1988).

A crucial question in the discussion of any magical there-and-back-again adventures is whether protagonists indeed mature through these exercises in liberation, whether they gain knowledge and experience, and draw conclusions: that is, whether these adventures prepare them for the definite step toward adulthood in the future.

Jungian-inspired critics often choose texts in which the events are dreamlike, a submerging into something dark and frightening, a wandering in a forest or a cave (*Divina Commedia, Alice in Wonderland*). But the nature of a dream presupposes waking up and discovering with relief that the disturbing dream is gone, and that at least this time you do not have to take the decisive step. J. R. R. Tolkien's skepticism toward *Alice in Wonderland* is based on the destruction of "Secondary belief" when a rational explanation of magical adventures as a dream is offered (see Tolkien 1968).

Conventional fantasy novels, whether they actually have an explanation of the adventure as a dream or not, let their protagonists remain totally unaffected by experience in the Otherworld. The adventure is nothing other than innocent play with a wooden sword and a rocking-horse, combating mother's green bathrobe thrown on an armchair. Naturally, play is also an important preparatory activity before the coming initiation. Still, play is not yet the real test of power, and the child does not know how he would have reacted in a real situation. To allow the protagonist to remain unaffected destroys the impact of the story. In *The Lion, the Witch and the Wardrobe*, we witness a noticeable regression: the children who have gone through trials in Narnia, who have proved worthy and have been crowned to be kings and queens, who have grown up and lived a whole life as wise and just rulers, return to their own reality as children, they lose their dearly bought knowledge and insights and therefore their accomplished initiation has no use.

In other novels, magical helpers may erase the protagonists' memory, as Merriman does at the end of Susan Cooper's *The Dark Is Rising* quintet. At best, they will remember their initiation as a vague dream. Although many fantasy novels have been analysed in terms of rite of passage, *The Lion, the Witch and the Wardrobe* among others (Walker 1985), the critics have ignored the "negation" of initiation in waking up or loss of memory.

Such a solution seems to be unsatisfactory for many contemporary writers. It is noteworthy that in a later novel, *Seaward*, Susan Cooper must have felt the insufficiency of her previous ending, allowing her young protagonists an option of recognizing each other in their future real life. The other option is to follow the magical agents to the island of eternal happiness, on condition that "you will go as children, as you are now, and you will never change," that is, the initiation will have failed, and a total regression is offered instead. Naturally, in a modern sophisticated novel, the author prefers the former choice: "... you will remember—and begin again. To live together through all the discoveries and lovely astonishments that go with the grief and the pain ..." (171).

The difference between the Narnia Chronicles on the one hand and *The Neverending Story* or *Elidor* on the other is that none of the many travellers to Narnia are affected by their involvement in the magical realm. It can naturally be argued that Edmund and Eustace are morally "improved"; however, since we do not know much about their lives in the primary world, we cannot judge whether the picnic has prepared them for the real trials in the real world.

The difference between *The Neverending Story* and *Elidor* is that Bastian is affected by his adventures in Fantasia quite superficially. The only thing we know about his life afterwards is that he is reconciled with his father. This is a conventional happy ending. We assume that Bastian has become wiser and more mature after his trials, but this is not the author's primary concern.

In *Elidor*, most of the events take place outside the magic realm. The threat from dark forces is felt much more strongly, since it concerns not the mythical Narnia, but the real England. Roland, one of the characters, is responsible for opening a passage between worlds, and he pays a high price for getting involved in the magical realm by going insane. This is a profound change from the carefree return from Narnia.

It is extremely seldom that children's writers describe the impact of a magical journey as negative, as Garner does in *Elidor*. Another example is Alison Uttley's *A Traveller in Time*, where the protagonist is permanently injured by her involvement with the past, which means that she cannot cope with her real life. I will return to this novel in my discussion of female initiation. In adult literature, on the contrary, it is highly probable that daydreaming, the creation of worlds of fancy, leads to a mental disturbance or at least to a total reevaluation of one's life. We may recollect, for instance, the reactions of Lemuel Gulliver upon his return from the land of giants or the land of horses.

In *Elidor*, we meet four siblings, as in the Narnia Chronicles, although not as gender-balanced: three boys and a girl. The didactic narrator of the Narnia novels is in *Elidor* replaced by strong focalization of just one of the four, Roland; besides, he completes the mission in Elidor while the other three fail (cf Propp's notion of "false hero"). Thus in fact we have an individual rather than a collective character, more similar to *The Neverending Story*. Unlike Lucy in *The Lion, the Witch and the Wardrobe*, Helen in *Elidor* is not a part of the collective character, but a "princess," similar to Jill in *The Silver Chair* or Polly in *The Magician's Nephew*. Her function in the story includes taming a unicorn, a traditional female role in myth. A shift from a collective toward an individual character is prominent in "there and back" stories, even though some master texts, including Narnia and *The Story of the Amulet*, have collective characters. Similarly, a change from a didactic and omniscient toward a focalizing and unreliable narrator is clearly felt in all later—after 1950s—texts.

AWFULLY BIG ADVENTURE

I have shown that there is no principal difference between Secondary World fantasy and time-shift fantasy—neither in the construction of the narrative nor in the function of time. I will go further still and maintain that there is no difference either between fantasy and the so-called "realistic" adventure.

Running away from home, the central motif of adventure stories, is merely another narrative device which takes the protagonist from the security of home and allows the same out-of-the-ordinary type of adventure as fantasy without losing the realistic anchoring. John Stephens has suggested the notion of "time-out" for this type of story (Stephens 1992, 132–139), which corresponds to Bakhtin's carnival theory. The events are not impossible, but often highly improbable and extraordinary.

However, the necessary condition of carnival is the reestablishment of the original order, that is, return to normal life. Carnival is always a temporary, transitional phenomenon—so is childhood. Like the carnivalesque fool, the child can temporarily, by means of magic or his own imagination, become strong, beautiful, wise, learn to fly, trick the adults, and win over enemies. The end of carnival means return to the everyday, but the purpose of carnival is not only entertainment, but a rehearsal of a future moral and psychological transformation.

Dennis Butts, among others, has pointed out that in their use of formulaic elements and stereotyped characters, adventure stories owe a good deal to the structure of traditional folk- and fairy tales in which similar patterns tend to repeat themselves (Butts 1992, 73). Butts refers to the ideas of both Propp and Campbell as possible instruments to examine the structure of adventure stories, and to those of Bettelheim to show the appeal of these stories. He also discusses *Treasure Island* in terms of folktale (74ff). I will take as an example another classical text, *Tom Sawyer.* It has been the subject of many examinations; however, since this book is as much a "master text" for adventure story as the Narnia Chronicles are for fantasy, I do not think I can omit it. The novel offers some valuable points for my discussion. The author's intention is stated in the Preface:

> Although my book is intended mainly for the *entertainment* of boys and girls, I hope it will not be shunned by men and women on that account, for part of my plan has been to try *pleasantly* to remind adults of what they once were themselves, and of how they felt and thought and talked, and what queer enterprises they sometimes engaged in. (5; my emphasis)

"Entertainment" for children and "pleasant" reminder for adults, bringing back to them the memories of their own childhood—this is what the author promises, and the first chapters of the novel certainly contain both. The setting could very well qualify for a domestic pastoral: a little village, happily isolated from the rest of the world, summertime, peace and harmony. The opening of Chapter 2 is reminiscent of many similar descriptions:

> Saturday morning was come, and all the summer world was bright and fresh, and brimming with life. There was a song in every heart; and if the heart was young the music issued at the lips. There was

cheer in every face, and a spring in every step. The locust trees were
in bloom, and the fragrance of the blossoms filled the air. (14f)

The function of this passage is, however, different from idyllic
fiction; in fact, it produces a contrasting background to the character's dark state of mind as he contemplates the work he is assigned
for punishment.

At first glance, *Tom Sawyer* is very different in its structure from
a typical quest narrative: there is no discernible home-away-home
pattern, and the plot is episodic rather than progressive, as in the
Narnia Chronicles. On closer examination there are at least two plots
intertwined in the narrative: one progressive (or linear), involving
struggle between hero and villain (Tom-Injun Joe), as well as treasure seeking and a princess; the other, indeed, episodic, where it is
possible *within* every episode to discern the circular home-away-
home movement.

In this episodic plot, Tom's adventures take him, in concentric
circles, further and further away from home, and into more and
more perilous escapades: from Aunt Polly's closet to the dangers of
the cave. If the first chapters depict harmless "pranks"—pinching
jam, playing hookey, getting other boys to do his work, blundering
in Sunday school—the murder in the graveyard is more serious,
since it not only initiates the second, linear plot, but also introduces
violent death into what has seemed a harmless idyll.

The disturbing effect of the murder is somewhat counterbalanced
by the restoration of paradise on the island. So far, Tom has always
returned home from his adventures. Playing hookey, he breaks the
rules, and going to the graveyard at night must be regarded as a
more serious violation. But his dependence on home, with its security, the warmth of the bed, Sid's presence notwithstanding, Aunt
Polly's overprotective love, and, not unimportant, regular meals,
has not been questioned yet.

Running away to Jackson's island is an attempt to escape from
civilization, which equals adulthood. Earlier, the boys go "grieving
that there were no outlaws any more, and wondering what modern
civilization could claim to have done to compensate for their loss"
(65). This may be a naive viewpoint, but it evokes the nostalgic
feeling which the author is trying, let us remember, to stir in adults
who are encouraged to recollect their childhood. The return to

nature is, despite its many joys, rather a failure. For one thing, its successful implementation is based on a serious crime: "It seemed to them, in the end, that there was no getting around the stubborn fact that taking sweetmeats was only 'hooking' while taking bacon and ham and such valuables was plain, simple stealing—and there was a command against that in the Bible" (95). The stolen food is a reminder that links with home have not been severed yet and cannot be for a while, that home is still a source of food, warmth and love, the absence of which they feel painfully during their voluntary Robinsonnade:

> The excitement was gone, now, and Tom and Joe could not keep back thoughts of certain persons at home who were not enjoying this fine frolic as much as they were. Misgivings came; they grew troubled and unhappy; a sigh or two escaped unawares. (101)

The young characters are not ready to leave their homes; yet they have clearly regarded both home and its two transformations, school and church, as prisons. The ambivalent status of home in adventure stories is especially clarified in comparison with its function in idyllic texts where it is unequivocally positive. In this episode, longing for home proves stronger than longing for adventure:

> … Joe's spirits had gone down almost beyond resurrection. He was so homesick that he could hardly endure the misery of it. The tears lay very near the surface. (108)

When Tom starts teasing Joe about being a baby and wanting to see his mother, Joe retorts:

> "Yes, I *do* want to see my mother, and you would too, if you had one. I ain't any more baby than you are."(109; author's emphasis)

Mothers are still important for the characters, and even though Tom only has a substitute one, her importance is evoked here.

After the idyllic interlude, the linear plot takes over, bringing about considerable changes in Tom's psychological evolution. Tom's witnessing against Injun Joe is a sign of maturity, especially given the fact that he breaks the childish "blood oath" he and Huck have sworn. However, since the author is writing for "entertainment" of the young, he must give Tom a palpable material reward, in the form of the treasure. It is a tribute to the genre, but also a ritual act. Like the fairy-tale hero, Tom gains riches and a princess. Becky's part in the story is worth a separate study, with all the intricate tools feminist criticism has offered us. In Jerry Griswold's essay "Desexualizing *Tom Sawyer*: What Really Happened in the Cave" the question of the author's self-censorship is discussed, as he promptly denies his character any signs of sexual awakening (Griswold 1996).

This question also brings about the other aspect of maturation: death. Tom is introduced to death in two widely diverse ways. The deaths of a peripheral character and a villain hardly raise the issue of his own mortality. More important are the wild fantasies about his own death (which apparently many readers recognize). Let us take another look at the island episode, this time from a mythical point of view.

In a rite of passage, young boys are removed from their normal surroundings and placed in isolation, where they have to cope on their own. During this isolation, they are considered to be dead, and are often earnestly mourned by their relatives. Thus, on the island, Tom and his friends go through a ritual death; they are also believed to be dead, and come back to their own funeral: a farce in terms of a "realistic" novel, but a marvelous illustration of the hero's symbolical death and rebirth. Without knowing it (and probably without the author knowing it), Tom restages the universal myth of the returning god.

In this scene, death is presented as being reversible, as it is apprehended in myth—"an awfully big adventure." Although Tom is old enough to come to the important insight of his mortality, the author prefers him to remain as innocent in this respect as in sexuality.

Let us contemplate the much quoted "Conclusion" of the novel:

> So endeth this chronicle. It being strictly a history of a boy, it must stop here; the story could not go much further without becoming the history of a man. When one writes a novel about grown people, he knows exactly where to stop—that is, with a marriage; but when he writes of juveniles, he must stop where he best can. (221)

That is, at the end of the novel, Tom is just as young, naive, and innocent a child as he was at the beginning, the linear development is again closed into a circle, the cycle is complete, and he is back to where he was—much like the Pevensie children. We have, however, another character, whose quest, although somewhat eclipsed by Tom's, is at least as much worth considering, and totally different from Tom's. Huck Finn's initial situation, as compared to Tom's, is lower social status, but greater freedom. I have a feeling that the author is ambivalent about the status of this character; societal rules demand that he be socialized, but all the other boys envy and admire him. I find it worth mentioning that even Huck is homesick on the island—for whatever hogshead he considers his "home." Huck is the "most orphaned" of the three boys, which makes him most free; still he is not prepared to retreat from the little comfort he is used to. When, in the end of the novel, Huck finds refuge in Widow Douglas's home, he regards it as a prison, because by this time he is ready to go further, as he will, in his own book. While Judge Thatcher has great visions for Tom as a lawyer or a military, Huck views his riches as a burden and escapes. Although he succumbs to Tom's arguments for a while, he will, as we know, soon start on a new journey. As Peter Coveney comments, *"Tom Sawyer* and *Huckleberry Finn* are essentially complementary, and should be read closely together" (Coveney 1967, 221; see further Molson 1985, 262). Tom capitulates and lets himself be socialized; Huck does not.

Huckleberry Finn deserves its own study, so I will only make some very brief observations. The novel was conceived by the author as another boys' book (see e.g. Coveney 1966). It may seem a sequel to *Tom Sawyer*, and has maybe functioned so in children's reading, in other countries especially, where the evaluation of *Huckleberry Finn* as "the great American novel" has hardly been acknowledged.

It is a novel about "freedom and integrity" (Coveney 1966, 15)— not a there-and-back story. A conflict between "sivilization" and freedom is the eternal theme of children's fiction, but in *Huckleberry Finn* it is resolved in a different way. In *Tom Sawyer*, home is a refuge and the little town an idyll, even troubled by murder. In *Huckleberry Finn*, home is to be left behind, and the town is cruel and hypocriti-cal. In the beginning of the novel, Tom is still playing, while for Huck "real life" is about to start. The rules of Tom Sawyer's Gang include much killing—because it is play, pretending. Huck sees no point in this. During his voyage, Huck sees many deaths and murders. While Tom stages his own death to have fun, Huck repeats the trick because he is in mortal danger; it is not play any more. Moreover, by the end of the novel, Tom still wants to play at "rescuing" Jim, while for Huck it is not a game. Huck knows that what they are doing is illegal, and there is no going away from it. As it turns out, Tom has known all the way that Jim has already been set free. This is beyond Huck's comprehension—not because he lacks imagination to play or because he has not read all the books where Tom gets his inspiration, but mainly because Huck has grown out of the mythical play-time. It is significant, as many critics have pointed out, that Huck's flight starts on the same Jackson's Island which was the setting of the innocent Robinsonnade in *Tom Sawyer*. It begins as a restaging of a ritual, but opens into a clearly linear progress. Although the novel has a sort of a "happy ending," it also suggests an aperture, because Huck is not going to stay with Aunt Sally and be "sivilized" once again. Huck has gained his passage into the adult world.

In Jungian terms, Tom is still at the stage of the primary unconscious, which keeps him happy and secure, while Huck has entered the second stage, the stage of split, which produces anxiety and longing. The image of the river offers wide possibilities for Jungian interpretations, as water is one of the most powerful symbols of the unconscious.

Aidan Chambers discusses *Huckleberry Finn* in terms of young adult fiction (Chambers 1986). Although he is right in his argumentation, the terminology itself is dubious. Just as childhood first emerged as a concept in the 17th century, and made children's literature possible as a phenomenon, adolescence as a notion is a 20th-century invention and a social construction, not an age category. Jane Austen's novels portray young women technically at the age under twenty; but they are socially in no ways teenagers (cf Tuman 1980, who treats *Pride and Prejudice* as a teenage romance). Adolescence denotes a marginal existence between childhood and adulthood, which can only appear under modern social conditions. However, it is true that *Huckleberry Finn* is a novel of adolescence in its intensive search for identity, which *Tom Sawyer* lacks.

The radical difference between the two novels is intensified by the use of the first-person narrator in *Huckleberry Finn*. It is generally believed that young readers prefer third-person narrators, which can be seen in the fact that most adaptations of adult novels into children's books have involved, among other things, a transposition from first to third person (*Robinson Crusoe, Gulliver's Travels* and many others).

There are several reasons for this assumption. A first-person narrative is more engaging, and it can be perceived as too frightening and emotionally involving, especially for a small child. Very small children have not yet developed a clear notion of an "I." They have problems identifying themselves with the strange "I" of the text. Many children's literature scholars have pointed out that young readers apprehend "I" as a real person and may start believing the role the "I" has in the story (see e.g. Lukens 1990, 129). Since early children's literature was written mostly for educational purposes, didactic third-person narrators were considered a suitable mode. I have already maintained that the majority of utopian texts use the omniscient third-person narrators. The transition to first person in *Huckleberry Finn* signals the more mature status of the protagonist.

A VARIETY OF PICNICS

No longer forced to make the artificial distinction between "realistic" and "fantastic" picnics, we can go through a variety of texts involving this pattern, noting similarities and dissimilarities. Each text would doubtless deserve a study of its own; for lack of space I can only briefly discuss some of them.

The protagonist may be sent on a journey in a historical setting, either in a "straight" historical novel, like Rosemary Sutcliff's *The Eagle of the Ninth* and Leon Garfield's *Smith,* or in a time-shift fantasy. The purpose may be entertaining, educational or psychological. The setting may be also pseudohistorical, for instance in Lloyd Alexander's Vesper novels. It is quite illuminating to compare Alexander's Prydain Chronicles (fantasy, magic), Westmark trilogy (adventure, pseudohistory), Vesper novels (adventure, pseudohistory, pseudo-geography) and his most recent novels, for instance *The Arcadians,* inspired by Ancient Greek mythology. Despite the difference in setting, they can all be described as "there-and-back" stories.

The instructive journey, such as *The Phantom Tollbooth,* takes the hero on an intellectual quest in a magical realm; but intellectual exercise may also be offered in purely realistic form, for instance *From the Mixed-Up Files of Mrs. Basil E. Frankweiler.* A variety of science fiction stories involve the "there-and-back" pattern, as do many post-catastrophe novels. A psychological quest for self can be found in many contemporary YA novels, for instance Gary Paulsen's *The Island,* a modern Robinsonnade (see further Nikolajeva 1994, where I investigate the pattern in some Canadian realistic and fantastic novels).

I will dwell very briefly on two widely different texts to demonstrate how the authors deny their characters any psychological maturation as a result of their journeys.

Erich Kästner's *The 35th of May* is often described in terms of "nonsense." In this, in its way charming story, Conrad who is assigned a school essay about the South Seas, is taken, together with his extravagant Uncle Ringel, on a journey assisted by a magical helper, a talking horse. Interestingly, they enter the magic world by walking through a wardrobe.[1] The travellers first come to the Land of Cockayne, which is exactly as it is described in all traditional stories, maybe with some additional imagination: for instance, a hen laying "fried eggs and bacon, or omelettes with asparagus" (45). The next stop is the Castle of the Mighty Past, where Charlemagne is a gate-keeper, Edward the Confessor a cashier, and where they further meet Julius Caesar, Napoleon, and a number of other valiant warriors happily engaged in sports, and Hannibal and Gustavus Adolphus of Sweden playing with toy soldiers. In the Topsy-Turvy Country, grown-ups go to school and have to learn to respect children's rights, and Electropolis is a high-tech utopia. Finally, in the South Seas they meet little princess Parsley, whose skin is chequered because her father is black and her mother white. After that, the uncle and the nephew return comfortably home, without having encountered any dangers, without any new knowledge or experience of a more profound kind. This funny, entertaining story has certainly been admired by many readers in many countries, but it has nothing to do with the idea of spiritual growth.

War-time stories have also been treated as a separate genre, in British children's fiction especially, with names such as Michelle Magorian, Nina Bawden and Jill Paton Walsh. Robert Westall's *The*

Kingdom by the Sea starts dramatically with a bomb attack in which the thirteen-year-old protagonist, Harry, loses his parents and his little sister. At least he believes that he has lost them. To escape being put into a home, Harry runs away and together with a stray dog wanders up the coast. It is a hard struggle for survival, described in every detail, where hunger and cold become tangible enemies, not merely easily-dealt-with elements in an adventurous robinsonnade. Harry meets a number of nice people and a number of evil people, and all the time something compels him to go further and further away from the lost home. But when he finally finds a new home, his happiness only lasts for a short while.

It is disappointing to learn that Harry's family has survived, not only because it is a sentimental "happy ending," but primarily because it mocks his sufferings and reduces a dangerous and serious quest to a naughty boy's prank, as his parents see his disappearance. If we consider Harry's adventure in terms of rite of passage, his peaceful homecoming is a regression into the security of childhood. Naturally, he has retained some of his newly gained insights: he now sees his parents from a new angle, and the dream of a different life is still with him. Yet, the pattern of the story if definitely "there-and-back-again."

The essential aspect of my approach is that I make no distinction between what is normally described as "genres" or "kinds" of children's fiction: historical fiction, fantasy, adventure, realistic everyday story, or "nonsense" (which I do not believe to be a generic category anyway, but rather a stylistic device). The difference is in setting, or more specifically in chronotope, the organization of space and time. In my typology, all these texts belong to the same narrative pattern: "semiclosed" in Peter Hunt's taxonomy, "Odyssean" in Lucy Waddey's. In Frye's mythical cycle, the closest description is romance.

It is, however, possible to see the difference within this scope of texts in terms of quest and picaresque. Quest has a goal; picaresque is a goal in itself. The protagonist of a picaresque work is by definition not affected by his journey; the quest (or Bildungsroman) is supposed to initiate a change. There is, indeed, sometimes a very subtle boundary between "there-and-back" and a definite, linear journey "there," which is best seen in the last volume of the Narnia Chronicles.

NOTE

1. I have investigated some novels using this motif in a variety of manners, see Nikolajeva 1996, 182ff. Kästner, writing his story in 1931, may have borrowed the idea from E. T. A. Hoffmann, or conceived of it independently.

Chapter 6

Where Have All the Young Girls Gone?

So far all the picnics I have discussed have either involved a collective protagonist or an individual male one. Apparently the reason for this is the predominantly male nature of the quest myth ("Odyssean"), which takes the hero away from home, into the wide world, in order to conquer new hunting grounds, kill monsters, or find treasures. Male initiation is constructed as a series of stations, where an adventure is offered at each, a task to perform, a test to pass. The pattern is linear and aimed at a goal.

Female initiation is totally different and obviously connected with circularity. The female body follows the lunar cycle, which is closely associated with the idea of death and rebirth (waning and waxing moon, cf Eliade 1955, 86). The cardinal function of the female body is reproduction. The female myths, describing female initiation, are aimed at repetition, rebirth, the eternal life cycle. Actually, very few genuine female myths exist in written—male, civilized, "symbolic" (Lacan)—form, due to many reasons. Connected with essential life mysteries such as menstruation and birth (both involving blood), female myths are more secret and sacred than male myths. They have mostly existed in oral form, as esoteric rituals. In Western civilization, they have been suppressed and muted by the dominant male culture. We can only discover traces and remnants of them, in the figures of the Progenitrix, the witch, the chthonic goddess (see Franz 1972; Birkhäuser-Oeri 1988; Lundell 1990; Warner 1994).

Writers who wish to describe a female initiation must therefore resort to various strategies, depicting girls in temporary, limited

situations: "time-out" or carnival. In adult fiction, two well-estab-
lished strategies are to describe the heroine either as mentally disturbed, the famous "madwoman in the attic" (see Gilbert & Gubar
1977; Felman 1985), or as a witch (Purkiss 1996). In both cases, the
implication is that the woman does not constitute the object of a
man's desire. Two strategies which are equally applicable in books
for adults and books for young readers are androgyny and fantasy.
In a "realistic" children's novel, running away, most often combined
with disguise as a boy, is a way to let the heroine taste adventure
before it is time to adjust to a traditional female role. Otherwise a
strong, independent woman or girl is still a character more common
in fantasy or science fiction, that is, text types which rely on time-out.
The carnival situation of both devices emphasizes the temporary,
the passing, the inverted—the girl is allowed to be strong and
independent on certain conditions and for a limited time. Just as the
fool during carnival is crowned and worshipped as a king, only to
be dethroned and humiliated as soon as the carnival is over, the
heroine can be temporarily superior to men, only to capitulate when
the original order is restored—or to perish. However, as Mikhail
Bakhtin demonstrates, the very depiction of carnival has a subversive effect.

Fantasy and science fiction offer writers considerable freedom
from societal conventions. As Rosemary Jackson points out, "fantasies have appeared to be 'free' from many of the conventions and
restraints of more realistic texts" (Jackson 1981, 1). Fantasy allows
wishful thinking impossible in so-called realistic fiction (see further
Russ 1995). But it also presents many dangers. A female protagonist
does not automatically make the novel a depiction of female initiation.

Carroll's Alice has been discussed as Anima, the female principle
(Bloomingdale 1971), but it is only true if we apply the author-oriented approach of Jungian psychoanalysis, viewing Alice as the
author's projected female side, which I am not inclined to do. Keep-
ing strictly to the text, there is nothing in the figure of Alice or in the
nature of her adventures which is not possible with a male hero. As
a *character*, Alice is doubtlessly female, as a *textual function* she is
absolutely gender-neutral. The same is true about Dorothy or princess Irene in George MacDonald's novels, two prominent individual
female figures in fantasy. As I have shown, when we are dealing

with a collective protagonist, the female component is either functionally neutral (Elfrida in *The House of Arden*, Lucy in *The Lion, the
Witch and the Wardrobe*) or performing the function of a "princess,"
in Proppian terminology, rather than hero (Helen in *Elidor*).[1]

Lloyd Alexander has been praised for his strong and independent
heroines: Eilonwy in the Prydain Chronicles, Mickle in the Westmark trilogy, Vesper Holly, and many more. A close examination of
these characters reveals covert sexism in their construction. Indeed,
all these active, strong girls are one of a kind, and very often they
despise their less lucky sisters. Instead of creating a genuinely
female character, the writer has made a simple gender permutation
allowing a girl to appear in a masculine role. This is a typical
example of tokenism.

In most contemporary fantasy novels of the "sword-and-sorcery"
type (Terry Brooks, Elisabeth Moon), female characters are tokens,
a female body set in a male role. Female attributes (most often long
hair!) do not create a female identity; the character could have been
male without the plot changing significantly, since the plot itself is
unmistakably male. Some exceptions are *The Darkangel* trilogy by
Meredith Ann Pierce or certain novels by Diana Wynne Jones, for
instance, *Howl's Moving Castle* or *Fire and Hemlock*. Ursula Le Guin
has attempted to counterbalance the male pattern of the Earthsea
trilogy in *Tehanu* (see e.g. Stephens 1992, 258; Hatfield 1993; Nodelman 1995). The result is a plot radically different from the dynamic,
linear plots of the three first parts.

A GIRL IN DISGUISE

Sandra M. Gilbert offers a fascinating exposé over the significance
of clothes and the motif of transvestism in literature, noting the
considerable difference between male and female writers (Gilbert
1980).[2]

It is quite amazing that within a period of ten years, between 1977
and 1986, at least five Swedish children's novels have made use of
an androgynous character, for very different purposes. Significantly, four of five are written by male authors. In *Anna-Carolina's
War* by Mats Wahl, a girl takes the place of her younger brother who
is drafted into army during the Thirty Years War. She plans to escape
after the first day but fails and after a while seems to be enjoying the

war adventure. The change of clothes brings about a change of mentality: Anna-Carolina thinks like a boy, feels like a boy, acts like a boy (among other things, she gladly participates in sexual abuse of other women), and tells her story in a typical male voice, registering external events in a rational, coherent and chronological manner. However, at the end of the novel, she suddenly undergoes a complete change, at the writer's whim, and patiently and submissively lets herself be married off. In Ulf Stark's *The Nuts and the No-Goods*, a similar unaccountable mentality change occurs in a totally different setting and for a different reason: the twelve-year-old Simone is mistaken for a boy, Simon, when she goes to a new school for the first time; the confusion is possible because she has a short haircut and is wearing gender-neutral clothes, jeans and a T-shirt. Simone accepts the game and for a week plays a boy's role, discovering that it is more exciting and gratifying to be a boy. Her thoughts and emotions reveal the male author's evident limitations; among other things, Simone in disguise immediately starts regarding other girls as "them" and commenting on their breasts and bottoms in a disgustingly sexist manner. As soon as Simone is exposed, she happily changes into a pink dress with strawberry-shaped buttons, once again accepting her role as a female, including that as a sexual object.

Still another male author, Peter Pohl, depicts a girl in boy's clothes in *Johnny, My Friend*, but the narrative perspective allows that Johnny remains "closed" and mystical, only described through the first-person narrator's eyes. The same strategy is to be found in Maria Gripe's *Shadow Over the Stone Bench* where androgynous Carolin is seen from the outside, through the first-person narrator's viewpoint.

In all these novels, it is promptly shown that by changing clothes, and thus trading her female identity for male, the girl can feel more independent as an individual and act on equal terms with men (cf Lehnert 1994). The androgyne also indulges in typically male occupations: war, sports, and risky nightly escapades. In all the novels, except *Johnny, My Friend*, the girl is forced to return to her traditional female role: the temporal nature of carnival is emphasized. In *Johnny, My Friend*, the androgynous heroine is brutally murdered. Death is also the outcome of carnival in *The Battle Horse* by Harry Kullman.

The Battle Horse is a gang book, describing some boys playing Ivanhoe in central Stockholm in the 1930s. It also depicts a social conflict, since only "preppies," Prep school students, rich men's kids, are allowed to take part in the tournament as knights, while "ordinary kids" are given the roles of horses: knights sit on their shoulders when they fight. As a gang book, it belongs in my category of domestic idyll, but for two details. First, it shows how two girls try to fight their way into a strictly male society; second, it portrays the way that harmless play suddenly turns into something serious, bringing about an irreversible change, that is, transforming idyllic time into a linear pattern.

The four main characters of the novel present a very complicated hierarchy. Henning, a preppie, is definitely on top: his father is a general, and he "wasn't only the best at all the subjects in school, he was best at *everything* (4, author's emphasis). Roland, the narrator, a poor worker's son, is inferior to Henning and painfully aware of it. "We took for granted that preppies were smarter than us, that being richer kids they'd been given extra or better brains at birth" (5). Roland's dream and ambition is to break away from his class, to leave his social background behind—he has no idea how to go about it, and his dream acquires a very material image: a fine Erector set, which becomes a status symbol, reverberating throughout the text. Rebecca, an upper-class girl, is superior to Roland because of her social status, but inferior to Henning because of her gender.

> Like Henning, she was best at everything in her school, but the strange thing was … that the same things which made Henning the unquestioned leader of the boy preppies made the girls avoid Rebecca. Actually, I thought they were just envious. Not because she was best at everything, but because she was so beautiful. (23)

Finally, Kossan (a nickname, which literally means Cow), the daughter of a poor unmarried mother, is supposedly the lowest among them. But although the author never mentions this explicitly, there are more intricate patterns in the hierarchy. Kossan, for instance, is a better reader than Roland, much to his irritation, as well as physically stronger. And Roland's mother regards herself and her son and even the otherwise despised Kossan superior to Rebecca, who is

Jewish. The implicit conflicts between the characters involve all of these aspects.

Kossan dreams of getting a proper education and becoming a teacher, since this is the only way for her to rise in society. Roland is much more ambivalent, he does not know where his loyalties are. For instance, he is eager to sit on the gallery and watch the tournament together with preppies (he is privileged because he lives in the same yard as Henning), but "horses" have good chances to earn easy money.

The central episode of the plot involves a mystery: after each tournament, an enigmatic hooded and masked Black Knight appears, and so far nobody has defeated him. Since Henning is the best in the gang, everybody expects him to challenge the Black Knight, which he eventually does. To everybody's amazement, he chooses Kossan as his horse. She accepts it as a great honor: it is the first time ever a girl has been allowed to participate in the boys' games. Again, Roland's feelings as he tells the story are ambivalent: he sees that Henning humiliates the girl, but he is envious of her part. Henning is defeated at the first joust and, infuriated, challenges the Black Knight to fight with bare weapons—so far they have put pieces of cork on their lances. They do, Henning wins, the Black Knight turns out to be Rebecca, and Kossan dies from a splinter of Rebecca's lance in her throat.

This tragic end to what seemed harmless play poses several questions. Rebecca is in love with Henning and wants to impress him, but she also wants to demonstrate that girls are no worse than boys. She has actually defeated every single knight before Henning. But she could only do it in disguise, in fact, could only participate in disguise.

The "horses" have hoped that the mysterious knight was an ordinary kid, one of them. Once again, Rebecca is superior as a rich man's daughter, but inferior as a girl. As soon as Rebecca is unmasked, nobody pays any attention to her.

Finally, Kossan, who seems to have found her own way toward her female and social identity, is killed by another girl—a tragic coincidence, full of symbolic meaning. Rebecca identifies herself primarily not as a girl, but as a better man's offspring.

For Roland, Kossan's death becomes a turning point. As the ambulance leaves the yard, he picks up the horse's head which

Kossan has been wearing, and, putting it on, identifies with Kossan—both her class and her gender. The day before the ill-fated tournament, Kossan has a prophetic vision, inspired by one of her favorite books:

> One day we horses are going to go over the ocean the way Gulliver did and leave the land of the Yahoos. And we'll get them to stop fighting, we'll abolish war, and nobody will have to be at the bottom of the heap. We'll take control and there won't be any words for lying, for rich and poor. No word for rich, no word for poor, no word for violence, no word for war—they'll be totally unknown! (163)

This is Kossan's legacy to Roland, as she indeed has sailed over to the happy hunting-grounds. If he had any doubt before about his true identity, now they are gone: "Carefully I climbed down from the paper bales without taking off the horse head and joined my fellow horses" (183).

TRAVELLERS IN TIME—FEMALE INITIATION

The epigraph of Alison Uttley's *A Traveller in Time*—"Time is. Time was. Time is not"—focuses the reader's attention on the notion of time, which is otherwise seldom touched upon directly in novels for children (cf my discussion of *Tom's Midnight Garden*). The metaphysical and philosophical aspects of the mystery of time are important for Alison Uttley who lets her character ponder on the nature of time shifts. In many other time-shift fantasies, for instance Edith Nesbit's *The Story of the Amulet* and *The House of Arden*, the characters take happy and uncomplicated rides in and out of history, very seldom having to worry about the consequences of their journeys. Uttley, on the contrary, depicts a complicated involvement with another historical epoch, which changes the female character's life.

A first-person narrator is quite unusual in fantasy (John Stephens maintains that it hardly occurs at all and views this as a radical difference between "realistic" and "fantastic" discourse; Stephens 1992, 251). In this case, a grown-up person is telling the story long after the events, remembering the things that happened when she was a young girl (extradiegetic, retrospective narrator). Thus she can reconstruct her feelings and comment on them from her adult perspective, with an adult's life experience and wisdom.

Further, unlike many time travellers, for instance Nesbit's five children or the Arden siblings, Penelope is an individual protagonist, and all events are centered around her, her feelings and sensations. This allows the author to go much deeper into the psyche of the character, to investigate her inmost thoughts and to register the minimal reactions of her senses.

Like so many fantasy novels, including *The House of Arden* and *The Lion, the Witch and the Wardrobe*, Alison Uttley's novel takes place in a very old house. The house itself, which existed already in the past where Penelope arrives, is in a way a mechanism of time shift. It is permeated with memories; even those who have never been allowed to enter the past believe that there are ghosts living here. It is repeatedly stressed that the air itself at Thackers is laden with memories and sorrows because of the tragical fate of the Babington family.

There are many typical time-shift patterns in the novel: Penelope makes repeated visits to the past, primary and secondary time go at a different pace, a door serves as a passage, Penelope cannot affect history or carry objects between times. However, unlike Nesbit's protagonists, who are comfortably transported in and out of distant epochs, Penelope does not at first realize that she has arrived in a different time. She comes and goes in a dream-like fashion, and she can never be sure when it will happen next time. Neither is she quite sure that she will be able to come back to her own time. The story acquires a more psychological note, as compared to Nesbit's time picnics, and a possible explanation may be visions as much as pure magic.

Often Penelope goes into the past in a kind of a dream, without clear memories of her visit: "I brought no consciousness of my travelling. I lost all as one forgets a dream on awakening" (129). She can also find herself in the past without warning. All in all there are some twenty descriptions of the passage in the novel, and the boundary between the two times is very vague:

> My visits must be outside time, for when I return I find I have been away for only a fraction of a second, no measurable period, not a heart-beat, but in that span I feel life more intensely and all my senses

are more acute. The grass is greener, the sky more translucent, as I
step light-foot and silent across the border. (164)

As Penelope becomes more and more involved in the past, her own
time seems remote and unreal to her.

> All memory of my mother and father had disappeared, I knew
> nothing about them. Only Thackers and the unchanging landscape
> remained, familiar and dear to me, as if I had known it from time
> everlasting, as if I were part of it, immortal soul of it come back to the
> loved place. (63)

Penelope returns to her own time with her identity changed. Time
travel, time paradoxes and historical facts are less important in the
novel than personal development. Penelope is obliged to choose
between her own reality and the past, which for her becomes more
real than reality. Back in her own time, she longs for the past:

> I longed to visit that great kitchen again, to listen to Dame Cicely,
> to be scolded by Tabitha, and perhaps to share that warm, intimate
> comradeship of the family that lived there. (95)

This passage reveals Penelope's problem with her own time and
identity: although she has parents and siblings, she is lonely and
unhappy. The past offers her something that she profoundly lacks
in her own time.

She becomes used to being transported through time, and when
she is in the past, she remembers less and less of her own reality:

> My mother and father, my sister and brother were forgotten as if
> they never lived, but Uncle Barnabas who seemed part of the soil itself
> and Aunt Tissie who was living in both centuries were ever present.
> They were made of Thackers earth, they were the place quickened to
> life and I remembered them. (118)

As her visits to the past proceed, Penelope becomes more and more
absorbed in it through her love for those she meets there, especially
young Francis Babington. But she also fears that she might get stuck
there and never be able to come back; she is aware of being displaced
in time. Unlike the Ardens, she does not have a magic agent at hand,

who can carry her back to her own time and security: "I knew there was a possibility I might not come back, and it was this knowledge which later tainted my experience with fear" (129).

Penelope's double life is a torment to her, and it makes her miserable in both times. She longs to be with the people she cares for, she has found her true love, but she is scared because she has no will-power over her transportations. "If I stay too long in this world of dreams, I shall die," she tells Francis (165). As the story progresses she also starts feeling a painful longing to go back to her own time, where she realizes she belongs after all:

> ... a flash of memory came to me, tearing my breast with pain. My mother and father, my sister and brother, and Uncle Barnabas and Aunt Tissie. Suppose I could never get back and those who loved me, those I loved, never saw me again. (189)

At one point Penelope is dying in the secondary time, locked up in a mine by the jealous Arabella. As it turns out, she is found in a deep faint in the primary time. Thus, the secondary time breaks through the boundaries; it has power over Penelope even when she is presumably safely back in her own time.

When Penelope is away from Thackers in her own time, she cannot any longer go into the past. During these two years Francis and the other people of the past "were more real than the people round me, and then they became phantoms, swirling in dim motion, disappearing like the summer mists" (146). But as soon as she is back she gets still more involved in the dramatic events of the past. Her love for Francis becomes stronger and more mature.

The end of the book is deeply tragic. One problem that Edith Nesbit ignored is what happens to identity once the magic adventure is over. How much of the experience is to be remembered by the characters and how has it affected them? Neither the Ardens, nor the Pevensies in the Narnia Chronicles seem to have undergone any change whatsoever. As shown earlier, in some fantasy novels the characters are promised in the end that they will forget about their experience. Like nonchalantly explaining away the extraordinary events by a dream, such a solution is surely an easy way out for an author who is less interested in the psychological impacts of the journey. But to many writers of fantasy, time displacement is a test, and its result a moral and psychological evolution.

The usual supposition is of course that the protagonists become morally better, wiser, stronger; that they acquire better chances of coping with their problems in the primary world. This seems, however, to be a typically male pattern. After her final return to the primary time Penelope feels miserable. Her love for Francis, the impossible love beyond time, makes her remain unmarried and true to him in her own time. Already before the adventure is over she tells her aunt: "I shall never marry, Aunt Tissie. I shall never fall in love with anybody in the whole world" (251). It may seem a young girl's folly, but for Penelope it is a solemn oath. The author never says explicitly that Penelope has kept her promise, but a keen reader may guess it by going back to the very first sentence: "I, Penelope Taberner Cameron, tell this story of happenings when I was a young girl" (13). As an old lady Penelope still has her maiden name. Penelope's identity is split, and she can never become her normal self. The only thing that she has left is hope that "some day I shall return to be with that brave company of shadows" (286).

Playing Beatie Bow is in many respects similar to Uttley's novel, and it has often been treated together with it (see e.g. Nodelman 1985b; Scott 1996a). However, there is one striking difference. The purpose of Abigail's going into the past is to change history, but not an event of overall historical importance, like the execution of Mary Stuart. Although Abigail's interference with history is on the individual level, still it is interference. She is supposed to intervene and save the life of one of the Bow children—in order that their special Gift may continue. But this is not the only purpose and perhaps also a very superficial one. On finding herself in the past Abigail gets another viewpoint on her own problems; when she returns she is capable of coping with them.

We meet Abigail when she is fourteen years old. Her parents have been divorced for four years. She blames her parents, especially her father, for all her problems, but at the same time "she knew that it wasn't the absence of her father that caused the empty place inside her" (6). Abigail's conflict is not with the surroundings, but with herself.

As a matter of fact her name is not Abigail—the name is a mask to hide behind. The name itself is an old witch name (originally

Hebrew, meaning "my father is my joy," but I am not sure it was Ruth Park's intention to give us that clue), and Abigail plays with the idea that she might be a witch. It is evident that she has some supernatural powers that enable her to cross the time boundaries.

The desire to change her name is prompted by Abigail's lack of identity. "The girls at school said she was a weirdie, and there was no doubt she was an outsider" (4). Being an outsider is another way of saying that Abigail is displaced; we are also told that she "felt a hundred years older and wiser" than her classmates (4), which anticipates her displacement a hundred years back in time.

Abigail's time travelling is not a joyful holiday, as it is for the Arden children. It is not an escape from a tiresome reality, as it is for Penelope. If anything, Abigail's journey is a discovery of herself. Unlike Uttley's novel, it is not a first-person narrative, but Abigail is focalized internally, with almost the same effect.

It takes quite a time until Abigail realizes what has happened to her, and she is more reluctant to admit it than Penelope. She thinks she must be dreaming, and only by asking a direct question and hearing that the year is 1873 does she accept the incredible truth. Unlike Penelope, Abigail is determined to preserve her identity. She keeps telling herself: "Abigail Kirk, that's who I am. I mustn't forget. I might sink down and get lost in this place—this time, or whatever it is—if I don't keep my mind on it" (45). She is keen on going back home, she feels trapped, especially since she realizes that she must wear her dress with the crochet in order to get back. But she is obliged to live weeks and months in the past, a hundred years before her own time, in a period which is alien and frightening. Unlike Penelope, she never feels at home and comfortable in the past. But she learns to know and appreciate it, and she learns to see that history is also a part of identity, her specific Australian identity.

Abigail lives with the Bow family and learns their life style that is so very different from her own and her mother's; she learns the art of adjustment. She learns to be kind and unselfish and consider-ate—something she was totally uncapable of in her own time. She discovers very soon that her arrival in the past has a purpose, but she does not know exactly what the assignment may be. Her most difficult moral dilemma will be to repress her own feelings in order to fulfil the purpose. Abigail's love for Judah is her real trial and rite of passage. It is a very fine portrayal of a young girl's first love, and the means Ruth Park uses are simple and subtle. "It was not possible," Abigail tells herself. "Love could not pierce one with a dart, envelop one with an unquenchable fire, all those things that old songs said, that the girls at school said" (123). Love makes her reconcile with this strange life; she no more longs to go back home to her own time and place. She does not think much about being loved in return, yet it is unbearable to know that Judah will marry Dovey. It is Granny who teaches Abigail to be unselfish. "If you love truly, you will also know how to live without your beloved" (134). In Alison Uttley's book, love is impossible because the lovers belong to different epochs. In Ruth Park's book, love is impossible because of a moral choice. It never crosses Abigail's mind that she may try to stay after the task is fulfilled.

In the epilog, taking place four years later, Abigail learns, contrary to what she had thought, that it was not Dovey but the abominable Gibbie she has saved for the future and the continuation of the Gift. She learns that Judah died young. She also meets Gibbie's greatgrandson. Abigail has changed a great deal in the meantime, she has become mature and emotionally stable, she is now able to see her involvement with the past from a new perspective.

It may seem too easy a solution of Abigail's problem to let her meet Judah's distant relative in the present, a substitute for the one she could never be united with, dead long before she herself was born. Also Robert's transcendental recognition of Abigail feels a bit forced. But it is a more satisfactory solution than in Alison Uttley's book. Penelope's experience in the past is catastrophic for her life, it is clearly negative. Abigail's experience is positive, it makes her strong enough emotionally to cope with the present, gain an identity, accept her parents and, in the long run, develop a normal relationship with a man, since in acknowledging Robert Bow as a substitute for the lost lover Abigail also finally gets free from her father.

AN ESSENTIAL LINK IN SOME UNKNOWN CONTEXT

In *Agnes Cecilia* by Maria Gripe we meet Nora, who lost her parents in a traffic accident when she was fours year old. As the novel starts, she is fifteen, so the years between their death and "now" are told in short retrospectives, like loose memories. Nora's relatives choose the worst way to handle this tragedy: they pretend it has not happened. "No one wanted to talk about it; she had to find out everything herself, bit by bit. It was confusing for her then, and nobody helped in the least" (12). "Bit by bit" is a key phrase; throughout the novel, Nora will discover, bit by bit, how she fits into the great pattern of life.

The adults around Nora are too cowardly or maybe too hypocritical to tell her the truth about her parents. "… Nora heard they had left quite suddenly. They'd gone far, far away, and no one knew when they'll be back" (13). In many children's novels, adults lie to children about death, revealing their own immaturity and inability to cope with it. At first Nora asks when the parents will come back, but nobody can tell: "After all, they were so far away" (13). She is placed with Anders and Karin, her father's cousin,

> for the time being. That is, until Mama and Papa came back from their long journey …It was one big lie that everyone participated in—including Nora … A long time went by before she realized that she ought to have forced everyone to confess that Mama and Papa were dead and that, in fact, she had a right to learn what had happened. She had a right to mourn and cry. But when she finally understood this, it was too late. Mama and Papa had become alien, distant beings. (14)

This death is quite different from the convenient withdrawal of Mary Lennox's parents in *The Secret Garden*. The death of Nora's parents is also an initial "absence," the prerequisite for the story to take place. But unlike Mary Lennox, Nora is deeply affected by their death, and although we first meet her ten years later, she has still not got over it. Moreover, the emptiness they have left makes Nora still more anxious about her own place in the world.

> She didn't belong in the family—she wasn't a part of it—even though Anders and Karin never made her feel that way, not consciously, at any rate. They did all they could for her. They were good people …. They tried to make her feel like a member of the family, but they didn't realize their efforts only showed that she wasn't. … They claimed that they thought of Nora as their own child. She had heard them say this to their friends countless times. And each time it sounded as believable as ever, but the unpleasant little thought im-

mediately flew through her head: If it were true, would they need to repeat it? (7f)

As children often do in such situations, according to psychological studies, Nora blames herself for her parents' death, thinking that they abandoned her because she was no good for them:

> Mama had been too pretty and Papa too smart. The accident was no accident. That's why they disappeared. If they'd loved me they would have taken me along in the car. Then I wouldn't exist now either, and no one would have to take care of me. (9)

Just before Nora is to start school, Anders and Karin take her to her parents' grave on All Saints' Day. It is a practical arrangement: Nora can be asked awkward questions in school. Suddenly the relatives want her to mourn, they tell her everything they can about her parents. She resents all this. She wants to keep her own memories of her parents, however vague.

Thus although the parents' death is a "function" (in Propp's terms) in the story, it has in the first place brought about an existential crisis which the protagonist goes through as we meet her. Some time before the novel starts, Nora's foster-family has moved into a new house. "… Nora and this house belonged together; she'd felt that the minute she arrived. It was as if she had always lived here. Even the first time she walked through the door it felt as if she had truly come home" (21). A strange house in which the protagonist moves at the beginning of a narrative is a commonplace in children's fiction. We meet it in novels such as *The House of Arden*, *A Traveller in Time*, *The Lion, the Witch and the Wardrobe*, *Green Knowe* books, *Tom's Midnight Garden*, and many others. It is especially significant in novels where it provides a setting for a time shift. The house is indeed an important link: Cecilia, the object of Nora's quest, used to live in the same room. The apartment is "haunted," not in the regular, ghost-story manner, but haunted by memories. It is noteworthy that Ludde, the family's dog, does not like the new house and runs away; it is a common belief that dogs possess the ability to perceive supernatural appearances.

However, *Agnes Cecilia* is not a regular time-shift fantasy, Nora does not actually travel in time, she only experiences the other time in a sort of vision.

> It's the same thing every time. The steps come as if they had risen straight out of the silence and slowly move in her direction. Nora knows there is nothing to be afraid of. Whoever is coming has never harmed her. She tries to ignore the footsteps and pretend that they don't exist, but this never works. The footsteps force themselves on her and make her take notice every time. (3)

Nora is Sunday's child who is supposed "to hear the grass grow." Incidentally, her foster-brother Dag is much more sensitive and ready to believe in all strange coincidences, maybe because they do not affect him directly. But he can help with comments like: "Of course, time doesn't move in only one direction. Time is like a sea with a thousand undercurrents. It must be able to move forward and backward and sideways" (113).

The plot is built as a series of coincidences. Nora "happens" to move into the same house where Cecilia once lived. Anders "happens," while putting up new wall-paper, to discover a sealed closet full of objects which become clues to the identity of the former inhabitants: a photograph, a dog's collar, a pair of worn ballet slippers, and an alarm clock. A clock as an amulet in time-shift fantasy is another commonplace (cf Uttley, Pearce, and Park). The clock, which is broken beyond repair, starts going backwards each time Nora has a vision or a sense of the past.

Further, Anders "happens" to arrange an outing to Stockholm with his school class immediately after Nora has had a mysterious phone call, ordering her to collect a parcel in a certain shop in Stockholm's Old Town. Nora's friend Lena's grandmother "happens" to have been born in the house where Nora lives now and can give her some valuable information. Nora "happens" to break a vase, discovering slips of paper which lead her investigation further. Ludde the dog "happens" to run away, leading Nora to an abandoned house and garden. Nora is forced to put the jigsaw-puzzle bits together, and so is the reader with her. Very soon, Nora stops viewing the events as coincidences. "It was more like an essential link in some unknown context" (30).

Dag has a strange dream, in which Nora is given an assignment: "Go, I know not where, to seek, I know not what" (32). She does not take it seriously. But later the same day, the volume of Russian folktales which Nora has found in one of the sealed closets falls off the shelf, twice, and both times is opened at the same page, where the hero is given a task: "Go, I know not where, to seek, I know not what!" (40). She tries to dismiss it as a coincidence, but cannot help thinking about it. When she tells Dag about the book and wants to show it to him, the book has vanished. When she finds it again, it "happens" to open on another passage:

> Store my last words in your memory. I shall die, and with my blessing I now give you this doll. Hide it well and show it to no one. But if some misfortune befall you, take out the doll and ask its advice. (50)

Both Russian folktales exist in a collection available in Swedish, which the author apparently had in mind. The first is a quite common type of tale about a king who sends his servant on impossible tasks to get rid of him; the "I know not what" turns out to be a magical invisible helper, who finally helps the servant to overthrow the king and take his place. This tale is of little relevance for the novel, except for the fascinating formula. On the contrary, the other folktale is an important intertext, being one of the very few known fairy tales depicting female initiation (see Franz 1972, 143–157). It is a well-known type as well, about the dead mother who helps and advises her daughter in difficult situations, especially against the stepmother's wrath. In most variants, the mother takes the form of a (totemic) animal or bird, so the Russian version, usually entitled *The Beautiful Wassilissa*, involving a doll, is quite unusual. Since the doll which Nora receives in a mysterious way from Hedvig, Cecilia's aunt, is an image of Cecilia, who is Nora's grandmother's half-sister, the relationship is more complicated than merely mother-daughter. The doll's function is not to protect Nora from evil, but to guide her on a spiritual quest. Nora really asks the doll for advice and seems to get answers; anyway, the presence of the doll helps her think. The doll seems to lead Nora in a certain direction. When the quest is over, the doll mysteriously disappears. Since only Nora has actually seen the doll (although Dag has collected the parcel from the toy shop), we may view the doll as purely symbolic, as a reincarnation of the dead Cecilia.

The intricate plot of the novel is centered around several generations. The patterns of fate have been passed down from mother to daughter, and there are at least four children in the story, besides Nora, who are abandoned in some way. First Cecilia, Agnes's illegitimate daughter, the hub of the whole novel. She is unwanted in the first place and abandoned by her mother who goes off to Stockholm, leaving Cecilia in her sister's care. When Cecilia is seduced by her ballet teacher and dies in childbirth, seventeen years old, her baby is sent away to an orphanage, because there is no one to take care of him. He in his turn gets an illegitimate child, who turns out to be Agnes Cecilia, Dag's secret love, Nora's distant cousin, and the main object of the quest.

What strikes one is that almost all participants in this tangled story are women, except Martin, Cecilia's son. However his fate is doubled by Carita's, the mother of his child. She also was abandoned by both her parents as a baby, and she has no relatives other than Nora's family. This is why she is eager that her child has a family to lean on. Being an orphan, and having heard all family stories, Carita wants to break away from the vicious circle. That is also what Nora feels an urge to do as she says to her grandmother: "It's true, you can't change things that have already happened. But you can try to prevent tragedies from being repeated" (226).

There are certain similarities between *Agnes Cecilia* and novels by Alan Garner, especially *The Owl Service* and *Red Shift*, where contemporary teenagers are caught in tragic patterns from the past and are forced to reenact events which happened long ago. In *The Owl Service*, Alison seems to have broken away from the vicious circle, transforming the circular pattern into linear. In *Red Shift*, Jan is strong enough to do so, while Tom presumably pays with his life for his spiritual weakness. Like Alison, Nora breaks the circular pattern. Nora's quest is a quest for self, and the identity she seeks and finds is unmistakably female. She does not go on big adventures and does not have to fight any external enemies. Her quest involves intuition and to a certain extent intellect. Apparently, this is the closest we can come to a "female" quest if we are to remain within the circular pattern of time, which restores the initial order for the protagonist or creates a new sort of order. The story has a "happy ending," the mystery is solved, and Nora has found a friend; but although she has also found her place in the complicated family tree, and in her search identified with a number of women, she has discovered herself as an individual, but not specifically as a woman. She has met death, and through her contact with the past she has met the sacred, but she has not yet been initiated into sexuality. We have to go further, beyond the point of no return, to find female protagonists who come to this insight as well. Incidentally, both in *The Owl Service* and *Red Shift*, the female protagonists have been initiated into the "feminine mystique." Jan more explicitly, since she has had a love affair with a grown-up man. Alison is suffering from menstrual pain in the beginning of the novel and is therefore more inclined to see blood than flowers in the intricate patterns of the past.

In all the discussed novels, the protagonist is allowed to investigate her specifically female identity under certain out-of-the-ordinary circumstances, either in male disguise or through an uncanny experience. In most texts, the protagonist is brought back to safety and the original order is restored. However, some contemporary authors, male and female alike, allow their protagonists to leave behind the innocence of childhood and proceed further toward experience and adulthood.

NOTES

1. Actually, as any linguist knows, the opposition male-female, like most culturally dependent oppositions, is a so-called privative opposition, which does not imply a presence or absence of a quality (+ or -) but a presence of a quality versus either presence or absence, that is, something neutral, marked versus unmarked (1 or 0, the principle of computers). Linguists often illustrate this by the opposition calf-heifer; a calf can be both male and female (unmarked), while a heifer is only female (marked). The whole notion of Otherness, which has become such an important instrument in literary criticism recently, is based on privative oppositions: the Other is everything that does not fulfil the criteria of Me. That is, unless a person is specified as "female" we perceive this person as "male=neutral," something that political correctness has taught us to avoid. Bearing this in mind, unless we can discover specifically female features of a quest narrative, we must regard all narratives as gender-neutral, which in our culture means male.

2. On the function of clothes see also Scott 1992, 1994 and 1996b.

Chapter 7

Breaking Away

THE PROMISE OF HAPPINESS?

While *Animal Farm* has been included as an animal story in children's reading, I have never come across a recommendation of *1984* as a science-fiction adventure for young readers. Dystopia has been by definition an impossible genre in children's fiction. However, a recent trend in children's fiction shows tangible traits of dystopia. We can see forerunners of this trend in post-disaster science-fiction novels, for instance, *The Prince in Waiting* trilogy, which combines high technology with medieval mysticism.

In the trend I am referring to, the dystopian idea is central, the kernel of the story itself, and the interrogation of modern—adult—civilization in these books is as strong as in Huxley or Orwell. It has taken children's fiction more than half a century to catch up with adult literature in developing this genre, which contradicts the view of childhood as a vision of a hopeful future. It is amazing that the genre has become so prominent, indeed one of the most prominent genres in British, American, and Australian children's fiction of the 1990s. An early representative of this trend may be seen in Robert Cormier's *I Am the Cheese,* where a ruthless totalitarian society is reflected in a mentally disturbed boy's mind. In Germany, Gudrun Pausewang has received much attention for her dystopian children's novels, especially *Fall-out,* a gloomy post-Chernobyl depiction of a nuclear plant accident.

In *The Giver*, the "brave new world" is portrayed in every detail. We meet a strictly regulated life with food rations and predestined working assignments for all citizens. We meet artificial family com-position and children reared in child factories; control over people's thoughts; executions—called by a politically correct euphemism "release"—of the aged, the sick, and the dissidents. More important, this, in our view, unbearable, colorless society is characterized by the absence of memory. The traumatic memory of the past, of war, hunger and misery is absent, but so is that of joy, love, friendship, of all emotions; one of the most significant lost memories is that of a Christmas Eve in the midst of a loving family. In this society, one and only person has the blessing—or the curse—to keep in his mind all memories of humankind, joyful as well as dark, which enables him to make moral evaluations. The protagonist of the novel, the twelve-year-old Jonas, has been chosen to become the next Receiver, a Savior figure who will take upon himself others' sins and pains.

The society in *The Ear, the Eye and the Arm* is different from that in *The Giver*, since the regulated paradise only involves a little part of it, the privileged upper class in Zimbabwe in the year 2194. The rest of the population lives in utter misery, which the three charac-ters, the upper-class children Tendai, Kudu, and Rita, discover when they by chance leave their protected world. Mostly the novel is an adventure in an exotic futuristic setting, but it contains the same ruthless criticism of adult society as does *The Giver*.

A number of recent British books have the same tone as the two abovementioned American ones. *The Disinherited* depicts an en-counter between an upper-class young girl and an unemployed boy in a totalitarian, dystopian society into which England has devel-oped during the early 21st century. *Foundling* is a futuristic Robin-sonnade in which a group of children escapes from new social structures where they are for different reasons doomed to die, more or less like the situation in *The Giver*. If these two examples out of several dozen are focused on the criticism of society, *Why Weeps the Brogan?* has more of a human dimension. In this post-nuclear-catas-trophe novel, irony and humor save it from didacticism, which is so irritating for instance in *Fall-out*. Gilbert and Saxon have lived for four years in what can be identified as the British Museum. It is once again a contemporary Robinsonnade, where the two siblings must survive on their own in a strange and hostile environment, getting food from the strategic store, and constantly fighting mutated spi-ders, the only other survivors. There is also a mystical creature, the

Brogan, who both threatens and helps, and who in a peculiar manner is connected with the vague memories which the children are trying to recover. Novels like these challenge our conventional views of children's fiction. However, unlike adult dystopias, there is always a slight hope in all the novels mentioned, an opening in the end, a promise of a solution. Jonas kidnaps his doomed little brother and escapes from his cruel world. What awaits him outside? Another society of the same kind? The three children in *The Eye, the Ear and the Arm* return, apparently unaffected, from carnival to their own secure life. Hugh in *The Disinherited* may eventually find a future life outside society, in a new idyllic setting. *Foundling* ends with the children having escaped their pursuers for a while and enjoying freedom. The siblings from the British Museum come out and recover their memories and their lost identity. In all these books, adults have betrayed children, but perhaps children are given another chance.

Although dystopia seems to be the opposite of idyll, it has in fact the same purpose: to conserve the children—as well as adults—in an innocent, unchanging state, comfortably freed from memories, emotions, affections, responsibilities—and from natural death. Breaking away from a safe and secluded dystopian society, children break out into linearity. However, quite a few authors depict a reverse process.

A Cry from the Jungle by Tormod Haugen is an extremely complicated and equivocal novel. One of its many intertwined plots describes a mad scientist who has constructed a machine which can extract people's dreams and transform them into energy. The scientist and his team kidnap children for their experiments. Another plot involves the sudden appearance of a jungle in central Oslo. The events taking place in a real city make the threat from the villain as well as from the jungle more tangible.

The adventure plot of the three first parts of the novel is merely a preparation for the characters' encounter with the jungle. Who is allowed to enter the jungle and why? Where does the jungle come from and what does it symbolize? It would be much too simple to apprehend the jungle merely as an element of popular culture, a horror story, a variation of aliens, dinosaurs, giant bees, or killer tomatoes.

The subject of the novel can be viewed within several discourses, such as world politics, children's rights or ecology. Haugen is trying to give us the illusion that the jungle is about anything other than the individual, that it is a global matter, that it "would change the whole nation." Nevertheless I find it more interesting and fruitful to interpret the jungle in terms of individual psychology. As a symbol, the jungle may signify a number of things, such as drugs or cyberspace (which, however, became a social factor several years after the publication of the novel). Most critics have interpreted the jungle positively, as a "sanctuary" (Breen 1995, 298), "a happy return to nature, which surpasses anything that Rousseau could imagine … evidence of the creative power of imagination" (Toijer-Nilsson 1991, 176). Actually, the jungle is much more complicated and ambivalent, which is clearly reflected in the various characters' attitudes toward it. The jungle is wild and uncontrollable, but natural. Is it a threat to civilization or a "happy return to nature"? Haugen portrays the attack of the jungle in a contradictory manner. He is trying to give us a sense of peace saying, for instance: "The strangest thing was that there was no panic," but the description of the jungle encroaching on Oslo is nightmarish, indeed like a horror movie, and the repetition of the words "homeless" and "fugitives" does not create any sense of security, but rather evokes reality with its wars, hunger and natural catastrophes. I cannot unequivocally accept the jungle as positive. It is undoubtedly destructive. Haugen shows the difference in children's and adults' attitude: the adults are thinking about various methods of "coping with" the jungle, struggling against it, stopping it, or the other way round, rather rationally "releasing our inner jungle." They also build "a new, extraordinarily efficient jungle committee." Children become curious and run away from home.

At the same time the jungle is definitely a liberation (as drugs and computer games can be), and it is summoned by imagination. The first description of it, a dream sequence, echoes Maurice Sendak's picture book *Where the Wild Things Are:*

> Miki put aside the heavy lianas and went through the knee-high, dripping grass. He went around the rocking-chair and a standard lamp partly covered by lavish greenery. He could hardly see the wardrobe behind a palm with moist leaves.

Later, Miki and the other children literally sing forward the jungle landscape which becomes more real with every minute. It is first described as a mirage, but very soon the children can enter it. The motif of entering a landscape created by imagination evokes the myth of Wu Lao-Tsu, the artist who enters his own picture. But who is the artist, the creator? We can suspect him to be Miki, since we apprehend him as a protagonist (subject); he is the one who encourages the other children to enter the jungle. But it turns out that the jungle is a collective creation (intersubjective), since everybody recognizes their own fantasy plants and animals in it.

We can thus view the characters of the novel as parts of the collective protagonist, a split personality longing to become whole again. The split character gathers in the jungle, but some parts stay outside. What is the passkey into the jungle? Is it every child's paradise? It appears to be more complex than that.

The word "betrayal" is one of the most frequent in the text ("lonely" and "loneliness" are two more). Miki's parents have betrayed him, each in their own way. Also the other children are described as betrayed by adults. Adults' betrayal of children is depicted in detail in the learned manuscripts of the Zhahdines, a fictitious archaic tribe that plays an important role in the story. A feminist activist sums it up in a lecture as: "… children who are not loved for what they are, who are not seen as the children they are, who are given the responsibility that they do not feel they can cope with." The jungle is a compensation for the lack of love and for the colorless, hopeless reality. It is open for both children and adults who have been betrayed and who are trying to forget their bitterness: "… dreaming, longing, but abandoned, *invisible*, lonely" (my emphasis). Invisibility as a consequence of betrayal is a recurrent motif in Haugen's books (see Metcalf 1992).

Among the children rejected by the jungle we find Veronica, who is at first deeply upset. The explanation is simple: "She had never felt lonely." The rational, pragmatic Veronica has no need to escape to the world of fancy. The evil scientist has not even tried to capture her, because she has no dreams. She stays in the real world and helps other children to "cope with" the jungle. One day she discovers that she can enter the jungle if she chooses to. But apparently she does not want to.

Is the jungle a symbol of the subconscious? Is it the dark, suppressed corner of our psyche which lies in wait and attacks us when we least expect it, and which feeds our dreams and fancies? We read for instance: "Miki felt the jungle inside himself" or "Somebody spoke of the jungle deep inside me." Also "an inner landscape similar to a jungle" is mentioned. The jungle is thus a part of the psyche. Is Haugen saying, like many children's writers inspired by Jung, such as Tove Jansson or Maria Gripe, that we have to meet our subconscious in order to become whole? But in this case there must be a way out of the jungle. If the Zhahdine messenger is The Wise Old Man, the guide in the Jungian model, he should not only lead the children into the jungle, but also out of it. Instead he abandons them. Haugen never says that the ultimate goal is to leave the jungle with a better understanding of life and one's own personality. For those who have chosen the jungle it seems to be the final destination.

In one of the Zhahdine legends, which must be seen as a key to Haugen's message, the Goddess characterizes the endless jungle as lack of variety. This can also be interpreted as the original, primitive wholeness of childhood—in a Jungian sense, the false wholeness which we must leave if we wish to develop and grow up. "… people are people exactly because they long for other places," the Goddess says. To stay in the jungle is not to live at all.

The jungle is thus conserving; to enter the jungle is not simply escape, it is regression, a frustrated attempt to return to the sorrowless idyll of childhood. If the jungle represents the Goddess, the good Progenitrix, then the children stay unborn in her womb. "A child must always be a reminder of man's wholeness," says a proverb from Zhahdine legends. But a man cannot be whole if the child is not allowed to grow up.

In another novel by Haugen, *Winter Place*, a young boy is trying to avoid taking the decisive step into adulthood by committing suicide. A young person's suicide becomes, strangely enough, a way to escape from death. *A Cry from the Jungle* starts with Miki's—then still Michael's—first encounter with death. "To be dead is the same as not being any more," he learns. At this moment Michael changes his name—a symbolical death and rebirth in a rite of passage—and also hears a cry from the jungle for the first time. The jungle has promised freedom but turns out to be a trap. After this first cry Miki enters "a new phase of his life," a phase where he is aware of his own mortality. After this, "nothing can be as it was before." The jungle calls him, and Miki, unable to cope with life and without help from adults, succumbs. Miki's father cannot accept death either—his mother's, Miki's grandmother's death—and is prepared to let the mad scientist free him from dreams or else to enter the jungle where death does not exist.

Entering the jungle is thus a circumlocution of suicide. In this case, the practical Veronica staying outside is both cleverer and more mature. Instead, she starts "a painful wandering which she would not like to be without," that is, movement toward adulthood. A positive example?

However, the children who enter the jungle have not much choice. The alternative is "to come home and be taken care of," that is get socialized into the norms prescribed by adult life. And this is exactly what the children are trying to avoid. Entering the jungle they believe that they are going home. They wish to stay in the jungle for ever and ever, while life outside the jungle goes on, with its light and dark sides.

Suggesting this interpretation of the novel rather than "the happy return to nature," I view it against the background of Haugen's other works. Many of them, especially *The White Castle*, depict the adults' attempts to prevent children from growing up, to preserve them as happily innocent, as eternal children. In *The Day that Disappeared* Haugen develops his own version of *Peter Pan*. But if this resuscitated Peter Pan tries to seduce children by promising them endless adventures, another figure in the novel, an old man called Sydenhjelm, may be apprehended as a study portrait for the mad scientist. Sydenhjelm gathers unhappy children and locks them up in his house, promising them happiness and peace. The motif of kidnapping in *A Cry from the Jungle*, which at first sight seemed an element of a criminal novel, appears to have deeper intratextual links. A novel published after *A Cry from the Jungle, The Lizards Are Coming*, depicts another dubious return to nature, involving children's transformation into monsters. A Norwegian scholar interprets this novel similarly to my reading of *A Cry from the Jungle*, that is viewing the transformation into giant lizards as ambivalent, but a regression rather than a positive solution (Bache-Wiig 1995).

Haugen's pessimism or rather a sense of resignation when confronted with the great mystery of life is something that he shares with many contemporary children's writers. Adults' oppression of children has become a commonplace, and the earlier happy endings have become unusual in serious children's fiction.

TOWARD LINEARITY

If the books discussed so far would normally be classified as dystopias, the next one, the *Mouse and His Child*, is most often referred to as toy fantasy. However, I would like to show that the central pattern in all these texts is similar: it depicts an attempt, successful or not, to break away from idyll, which is often expressed by the change in temporal pattern of the novel from circular to linear.

The Mouse and His Child starts with a perfect image of childhood, a doll house, a self-sufficient world existing wholly in the cyclical time:

> ... the dolls never set foot outside it. They had no need to; every-thing they could possibly want was there ... *Interminable*-weekend-guest dolls lay in all the guest room beds, sporting dolls played billiards in the billiard room, and a scholar doll in the library *never ceased* perusal of the book he held .... In the dining room, beneath a glittering chandelier, a party of lady and gentleman dolls sat *perpetually* around a table ....
>
> It was the elephant's *constant* delight to watch that tea party through the window ... (4f; my emphasis).

The very idea of a windup toy is repetition, predestination, things going on forever. Another aspect is absence of change and free will. But the mouse child is at once anxious about linearity:

> "What happens when they buy you?" he asked her.
> "That, of course, is outside of my experience," said the elephant, "but I should think that one simply *goes out into the world* and does whatever one does. One dances or balances a ball, as the case may be."
> ... The doll house was bright and warm; the teapot gleamed upon the dazzling cloth. "I don't want to go out into the world," he said. (6; my emphasis)

The elephant is displeased: "... it is expected of this young mouse that he go out into the world with this father and dance in circles" (6). This statement contains a contradiction. Going out is linear, dancing in circles by definition circular; this contradiction sets up the whole movement of the book.

> ... the windup toys were not presents for the children; the grownups brought them down from the attic *every year* with the Christmas ornaments, and *every year* after Christmas they were packed away again. (8f; my emphasis)

This passage, more than any other, accentuates the adults' nostalgia. It is no coincidence that the novel starts at Christmas, the time of year when most adults get nostalgic. But for the toys, representing children, eternity does not seems attractive:

> The monkey complained of being made to play the same tune *over and over* on a cheap fiddle; the bird complained of having to peck at a bare floor; the rabbit complained that there was no meaning in his cymbals. And soon the mouse and his child complained of the futility of dancing in an *endless* circle that led nowhere. (9; my emphasis)

The regularity of the two mice dancing in circles is reminiscent of the wonderful mechanical toys in *The Nutcracker*: after a while, the children ask their godfather to make the figures in the windup castle do something else, for instance go out from another door, and when this proves impossible, they get bored. This is a perfect metaphor of the adults' *idea* of what children might enjoy—far from the real perception.

Thus if the mice were to dance Christmas after Christmas until the end of the world, there would be no story. "So it was that four Christmases came and went, until there came a fifth Christmas that was different from the others" (9). This is a step away from circularity as well as from the iterative. The mouse child breaks the rules, and the expulsion from paradise follows immediately. As always, this is an ambivalent action: tragic, but necessary. All the further events of the novels are stations on the toys' linear (or rather pseudo-linear, as I will show) journey. Joanne Lynn, reading the novel as a pastoral, observes: "Each subsequent escape is toward a more pastoral scene—or so it seems" (Lynn 1986, 21). Indeed, the pastoral elements of the novel are more than dubious.

The tramp, who throughout the novel acts a *deus ex machina* toward the toys (and most probably personifies the covert, omniscient narrator), repairs them, but they cannot dance any more, they go straight, the father pushing the child backwards in front of him. This is of course *physically* a linear progress, but only a token one for the psychological dimension of the story. The mice cannot go further than one winding-up takes them, yet they like walking better than dancing in circles. When the fortune-telling frog tells the mice: "You have broken the circle ... and a straight line of great force emerges. Follow it" (28), the author seems to be telling us that linearity is preferable. The idea is reinforced repeatedly in the text: "There is no going back," said the father; "we cannot dance in circles anymore" (34).

At the same time, the idea of circularity continues to be central. The mice watch the circle of nature: weasels eat shrews, the owl eats the weasels, and carries away Frog. Muskrat makes the mice more or less walk in a circle again, in his crazy endeavor to fell a tree. The enterprise can take a long time:

> Day after day the Muskrat and the mouse and his child worked at the tree ...
> While Muskrat's project trudged ahead, the life of the pond went on as always ... Above the mouse and his child waxed and waned the icy moon, and bright Sirius kept his track across the sky while they trod theirs below. (88f)

This is a temporary return to circularity and iterative. The unique feature of this novel is that its linear time, chronos, can be infinitely long, because the toys do not grow up, do not have to eat and are not in a hurry. Therefore, story time takes many years, which is normally impossible in a children's book. But it emphasizes the sense of kairos.

Further wisdom is preached by Serpentina the turtle:

> This mud being like other mud, we may assume that other mud is like this mud, which is to say that one place is all places and all places are one. Thus by staying here we are at the same time everywhere, and there is obviously no place to go. Winding, therefore, is futile. (102)

Serpentina translates mythic time into mythic space. Amplified by the idea of infinity, expressed by the famous can of Bonzo Dog Food, this is a perfect philosophy of mythic existence.

The world the toys have come to is as far away as possible from childhood paradise: dump, commercialism, violence (Manny kills the donkey who is too feeble to work), crime (bank-robbing), hard work and exploitation, frauds (the fortune-teller), war (between shrews), incomprehensible art forms, pure-thought philosophy— definitely the world of adults.

The novel is also very much about eating and being eaten up— amazing, given the fact that the main characters do not eat at all and cannot be eaten, or, as the hawk remarks, they are not part of the balance of nature (119). Many critics have observed (and objected to) the violence in the animal world, especially the episode with shrews, weasels, and owl. However, all these violent deaths do not affect the toys, just as "adult" deaths most often do not affect children. The mouse child is not frightened by being carried away by the hawk, since he knows that the predator will soon discover that they are inedible. Being inedible (as well as not having to eat) is a tragedy much worse than not being self-winding, although this aspect is deliberately omitted by the author. Toys are not part of the circle of life and can never be. In a totally toy (idyllic) world, it would not matter; but since there is a constant juxtaposition between nature and culture, flesh and tin, we cannot wholly neglect this aspect. Unlike *The Velveteen Rabbit*, the toy mice have no objective of becoming alive. They are inanimate (literally: lacking soul!) objects and so they remain, even though the father says: "We aren't toys any more … Toys are to be played with, and we aren't" (131).

Therefore the author introduces a special form of death for the toys, which they go through, as ritual prescribes, three times. Since death, for toys, unlike all other deaths in the story, is reversible, they are reborn like the returning gods. In her most illuminating essay, Valerie Krips notes that after each destruction and resurrection, the mouse and his child reemerge with new qualities: first they go straight instead of dancing in circles, after the second remaking they are separated from each other, and finally they are made self-winding, or so it seems. Krips maintains in her Lacanian reading that they acquire a new identity each time, which she views as a problem, since the identity which the mouse child has discovered in his reflection in the tin can—going through the "mirror stage"—is no longer there (Krips 1993). For me the question is less relevant since the toys always remain essentially what they are. Therefore they seek their paradise in the company of other toys, and in the constrained world of the doll house.

The novel invites a Jungian interpretation with its many symbols and images, descents and reemergence, the Dante-like wandering through the circles of Inferno, Manny Rat as the dark Shadow, the seal as Anima, the three uncles as the Wise Old Men, the guides, the helpers, the three clever adults, without whose assistance initiation is not possible. Ironically, but quite consistent with the Jungian model, escaping from Manny Rat the mice get farther away from the elephant, one of the objects of their quest. The Shadow has to be met face to face, which also happens in the end. The most problematic aspect is that according to Jung, the final goal of the process of individuation is to become whole, while the two mice are instead separated. Does this mean that individuation has failed?

For a Jungian, the essential question is who is going through individuation. What is the implication of a father and child stuck together? Lois Kuznets views the mouse child as the protagonist since it is a children's story (Kuznets 1994, 171), which for me is a circular argument. Are we once again dealing with a collective hero, in an unusual combination of child and adult? The focalizing pattern of the narrative rather suggests the notion of intersubjectivity. What do the mice represent? Does the child bring back childhood to his father—a motif observed by many critics of Arcadian fiction?

During the journey, the father is looking forward, while the son is looking backward, although logically it should be the other way round. Apparently, the mouse child does not wish to grow up and become independent, but on the contrary seeks to go back to the security of his early childhood, symbolized by the doll house. His faith in this paradise is unshakable:

> He had never been so happy, had never felt so lucky. He had never doubted that he would make his dream come true, and all the remaining difficulties shrank before him now—the doll house and the seal would certainly be found, the territory won, and he should have his mama. (95)

The father, forced to look forward, is much more skeptical about the future: "Our motor is in me. He fills the empty space inside himself with foolish dreams that cannot possibly come true" (35). The father is repeatedly prepared to give up, while the child never loses hope. But it is not hope for future, but hope to return to the mythic past, which the father, an adult, does not believe in. However, when the father sees the seal, the elephant and the house, after his second rebirth, he is prepared to fight for his territory. In a way, the father takes over the child's role as protagonist (like Colin's father in *The Secret Garden*), because now he also wants to retreat into the mythical world of childhood. Paradoxically, this wish is combined with a clear erotic desire:

> The elephant was shabby and pathetic; her looks were gone, departed with the ear, the eye, the purple headcloth and her plush. The father saw all that, and yet saw nothing of it; some brightness in her, some temper finer than the newest tin, some steadfast beauty smote and dazzled him. He wished that he might shelter and protect her … He fell in love … (95f)

The erotic subtext of the novel is obvious, especially in the rivalry between the mouse father and Manny Rat, and the elephant's open aversion for Manny, who has, we might say, raped her. However, the intersubjective construction of the protagonist allows the author to subdue the sexual undertones by shifting the focus to the child and his need of a mother, rather than the father's need of a sexual partner.

The idea of self-winding—linearity—is suddenly overshadowed by the idea of home, security, peace, idyll, circularity. The notion of home is reinforced by the notion of territory which the mice learn from the war of the shrews (45). The recovery of the doll house is the foremost symbol of the restoration of paradise: "The house was *firmly* nailed to the platform" (156; my emphasis); "… phoenixlike, the place seemed reborn of itself" (157). However, the author hurries to admit that the restoration is only partial:

> The doll house would never again be what it once had been; its stateliness and beauty were long gone, but something new and different emerged from the concerned efforts of the little family. (157)

The end of the novel depicts a final acceptance of a paradise substantially inferior to the initial dream. The setting is still the dump. The house and its inhabitants are worn out and shabby. The flow of time is irreversible. Joanne Lynn maintains that Hoban pictures a sort of compromise of Utopia, "accepting the limitations of human nature," yet a "place in which human society rises above the junk-heap of technological civilization and creates from however disparate material and human capacities a world that glows with possibilities of the worth of human existence" (Lynn 1986, 23). In terms of social or even psychological values, it may be true. In terms of restoring archaic, mythic time, the ending shows the futility of every attempt to recreate Utopia.

Manny Rat makes the mice self-winding, which turns out only to mean going on forever without change: "... self-windingly and interminably walking ..." (167). This may be seen as Manny's last attempt at revenge. When the winding stops, the mice only feel relieved. The last pages of the novel bring back the iterative, stretching into the eternal future: annual drama festival, yearly Deep Thought Symposium, etc. "Your fortune has been made," said Frog, "and needs no more telling" (181). That is, the toys have no future, they are dead. The mouse child will forever be a child. Paradise is regained. The child creates this paradise according to his childish visions, even though they challenge common sense: his father marries the elephant, the seal becomes his sister. This is also communal rather than individual happiness, involving both animals and toys, which is a dubious message from the author. A very important question remains unanswered at the closure of the book: what happens to the animals, the kind uncles, who, being mortal, cannot possibly become part of this eternity? Are they disposed of when no longer needed? Apparently, the little child's vision cannot reach that far.

The mouse child's dream of paradise is expressed by the iterative at the beginning: " ... will you sing to me *all the time*? And can we all *stay* here together and live in the beautiful house where the party *is on* and not go out into the world?" (7; my emphasis). The elephant explains that it is impossible. In the end, they seem to have achieved the impossible, but it is an illusion. There is no regular happy ending to the story, no reward for suffering, no punishment for the villains.

It is more like the story of the Steadfast Tin Soldier, who, after a long time of trials, is united with his beloved ballerina in death.

The tramp's farewell to the toys: "Be happy" must be viewed as the narrator's comment. Is the essential component of the fairy-tale formula "happy *ever after*," with all its implications, truncated? As Lois Kuznets remarks, "Be happy" makes no promises about the future. Kuznets goes on to: "And this relatively happy ending acknowledges the necessity of endless remaking, virtual recycling of the world to meet human desires. Hoban uses his toy narrative to mirror and exploit the uncertainties of human life ..." (176). I would add—adult life.

MEETING SHADOWS

Although the two fantasy novels by Astrid Lindgren, *Mio My Son* and *The Brothers Lionheart*, show some superficial similarities with my master text of fantasy (and thus of the there-and-back-again pattern), *The Lion, the Witch and the Wardrobe*, they are radically different in some essential aspects.

To begin with, they involve individual rather than collective protagonists, common in traditional fantasy. A very brief comparison between the collective character in *The Lion, the Witch and the Wardrobe* and the individual character in *Mio My Son* demonstrates clearly how the central message of fantasy is amplified by means of a complex character. Mio is at times ready to give up, and he almost becomes a traitor, like Edmund. The most important battle takes place within himself. The individual character in *Mio My Son* is much more complex than any of the four Pevensies, and we apprehend him as an ordinary human being rather than as a fairy-tale hero. The Pevensie children are quite pale, they merely perform the actions the plot demands of them.

Further, unlike traditional fantasy, *Mio My Son* and *The Brothers Lionheart* use first-person narrators. First-person narratives are extremely rare within fantasy genre (among my corpus of 250 texts studied in *The Magic Code* there were hardly a dozen; see Nikolajeva 1988). The reason is probably purely educational: a first-person narrative, implying a stronger identification, can be considered too frightening for young readers when confronted with evil forces in a magic realm. However, this confirms my argument about the predominance of third-person narratives in combination with circular patterns. Both *Mio* and *The Brothers,* breaking away from the circular pattern, involve a more engaging first-person narrator.

In fact, the narrative structure of both novels is extremely complicated as compared to the omniscient, didactic narrator of *The Lion, the Witch and the Wardrobe,* who can switch between Edmund and the other three children when they part, or can render all the four children's thoughts and feelings, contrasting them. He can even enter the mind of the evil White Witch, their enemy. In doing this, he destroys some of the suspense of the story; it would have been a more powerful story if the readers were to discover the effect of the evil forces by themselves, together with Edmund or maybe before him. This is exactly what happens in *Mio* and *The Brothers* where the naive, innocent, ignorant child narrator is by definition unreliable.

Another principal difference between traditional fantasy and Astrid Lindgren's two novels is their firm anchoring in reality. In *Mio,* the narrator models his imaginary world on his own reality, furnishing it with the brilliance of a fairy tale. The only thing Andy knows about his real father is what Aunt Hulda has told him, that his father was a good-for-nothing. Therefore Andy must model his imaginary daddy, My Father the King, on his friend Ben's daddy: "His face was like the face of Ben's daddy, only more handsome," adding some fairy-tale glory to it: "his clothes glittered with gold and diamonds" (19). Andy has no mother, therefore Pompoo's mother takes over the role, but the model is Mrs. Lundy from the fruit shop: "she was just like Mrs. Lundy, except perhaps a little prettier" (29). Even Charlie the brewer's horse acquires his rightful place in the imaginary country, transformed into Miramis the wonderful flying horse. The most important figure is naturally the friend and squire Pompoo: "he had just the same brown dark hair as Ben and just the same brown eyes" (25f).

The other figures in the Farawayland come from fairy tales, for instance Nonno's granny: "you'd think she had come straight out of a fairy tale, though she was a real live granny" (46). Also Totty and his siblings live in "just the kind of cottage you read about in fairy tales" (58), and all children are nice, the way they never were back at home: "They were always against somebody, and that one was left out of all the games. Usually that was me" (59). Creating the nice children, Andy the narrator counterbalances his bitter experiences. The magical helpers—the genie in the beer bottle, the Weaver, the hungry Eno, the Swordsmith—all come directly from fairy tales that Andy has read.

As to the evil characters, they are products of imagination rather than of the immediate surroundings. Sir Kato is never directly associated with Andy's foster-father, but the connection is obvious. However, Andy seems to be more bitter toward his foster-mother, Aunt Hulda. Why does he create a male object for his hatred? According to the Jungian model, writers project their dark feelings, the Shadow, into characters of the opposite gender (see Veghlan 1987; I refer to this essay and expand it in my study, Nikolajeva 1996, 76–79). C. S. Lewis, a male writer, creates the White Witch as the image of ultimate evil. It is therefore logical to assume that Astrid Lindgren, a female author, should portray the evil as a male figure. Besides, according to the same theory, literary characters often meet their Shadows in the form of figures of the same gender. Sir Kato represents the dark, animalistic traits in Andy/Mio himself. This is especially clear from the fact that Mio chooses to meet Sir Kato in an open combat rather than sneak up on him in a trickster manner, wearing his invisibility mantle. Mio must meet his Shadow face to face. Further, at the last moment, Sir Kato begs to be killed and liberated from the burden of his own evil:

> "Make sure you pierce my heart! Make sure you thrust straight through my heart of stone. It has chafed there for so long, and hurt me very much." (158)

Similarly, Nangiyala is a product of Rusky's imagination, inspired by his brother's stories, in particular, his formula "still in the days of campfires and sagas" (9). Unlike Andy, Rusky is not a reader, so he has to fill in the gaps in his brother's stories himself. There are no characters, except his brother, and no episodes or situations that Rusky transposes from his real world to Nangiyala. Besides, the evil is depicted in two stages. Katla the female dragon is a traditional monster, evil by nature. But the real villain of the story is Tengil, a human being. Rusky's exploration of evil becomes, unlike Mio's, a discovery of a treacherous human mind. Further, his adored brother Jonathan is by no means a fairy-tale hero; for one thing, he refuses to fight or kill. The constellation of characters in The Brothers is more

intricate and ambivalent than in *Mio* with its clearcut depiction of
evil and its servants.

The principal difference between the construction of "reality"
and the imaginary world in C. S. Lewis's and Astrid Lindgren's
fantasy novels can be described in Tzvetan Todorov's terms of
marvelous versus fantastic. The essence of the fantastic lies in the
hesitation of the protagonist (and the reader) as confronted with the
supernatural (Todorov 1973, 25). Traditional fantasy, represented
by C. S. Lewis, will fall under the category of the marvelous. His
characters feel no hesitation when confronted with the inexplicable,
but Astrid Lindgren's do, and so do the readers. Both Andy's and
Rusky's experience may be "real," but they may also be dreams,
fancies, or hallucinations. The boundaries between "reality" and the
Otherworld are more elusive in *Mio* and *The Brothers*, and the
passage more subtle. The there-and-back-again pattern, meant to
create a sense of security, stability of the universe, immutability of
identity, and certainty of a "happy ending," is contrasted with
uncertainty, instability, duality, and hesitation.

In both novels, the transportation to the Otherworld implies a
complete restoration of Paradise. The initial situation for Andy as
well as Rusky is a neverending misery. Andy's life with his foster-
parents is colorless and uneventful. In Andy's home, they never
laugh or show any emotions. Andy is not allowed to bring friends
home. The season when the story starts is autumn, and the time of
day is dusk—both are the time of decay and death.

By contrast, the Farawayland is, like every Arcadia, a country of
eternal summer and sunshine. The lavish imagery is transparent:
Garden of Roses, green pastures, silver poplars, singing birds, beautiful music, shepherds, lambkins, campfires. Mio has his beloved
father, who holds his hand, providing a body contact he has always
lacked, and he is surrounded by friends. He gets his own horse. He
is treated to food, and not just any food, but pancakes—which for
Astrid Lindgren is always the foremost symbol of home and love:
"I like pancakes more than anything. Ben's mummy used to make
them, and sometimes gave me one, but these that Pompoo's
mummy had cooked tasted even better" (42).

The ritual function of food is still more prominent in *Mio* as
compared to the Narnia Chronicles. Mrs. Lundy from the fruit shop
"used to give me sweets and fruit" (11), a detail with several mean-

ings. It is a sign of generosity, in sharp contrast to the stinginess of the foster-parents. Andy is generous himself: for instance, he gives sugar to the old brewer's horse. But "sweets and fruit" are also a sign of a secret covenant between the boy and Mrs. Lundy, the magical helper, donor and sender (Propp's terms). With her food, the good fairy prepares the boy for his life in the Otherworld. Sweets and fruit also anticipate the magic apple, the sign by which Andy will be recognized as prince Mio. Apples often have a symbolic meaning in folktales and myth.

The plot is set in motion by Aunt Hulda sending Andy to get her some *dry* biscuits (unfortunately translated into English as buns) "that she specially liked" (12). This act characterizes her as selfish; besides dry biscuits symbolize her attitude to life (cf Edström 1992, 169). It is never mentioned explicitly that meals in Andy's home are dull. But sitting alone on a park bench, he longs for the joy of a shared meal: "Everybody had gone home for supper. ... [Ben] was sitting inside eating pease pudding and *pancakes* with his daddy and mummy" (14, my emphasis).

Among the magical objects the hero is given for his quest are Bread that Satisfies Hunger and a little spoon which used to belong to Nonno's little sister, kidnapped by Sir Kato. Mio gives the bread to the hungry Eno—a very common fairy-tale motif—who shows him the way. But the bread is not merely a magical agent, since, unlike fairy-tale heroes, Mio and his squire must eat. Andy, who is telling the story, knows very well what it means to be hungry, and he can easily imagine Mio's wandering inside the Blackest Mountain and knowing that soon there will be no food left: "We ate only a little, because we didn't know how long it had to last" (115). After crossing the Dead Lake, they eat the last piece of bread and "we didn't know when we should get any more to eat" (133). Somehow, fairy-tale heroes never bother about eating!

Finally, when choosing punishment for Mio and Pompoo, Sir Kato decides to let them starve. "In my castle," he said, "you die of hunger in a single night, because the night is very long and the hunger is very great" (145). There are several implications in this scene. It expresses once again a child's subconscious fear of hunger. Death as such is an abstract notion for most young readers. Hunger on the other hand is something everyone has experienced, at least on a very modest scale. To be hungry, not to get food is a tangible

threat. However, it can also be translated into more symbolic notions. Hunger in Sir Kato's castle is hunger for love and warmth. The
lack of these has caused Mio's quest. When the terrible hunger
comes, Mio thinks "longingly of the porridge which Aunt Hulda
used to give me for breakfast and which I had disliked so much"
(150). Here comes the first sign of forgiveness and reconciliation
with the foster-mother. The rescue appears in a fairy-tale manner,
from the spoon which has been given him with love by his friends.
The magical food he gets from the spoon provides him with physical
and spiritual strength to go into the final combat.

Rusky's earthly life is still more miserable than Andy's: he is ill
and knows that he is soon going to die. He describes himself as an
"ugly, stupid, and cowardly boy, with crooked legs and all" (9). His
father has gone to sea and never comes back; and his mother is too
busy earning her living. When his brother Jonathan dies in a fire,
Rusky loses his last foothold in life.

In contrast, Nangiyala is presented as the most beautiful country
in the world. The young brothers live in a house of their own in
Cherry Valley, surrounded by gorgeous mountains. The air is clear.
All Rusky's dreams come true: he can run and swim and ride a
horse, he can climb mountains and fish in a stream. He has become
healthy, strong and brave. Sofia, the good fairy, comes with food,
including pancakes, because in Nangiyala everything is free, and
everybody helps everybody else. The happiness seems to be eternal.
Nangiyala also has mythical time: "... there was no *time* in Nangiyala the way it was on Earth. Even if he did live until he was ninety,
it wouldn't seem like more than two days at the most before he
came" (12, author's emphasis).

Into these two idyllic realms, evil is introduced by subtle means.
Unlike the folktale hero who is promptly told that he has a task to
fulfil and likewise promptly agrees to perform it, Mio is both hesitant and scared, and it takes a long time for Rusky to realize and
accept that there is evil in Nangiyala.

Unlike fairy-tale kings, Mio's father does not explicitly tell him to
go and fight Sir Kato. Mio must make the decision himself, and
when he does, the father says: "Ah! So soon?" (69), while Pompoo
the squire says: "Ah! At last!" (71). Everyone knows that Mio has a
predestined task, but it is part of his trials to come to the insight on
his own: "I was going there to fight Sir Kato, though I was afraid,

terribly afraid, and I wanted to cry when I thought of what I had to do" (81). This is a long way from the rational matter-of-fact manner in which the Pevensie children accept their task. Mio is more like Christ in Gethsemane than a folktale hero when he begs his Father: "I know you want me to fight Sir Kato, but won't you please let me off?" (100). Despite overt Biblical parallels in *The Lion, the Witch and the Wardrobe*, Mio displays more profound links with Christian motifs. Mio the Savior will repeatedly be tempted by Satan.

Mio's destiny also involves mythical time: "a thousand, thousand years" (passim). The prophecy about him is told in the fairy-tale form: "Once upon a time there was a king's son riding in the moonlight ..." (65f). With available grammatical categories, it would be told in the iterative: a king's son has always been riding.

Notably, Rusky does not have to meet his antagonist in a combat; nevertheless he has enough occasions to show courage. Possibly, the impact of this novel is stronger because its character has less of a valiant fairy-tale hero about him. This role is taken over by his brother, while Rusky constantly underlines how scared and helpless he is. However, his ultimate task is if possible still harder than Mio's, and much more of a self-sacrifice (cf Metcalf 1995b).

Why is it necessary for the characters to undergo more trials? Haven't they suffered enough in their earthly life? A sentimental Victorian fantasy story, like *The Water Babies*, would be satisfied by rewarding the deprived heroes with a glorious afterlife. This happens in Astrid Lindgren's own short story "The Southern Meadow" where two poor children escape from their miserable life into the eternal happiness of a heavenly garden. However, both Andy and Rusky have acquired their new positions in advance. The orphan boy Andy becomes prince Mio, his father's beloved son. Rusky the sick, unhappy boy becomes Karl Lionheart, healthy and strong. As in a rite of passage, they receive new, adult names to go with their new identities. Giving him the apple, Mrs. Lundy says to Andy: "Good-by, Karl Anders Nilsson" (12), meaning that the old identity will soon be left behind. But deep inside, they remain unchanged. They still have to go through their initiation.

Transportation to the Otherworld is in both novels a depiction of ritual death. *The Brothers* is more explicit: the passage to Nangiyala is described in plain language as death. But Andy's journey to the Farawayland can also be interpreted as death. On the "realistic" (low mimetic in Frye's terminology) level, he may freeze to death on his park bench, like Andersen's little match girl; he may commit suicide in despair; he may even get murdered by some maniac whom he in the last second imagines to be a genie from a bottle. On the mythical level, Andy must go through ritual death and resurrection. His initial euphoria in Paradise must necessarily be followed by trials before he can emerge from the realm of death. John Stephens insists that characters cannot focalize their own death (Stephens 1992, 225); however, the narrative structure of both novels successfully defies this challenge.

Mio's entrance into Sir Kato's country and Rusky's entrance into Wild Rose Valley exemplify the second ritual death, descent to the next level of Inferno. The landscape Mio and Pompoo meet in Sir Kato's country is more reminiscent of the realm of death than the pastoral Greenfields Island: Dead Forest, the Deepest Cave in the Blackest Mountain—there are enough symbols for both Jungians and Freudians to operate with. In *The Brothers* there are also caves, caverns, cellars, and narrow underground passages. Both heroes emerge from their infernal descent as the myth prescribes.

There is, however, a significant difference. In a traditional narrative of death and rebirth, the character returns to his ordinary realm after having gone through trials and performing his tasks, as do the Pevensie children. True, Mio returns from Sir Kato's country to the Garden of Roses. The paradise is regained. There are green leaves in what used to be Dead Forest. The enchanted children are transformed back into human form. Mio even conquers death: the little girl Milimani who sacrificed her life in a bird's disguise to help Mio, is miraculously resurrected. The cyclical, mythical time is revived. However, Mio does not return home to become Andy again, at least not if we interpret his story as "true."

Rusky never returns to the paradise of Cherry Valley. Instead, he must go further, into another abyss of death, where a new Paradise, still more beautiful than Nangiyala is waiting. At least this is what Jonathan promises him. A possible interpretation of *The Brothers* is that the adventures in Nangiyala are products of Rusky's agony as he is dying, alone and miserable, and grieving his dead brother, at home on his kitchen sofa. In any case, his journey has definitely become linear. A similar interpretation of *Mio* suggests that Andy invents a story to comfort himself in his loneliness on the park bench. We can turn to the narrative situation to get some clarity. In the end, the narrator is trying to give us the illusion that the protagonist has stayed in the Otherworld: "There is no Andy on any seat in the Park. He's here in Farawayland, you see. *He is in Farawayland, I tell you*" (179). The author's emphasis reveals the narrator's frantic attempt to persuade the narratee. Apparently, Andy has been telling the whole story to himself, the narrator and the narratee thus being identical, while neither of them is identical with the protagonist, prince Mio. Some features of the text expose the relationship between the two: now and then, the narrator makes a blunder and is forced to correct himself:

> There were so many hiding places! If there had been one-tenth as many in the Park, Ben and I would have been thrilled. I mean, Ben would have been thrilled. *I* shall never have to look for hiding places in the Park again, thank goodness! (31; author's emphasis)

A more ambivalent interpretation is suggested by the many questions appearing throughout the text in the form of free indirect discourse, for instance:

> Was he [sir Kato] then so frightened of me that he needed so many guards? Was he so frightened of one who had no sword, and who would be behind seven locks, with seven and seventy guards outside? (147)

Is it the protagonist's thoughts at the moment or the narrator's comment afterwards? The situation is crucial, since the insight about Sir Kato's fear of him makes Mio realize his own strength. If Andy the narrator is telling the story to Andy the narratee, sitting on a park bench, this is the most powerful turning point of the psychodrama.

If Andy has only made his journey to the Farawayland in his imagination, and is in fact sitting on a bench in Stockholm when the narrative ends, then the pattern of his journey is circular, carnivalesque, while his imaginary trials have made him better prepared to cope with his situation in reality, in a sort of self-therapy. The struggle against evil has not been a purpose in itself, but the reason for Andy's knowledge of self. Similarly, Rusky's experience of evil in the Wild Rose Valley is merely a preparation for his acceptance of his own mortality.

Both novels may remind us of the final part of the Narnia Chronicles, *The Last Battle,* where the circular pattern of the previous parts is changed into a linear one, and the eternity of Narnian paradise is destroyed for ever. As in *The Brothers Lionheart,* the passage into linearity is through death. However, if C. S. Lewis's characters are as unaffected by death as they once were by the adventures in Narnia, for Andy and Rusky their experience of the Otherworld is an act of maturation. And Rusky, having been introduced to death, has gone one step further.

MOTHER'S BREAD

Ronia, the Robber's Daughter is a story of a young girl gaining freedom and independence from her parents, a true rite of passage. However, as we have seen, female initiation is radically different from male, since it includes at least one additional stage. Like Mio and Rusky, Ronia must leave the security of home. But in order to acquire her female identity, she must also liberate herself from her oppressive father and reestablish links with her mother, if she is ever to develop a normal and healthy relation with a man. Ronia's objective is not to become a hero, which is probably the main merit of this book. Unlike so many female characters in fantasy novels, who are forced by the authors into traditional male roles as dragonslayers or spaceship pilots—a simple gender permutation, tokenism— Ronia's dilemma is to reconcile her independence with a female identity, which among other things will not permit her to become a robber chieftain.

Unlike Mio and Rusky, Ronia's trials are not caused by lack of anything. Ronia has everything a young child can dream of: a secure home (in fact, symbolically enough, a stronghold, a fort), food, clothes, and loving parents. She takes all this for granted: "she wondered about it no more than she wondered where the rain came from. Things were just *there*—she had noticed that before" (18; author's emphasis). Her horizons are limited, as they always are for a young child: "For a long time she had believed that the great stone hall was the whole world" (10). The phrase is echoed later:

> She soon realized how stupid she had been: how could she have
> thought that the great stone hall was the whole world? Not even the

huge Matt's Fort was the whole world. Not even the high Matt's
Mountain was the whole world—no, the world was bigger than Matt.
(13)

The child's successive insight that the world is big includes the
realization that parents cannot provide everything. Her enemies, the
shadows she must learn to fight are overprotective adults, in the first
place her adored father. Thus, although the setting of the novel is
vaguely medieval, with some fairy-tale elements, the psychological
implications are closer to "reality" than in *Mio My Son*; or in Frye's
terminology, the myth is more displaced in *Ronia*.

Of Ronia's parents, her mother clearly realizes the necessity of
initiation, while Matt, the father, would prefer to keep Ronia in the
state of innocence forever. The reason is that Matt is a grown-up
child himself: spoiled, selfish, and narrow-minded. His immaturity
is especially evident in his childish refusal to accept death. "He's
always been here! And now he is not!" he laments when Noddle-
Pete dies (173). But just as Ronia's birth comes as a reminder of
changes, so Noddle-Pete's death, reducing the magical number of
twelve robbers, is a necessary part of life. Also Ronia will be confronted with death, when she sees a bear kill a foal. As in *The Mouse
and His Child*, death is presented as a part of the natural life cycle:
"Those are the kind of things that happen in Matt's Wood and in
every wood" (129). The cyclical character of time in Ronia is emphasized, among other things, by her recurrent spring yell. Ronia's
affinity with nature is one of her most essential features.

Ronia's maturation is echoed in Matt's; it is a reciprocal process
where Matt's insights are equally important for Ronia's independence. Very early in the novel, the initial idyllic state must be
interrupted:

> And one fine day Matt realized—however little he liked it—that
> the time had come.
> "Lovis," he said to his wife, "our child must learn what it's like
> living in Matt's Forest. Let her go!"
> "Ah, so you've seen it at last," said Lovis. "It would have happened
> long ago if I'd had my way." (11)

The first confrontation between Ronia and Matt comes when Ronia
happens to overhear that Matt takes things without asking. In this

scene, her naive perspective is reflected, since even young readers
are supposed to know what robbers do for a living. When Ronia
takes up the issue, the point of view shifts toward Matt for a short
while:

> Matt had no need to be ashamed. ... On the contrary, he usually
> blustered and bragged that he was the greatest robber chieftain in all
> the woods and mountains. But it was a little harder now that he had
> to tell Ronia about it. Of course he had intended to tell her all about
> it sooner or later when it was necessary. But he had wanted to wait a
> little. (45)

This shift does not only indicate the central conflict of the story—
that between father and daughter—but also reveals Matt's immaturity. In the depicted process of growing up and liberation, Ronia
and Matt are almost interchangeable. This is clearly shown in every
situation when the tension between the two occurs. When Ronia is
sick with fever, we share Matt's point of view: "He knew what was
going to happen! Ronia was to be taken from him; she was going to
die ..." (58). Matt is right, Ronia is to be taken from him; however,
not by death, but by a young man.

Ronia's progress is easily described in Jungian terms of individuation, going from harmony through split toward a more genuine
harmony; the split fort anticipates Ronia's split personality and
divided loyalty. The text also offers a number of transparent symbols used in the Jungian model: woods, water, cave, and wild horses
to be tamed. The description of Ronia's initiation could have been
taken directly from an anthropological study. She is left to cope on
her own in a deep dark wood, she must learn everything about the
wood, she must meet all the dangers and all the joys. Characteristically, some of the dangers are depicted in fairy-tale forms:
harpies, apparently representing dark female powers, and goblins,
representing male forces, projections of mother and father. At one
point, Ronia is also tempted by death, lured by the Unearthly Ones
to enter their underground realm.

As in many similar stories, food from home accompanies the
novice during seclusion in the wood, and although the final goal is
to break away, for a long time food provides the strongest link back
home. One of many signs of Matt's immense love for his baby

daughter is his stubborn wish to feed her with porridge. He wants to take over Lovis's role as the nurturing mother, in order to bind Ronia to himself. It is, however, Lovis who packs the food for Ronia when she is to go out in the wood.

The most serious trial with which Ronia is confronted concerns human loyalties. The very first time Ronia is in the wood on her own and is attacked by gray dwarfs, Matt comes to the rescue. But soon the role of the rescuer is taken over by Birk.

Among the many episodes where the two children save each other, Ronia saves Birk from hunger. There is enough food in Matt's Fort, while Birk and his parents are starving. The sharing of food is a violation of a very strict prohibition: "Borka would be beside himself with fury if he found out that I was taking bread from you" (71). To share food with the enemy, to take food from the enemy— the children's dilemma is really difficult. Ronia even gives Birk food to smuggle into his mother's larder. This action demands more courage than inviting friends to a meal, as Pippi does. The shared food confirms that the bonds of friendship—or love—are stronger than the bonds of blood. This insight is essential for a child's psychological development, as well as for the emergence of gender identity. Even though Ronia will eventually return to Matt's Fort, by giving food to Birk, the enemy's son, she has made her choice, long before she jumps over Hell's Gap to betray her father in order to save her beloved. The Romeo-and-Juliet theme is played on a more mundane level.

The broad scale of Ronia's emotions toward Birk and the tension between Ronia, Birk and Matt are brilliantly built up by the focalizing pattern of the text. In the scene when Ronia first meets Birk, the narrative method of "estrangement" is used: describing familiar objects as if they were unfamiliar. Instead of saying that Ronia saw a boy, the author paints this emotionally charged picture:

> … Lovis had said that there were plenty of children in other places, and of two kinds: those who would turn into Matts when they were big, and those who would turn into Lovises. Ronia herself would turn into a Lovis, but she knew in her heart that the one who was sitting dangling his feet over Hell's Gap would turn into a Matt. (22)

To begin with, Ronia sees her future lover merely as a substitute for her father. She takes a long time to admit that she is attached to Birk by much more than the symbolic rope. "Birk never appeared in her woods, and of course she was glad of that," states the narrator, but goes on at once: "Or was she? Sometimes she was not sure how she felt" (50). Later, Ronia suddenly discovers that she "longed for him. How that had happened she had no idea" (63). Proposing Birk to be her brother is just another act of self-deceit, and the author puts the comment into the mouth of Birk's mother: "Sister! ... Oh, yes, we know what that will mean in a year or two!" (97). However, both Ronia and Birk continue to pretend that their emotions do not go beyond those of siblings.

In the quarrel scene, the point of view shifts to Birk. But it is not in any way like Colin coming to the foreground in *The Secret Garden*. Why the author chooses to present this incident from the male, rather than female perspective, is not made clear. Probably, since Ronia is unfairly accused, the depiction of her hurt feelings would be too strong. More likely, the author tries to give us insight into Birk's immense devotion for Ronia, in order to make him a worthy rival of Matt. Matt has not been focalized for a long while at this point in the story, so Birk has taken his place as the second focalizer, alongside Ronia. The scope of emotions described on a mere four pages (115–118) is vast, and the succession quick—rage, regret, more anger, anxiety, longing, jealousy, more regret, and finally joy at finding Ronia again. At this moment, the point of view shifts back to Ronia. We never learn what she felt during these hours.

For the rest of the book, we get short glimpses into Birk's mind, just to remind us that we have once shared his point of view and therefore should be able to empathize with him. It is Birk's grief we are forced to share in the end: "And Birk knew as he stood there that now it was time. Time to say good-bye and let Ronia go back to Matt, with thanks for the loan ... And he had known it for a long time, so why did it hurt so much?" (153). Again we may ask why the author chooses to describe this from Birk's perspective. Ronia's joy of reconciliation with her father is mixed with the anxiety of losing Birk. Birk is just profoundly unhappy. As readers, we are spared the ambivalence of Ronia's emotions. Also Matt's point of view comes momentarily forward in this scene, and he realizes that from now on he must share his daughter with another man. This is the moment of Matt's maturation.

When the two children decide to leave their childhood homes, they build a home of their own in Bear's Cave and consecrate it with a ceremonial meal. They have taken bread from home, as they always used to, but very soon they have to start providing food themselves by fishing. Bread is "culture food" associated with home, fish is "nature food" associated with freedom and independence. Perhaps the author suggests that both Biblical symbols, loaves and fish, are necessary for human well-being.

In their make-believe adult life, Ronia and Birk dutifully perform their gender-related roles: Birk provides food, Ronia collects herbs and tends the fire. In a way, their life in the cave is a restoration of Arcadia: the woods are beautiful and peaceful, they have each other, and "… it was summer. More and more summer every day, clearer, warmer than any summer they could remember" (135).

A dramatic event interrupts this summer idyll. Ronia discovers a mare who is torn by a bear and bleeding heavily, making Ronia extremely anxious. With a risk of being over-interpretive, I view this scene as a depiction of Ronia's first menstruation. She is eleven and turning into a young woman, and the sight of blood fills her with fear and dismay. She administers dried moss to the bleeding mare— in Sweden, a once well-known popular sanitary protection. This step in Ronia's growth is essential in her relationship with Birk, as she becomes aware of herself as a woman. The episode is preceded by a quarrel between her and Birk, where she loses her temper and runs away—a good description of PMS.

When there is no bread left, the children become more dependent upon their own provision. They milk the mare, snare fowl, fish, gather roots and berries. As long as it is summer they do not starve. "… it was a long time until winter—what did she care about it now?" (113). This is a young child's attitude toward life, as the happy feeling of "here and now" suppresses every thought of future troubles. Still, there are momentary fears, especially in Birk's thoughts, that sooner or later they will have to return home in order not to starve. In other words, they are still too young to survive on their own, so their Robinsonnade is merely training for the future—a picnic.

Birk becomes desperately aware of their vulnerability when
Lovis sends them bread. Superficially, this is bare necessity, since
they have run out of their supply. On the symbolic level, this is a
reminder that Ronia is still heavily dependent on home. Ronia longs
for "Lovis's bread," not simply any food: "Lovis's bread! I'd forgotten there was anything so wonderful" (132). The bread symbolizes
mother's milk which Ronia longs for: it tastes "like a blessing in her
mouth, and it made her miss Lovis" (132). She eats it eagerly and
wants to share with Birk, but he rejects it, since he does not need
food from home. Birk has come much further in his liberation from
his mother, for instance, he cannot stand his mother's touch, while
Ronia wants both to sleep with her head on Lovis's knees and sit
comfortably hugged by Matt. Birk is painfully aware that Ronia is
still very much attached to the nurturing mother's breast.

Lovis knows what she is doing. Appearing in the cave she says:
"You'll get bread when you come home" (144). The bread she earlier
sent to Ronia was a decoy, to give her a taste of home. It is not a
coincidence that she comes when Ronia least wants to see her, since
she interrupts the wonderful feeling of unity between Ronia and
Birk as they have just faced and escaped death. The two have
reached a higher stage in their development, where food is no longer
the most essential thing. The extremely intensive and sensual episode when they are drowning may be interpreted as a coition, an
initiation into sexuality:

> ... although neither of them could hear a word, they spoke to each
> other. They said what must be said before it was too late. How good
> it was to *love* someone so much that there was no need to fear even
> the most difficult thing. (140, my emphasis)

This is actually the only occasion in the novel when the word "love"
is used about Ronia and Birk. The emotion which they have pretended was only foster-sibling friendship is given a verbal expression. The two young people have gone over the threshold into a
higher spiritual life. But Lovis is tempting Ronia to return to the
security of childhood, just as the smell of food forces Sendak's Max
to abandon his wild fantasies. So when Ronia comes home to eat
Lovis's bread she has undergone a regression in her development,
intensified by the picture of her sleeping in Lovis's arms in a fetal

position, when she "sank into the deep peace of childhood" (145). She has come a long way, but she is not totally free yet, because otherwise it would not be a children's book.

Significantly, the novel ends in the present tense, denoting the iterative:

> It is early morning. As beautiful as the first morning in the world....
> And they come to their cave, their home in the wilderness. And everything is as before, safe and familiar. ... Spring is new, but it is still the same as ever. (176)

Thus, although the author has allowed her character to break away from idyll, represented by home and protective father, she feels obliged to bring her back into temporal security, because otherwise the conventions of a children's novel would be broken.

BRIDGES INTO ADULTHOOD

Bridge to Terabithia has been subject to a fate similar to that of *The Brothers Lionheart*, since it has been repeatedly referred to as a good novel to introduce death to young readers. However, it is not a book about "coping with death," but rather about the hard work of growing up, told not from the point of view of an omniscient and didactic adult, but that of an inexperienced and therefore vulnerable child.

As readers, we may apprehend very quickly not only the fact that Jess becomes friends with Leslie, but also why. For Jess, the focalizing character, it takes some time to acknowledge that fact, and not until the end of the story does he realize what Leslie has meant to him. Seemingly, the author uses quite banal devices to portray Leslie's otherness: she is a newcomer, the family is somewhat odd, both parents are writers, they have no television, but lots of books. Leslie wears wrong clothes, she is bullied in school, and the fact that she can run faster than even the older boys does not add to her popularity. However, the shift in point of view between Jess and the readers—a device called *filter* in narratology—makes us see what Jess himself fails to see: not only is he curious about Leslie because of her otherness, but it is the very nature of otherness, its spiritual and intellectual value, that attracts him. "The word 'beautiful' came to his mind, but he shook it away" (28). It is the spiritually under-privileged child's first encounter with the boundless universe of spiritual life.

To his own surprise, Jess finds himself in a totally new world together with Leslie, not only a world where his reading and drawing interests have a value, but literally a magical world which Leslie creates with her imagination, drawing inspiration from her exten-sive reading. What may seem innocent play—and what Jess at first apprehends as play and make-believe—is in fact a powerful descrip-tion of a rite of passage, which Jess eventually will realize. Terabithia could just as well be a magical Otherworld, like its model Narnia.

In Terabithia, Jess becomes, with Leslie's help, a king and a glorious knight, strong and brave and a match for any enemy. Constructed as a spiritual quest, his transformation into a hero at the same time creates in Jess a self-delusion. What readers might see, and what Paterson conveys by small, but effective means, is Jess's total immaturity and inability to leave his own dull and confined, but secure world. Since the actual passage to Terabithia is connected with a certain physical danger, Jess makes excuses of a substantial rather than a psychological nature to explain his reluctance. When the river, which is the boundary to Terabithia, bursts its banks, Jess happily seizes upon this pretext for not crossing over.

I find it significant that the person who involuntarily lures Jess away from Leslie and Terabithia is his music teacher who has encouraged his artistic aspirations. Another detail of Jess's shifted point of view is his evident erotic attraction to Miss Edmunds, which he of course cannot acknowledge, still less verbalize, and which probably also lies beyond young readers' grasp. The portrayal of subconscious rivalry on the teacher's part becomes understandable if both she and Leslie have the same function in Jess's initiation, namely as a mother substitute (or Anima if we so wish).

Filter is used in an equally skillful way to describe Jess's accep-tance of Leslie's death. Just as the readers clearly see that Leslie has become his friend, while Jess himself does not acknowledge it, he also refuses to realize that she has left him. Unlike most interpreta-tions of Jess's reaction to Leslie's death (e.g. Chaston 1991), I see his resentment mostly as anxiety at having to grow up without her female guidance, which is the natural consequence of my reading the text at a ritual, rather than a realistic ("mimetic") level. Like

Holden Caulfield's younger brother, Leslie does not have to go through the painful process of adolescence, and Jess is subconsciously envious of her. If the psychological aspect, developed by Joel Chaston, suggests that a child often cannot "forgive" a relative or a friend for being dead, the ritual aspect emphasizes the confusion of a novice left without his guide and feeling betrayed. Further, as Chaston has pointed out, in all the intertexts—Narnia Chronicles, *Hamlet*, *Moby Dick*, and especially the Bible—death is presented as something noble and, significantly, as transient. Death in *The Last Battle* is simply the beginning of "Chapter One of the Great Story ... in which every chapter is better than the one before" (165). Therefore Jess is not prepared, or rather thinks himself not prepared, to experience "real," that is, irrevocable death: "Leslie could not die any more than he himself could die" (106)—a typical immature child's attempt at self-deception. However, Jess's feelings are not exposed directly to us, but the point of view is once again filtered, shifted, so that we realize long before Jess that Leslie the guide has served her purpose—to open the world for Jess, thus enabling him to go further.

> Now it occurred to him that perhaps Terabithia was like a castle where you came to be knighted. After you stayed for a while and grew strong you had to move on. For hadn't Leslie, even in Terabithia, tried to push back the walls of his mind and make him see beyond to the shining world—huge and terrible and beautiful and very fragile? (126)

If we only read the novel on the mimetic level, it is a tragedy that Leslie is dead, and the novel indeed offers consolation to a reader who has in the same manner lost a relative or a friend. However, Katherine Paterson has herself rejected this reduced view of her work. On the symbolic level, Leslie has played out her role, and it does not really matter any more. What she has given Jess, nobody can take away from him. Moreover, he can carry this insight further, which he actually does in the very last chapter, when he builds a real bridge across the river and invites his little sister to enter Terabithia as a new queen.

The motif of a self-deceiving child is amplified in Paterson's two most prominent quest novels, *The Great Gilly Hopkins* and *Park's*

Quest, which can be treated as variations on the same theme, a girl seeking her mother and a boy seeking his father. However, for Park as well, the emotional betrayal of the mother proves more important than the physical absence of the father.

Gilly is strong, independent and impudent on the surface, while deep inside she is profoundly insecure and unhappy. The title does not reflect the author's seemingly impartial judgment of the character (cf "traditional" titles such as *Curious George*), but rather the character's predisposed judgment of herself. The gap between the two points of view challenges readers to investigate them more closely and to take a position of their own, most obviously seeing through Gilly's self-imposed greatness.

Like *Bridge to Terabithia,* this book could easily be perceived as an ideal illustration of the so-called issue-oriented children's literature: a problem child placed in a foster home after a long row of earlier failures, which have all contributed to her profound insecurity. However, the plot itself would evidently never be sufficient to create a narrative of such intensity. The events do not come to us directly, but are refracted through Gilly's self-assured, but immature mind. While Gilly believes that she is witty and cunning, and that she is in complete control of the situation, the readers see that she is getting more and more emotionally dependent on her ugly, fat foster-mother, the blind neighbor and the young, helpless foster-brother. When the ideal image of the absent mother fails, this peculiar trio becomes Gilly's first real family, even though she is not allowed to stay with them. Actually, by the time Gilly's grandmother turns up to "save" Gilly from the horrible place she has been put into, Gilly is as devoted to her foster family as can be, without the narrator ever mentioning the fact. And when Gilly realizes that her grandmother is determined to take her away, her reaction is: "No one could make her leave here" (113). The crucial point comes when Gilly says proudly to a classmate: "My family ... My brother. ... My mother. And my—uncle" (118).

The superficially "happy" ending, in which Gilly finds both her biological mother and her grandmother, is apprehended by a keen reader as an obvious irony. The narrative structure of the novel reinforces its psychological movement toward the character's spiritual wholeness; however, the complete fulfilment of the self is never achieved.

In *Park's Quest* we also meet the naive perspective where the readers are several steps ahead of the character in accepting the uncomfortable truth. Park is trying hard to shut his eyes to something obvious. He knows that his father was killed in Vietnam. But his mother refuses to discuss the father; she would not even accompany Park to the Vietnam memorial. Reading the father's name on the stone becomes the first phase of verbalizing the suppressed emotions.

When Park goes to see his grandfather it appears that his mother has concealed more important facts from him. Not only does he have an uncle, but also a half-sister, almost his own age, and Vietnamese. It is because of this girl that Park's mother divorced his father, not long before his death, which she has also kept a secret. Again, the truth about the girl, Thanh, is obvious to the reader long before Park is emotionally strong enough to accept it.

Since the author chooses to let her narrative voice remain in the background, the readers are left without any guidance as to the characters' inner qualities or external behavior. The readers must themselves decide whether Jess has betrayed Leslie, or whether Gilly is as great as she imagines. This may appear a more generous attitude toward the reader, since the adult author addresses young readers on equal terms. On the other hand, we are trained to identify with characters, most often by sharing their point of view. When this reading strategy is deliberately impeded, readers may feel frustrated, or on the contrary, they may find satisfaction in their superiority over the character. The delicate balance between having confidence in young readers' ability to disengage themselves from characters and stimulating enough empathy to involve the reader is one of the many dilemmas of contemporary children's fiction (see further Nikolajeva 1997a).

The narrative device of filter is used to emphasize the dominant theme—the neglected child and the betrayal of the mother. The child's desire and frustration are both expressed and suppressed by means of language, or rather, the "preverbal," the "imaginary," in Lacanian terminology. According to Jacques Lacan, the early stages in a child's development, when the child is strongly connected with the mother, are based on preverbal structures (images, therefore "imaginary" stage). At later stages, children must learn to express their emotions verbally and structure them in compliance with existing norms (which are conventional, "symbols" in semiotic terminology; therefore "symbolic" stage or order), which Lacan attributes to the father and calls "Father's Law" (Lacan 1977).

Without attaching too much significance to this rather mechanical model, I would like to draw very superficial parallels between the way the texts discussed are constructed narratively and their possible psychological implications. Basically, the characters' inability to verbalize their suppressed emotions, reflected in the narrative structure, may signal that they are stuck at the preverbal stage. The mothers' negative role thus implies conserving the child at this stage.

Further, intertextual links give us additional guidelines to the messages of the novels. They have been praised as "the ultimate realism" (Huse 1984), but the author has stated that they often have traditional myths as "hypotexts," that is underlying textual structures, and that her characters are each in some way a reincarnation of the traditional mythical hero, "a hero with a thousand faces" (see Paterson 1995, 146ff). In *Bridge to Terabithia,* Paterson offers Jess and the readers Narnia Chronicles as a matrix for interpretation. Functionally, there is no difference between Narnia and Terabithia, for both are sacred places where the hero is taken to be initiated. The passage, represented in the Narnia Chronicles by the wardrobe, among other things, is in Paterson's novel just as clearly marked and just as dramatic.

Intertextual links in *Bridge to Terabithia* have been investigated by many scholars (see e.g. Bell 1982; Smedman 1989; Chaston 1991). Among the many possible intertexts, the Narnia Chronicles are the most evident. By alluding to Lewis, Paterson provides the readers with an interpretative strategy. However, since Jess is not familiar with the intertexts, Leslie's stories, which rather act as a reading guideline for the readers, acquire for Jess a pronounced character of spiritual guidance initiating the novice into a mystery. The discrepancy in point of view gives the readers a sense of superiority over the protagonist.

In *The Great Gilly Hopkins* there is a variety of fairy-tale intertexts, Rumpelstiltskin being the most tangible. But there are others, which each in their own manner, push the readers toward a desired interpretation: "Like Bluebeard's wife, she opened the forbidden door and someday she would have to look inside" (115); "To be herself, to be the swan, to be the ugly duckling no longer—Cap O'Rushes, her disguise thrown off—Cinderella with both slippers on her feet—Snow White beyond the dwarfs—Galadriel Hopkins, come into her own" (124). The irony is that "Galadriel" is just as much a borrowed identity as everything else.

Also, Park keeps translating his quest into the mythical dimensions of the Parsifal legend, because he is too immature to find his own words. Another intertext is Conrad's *Heart of Darkness* which most probably only works on the adult level.

Quite a few critics have objected to the fact that Katherine Paterson's novels do not offer young readers any hope. Paterson has refuted criticism by saying that "there is no way that we can tack [hope] on the end of the story like pinning the tail on the donkey" (Paterson 1995, 324). Hope and future are very abstract notions for a young child, and in a filtered narrative, where the protagonists' ability to judge their own situation is limited, a happy ending would feel unnatural. The completion of the narrative does not automatically indicate a satisfactory closure of the story. Instead, we meet a disharmonious ending which almost always suggests that the character has gained something, but lost something else. There is a sort of illusionary promise of hope, expressed through the characters' filtered perception, but since their point of view is different from ours, as readers we may wonder whether Jess can indeed cope without Leslie or Gilly without Maime Trotter. We wonder whether a new-found sister can compensate for Park's eventual—spiritual— loss of his father. Here the more general, mythical levels of texts give us a clue, suggesting a more or less imperative reading strategy, or even, I might add, a metafictional comment on the story. At the same time the narrative filter allows us to make inferences beyond the characters' perception. Despite all failures, we are made to believe that Paterson's characters can go on. They have been dubbed knights in their sacred places. They have drunk from their holy grails. Then they can continue their life quests.

In Paterson's novels, the self-deceiving child is reluctant to verbalize the suppressed desires, rather preferring to disguise them in images. These preverbal, "imaginary" (Lacan) expressions of suppressed feelings precede the "symbolic," articulated statements. In many traditional children's novels, where the narrative strategy forces the readers to share the protagonist's point of view, the authors find themselves obliged to articulate the insight gained by the protagonist—and thus by the reader. Contemporary writers of Katherine Paterson's caliber rather choose to let the protagonist remain, at least partially, at the preverbal stage and instead let the readers train their ability to express their feelings with words.

Chapter 8

Beyond the Point of No Return

The young adult novel as a contemporary phenomenon, basically originating in J. D. Salinger's *The Catcher in the Rye*, portrays a person in a marginal situation.[1] Childhood is over, and adulthood will begin any moment. This creates anxiety, the dominant emotion in young adult novels, since the protagonist realizes that there is no way back, that this is no longer a dream, play or a fancy-dress ball when it is sufficient to wake up, cry "pax!" or pull away the mask in order to return to the security of a childhood paradise.

The protagonist of the adolescent novel looks back at his childhood as a carefree idyll, while he is at the same time curious about the strange, previously forbidden adult life, which he often apprehends as threatening. Holden Caulfield watches with excitement and sorrow his younger sister riding the merry-go-round, while he himself stands beside, knowing that he has become too old to participate in the joys of childhood. However, he does not dare to take the step into adulthood, to start a sexual relationship, or to adjust to the demands of adult society. The adult temptations, typically enough depicted as alcohol and sex, both allure and disgust.

The adored dead brother becomes a powerful symbol of the happiness of not having to grow up (cf Haviland 1990). The cruel insight about the inevitability of adulthood leads Holden to a nervous collapse. The open ending of the novel does not give us any guidance to the question of whether Holden is now ready for initiation: his time of trials has just started. However, he has definitely stepped off from the circular merry-go-round of childhood into linearity.

Strange as it may seem, I will begin my discussion of the young adult novel with Hans Christian Andersen's *The Little Mermaid*. All Andersen's "original" tales, those not based on folktales, have a linear ending. Also some that are loosely based on folktales or local legends, like *The Little Mermaid*, have a linear ending. The tale invites psychoanalytical interpretations, which also have been made (e.g. Duve 1967, Barlby 1995). I will discuss it in terms of linear time and initiation into death and sexuality. It starts with a typical depiction of idyll:

> … here grow the strangest plants and trees; their stems and leaves are so subtle that the slightest current in the water makes them move, as if they were alive. Big and small fishes flit in and out among their branches, just as the birds do up on earth. At the very deepest place, the mer-king has built his castle. Its walls are made of coral and its long pointed windows of amber. The roof is oyster shells that are continuously opening and closing. It looks very beautiful, for in each shell lies a pearl, so lustrous that it would be fit for a queen's crown. (57)

The mermaids also have their *gardens* on the bottom of the sea. The little mermaid is kept in innocence (= childhood) until her fifteenth birthday, her coming of age. She is eager to investigate the world of humans—adults. So strong is her longing for this world that she is prepared to sacrifice anything to experience it. "Every time your foot touches the ground it will feel as though you were walking on knives so sharp that your blood must flow" (68), the sea witch warns her. The pain and blood suggest defloration: "It will hurt; it will feel as if a sword were going through your body" (68). Naturally, getting rid of her fish tail and acquiring legs also implies genitalia. She is naked when the prince discovers her; of course she had been naked all the time in the sea, but now her nakedness has a new significance. She uses her long hair to hide her body—apparently also her sex.

It is tempting to see the little mermaid's desire as primarily sexual, and superficially her frustration only concerns the prince's sexual indifference: "Day by day the prince grew fonder and fonder of her; but he loved her as he would have loved a good child" (71).

Let us, however, not forget that the main reason for the little mermaid's decision to leave the sea is her fear of death:

> I am going to die, become foam on the ocean, and never again hear the music of the waves or see the flowers or the burning red sun. Can't I do anything to win an immortal soul? (66)

Eternal life, not the prince's love, is her goal. Contrary to what the witch has initially told her, the transformation is reversible: the little mermaid can, by killing the prince, return to the sea, but it means that she has to refrain from adulthood and return to childhood. Although she is promised three hundred years—an eternity for a child—she is not tempted by it and prefers to die. The child has taken a definite step into linearity.

DEEPER AND DEEPER INTO DARK MYSTERIES OF LIFE

Johnny, My Friend by Peter Pohl has been discussed by a number of Swedish critics, mainly in terms of its ruthless realism and criticism of society, both in depicting Johnny's life conditions and his[2] violent death. According to the author, the theme of the novel is adults' exploitation of children; however, even a "mimetic" reading easily discovers that it is impossible to reduce the novel to the theme of underprivileged children alone.

The narrative structure of the novel is a very detailed description of a rite of passage. Chris's life is ordered and regulated, and it is also secure and protected from all evil. He has just started secondary school, a privileged school in the center of Stockholm. Unlike most of his former classmates, whose parents could not afford to send their boys to this school, Chris comes from a well-off family: "... everybody else's dad was a welder or a glazier or a bricklayer, apart from Bert's who was a wino. But mine was a chief clerk" (45). There are no conflicts in the family. It is in a way a perfect, balanced family: a father, a mother, two children, a boy and a girl. Nothing can threaten this idyll.

Chris is a diligent student, as is expected of him, and he is also pedantic and interested in facts, which has gained him the nickname Catalogue Chris. He is also extremely verbal: "Words are my favourite meal" (14). He likes what he calls "clear, straightforward language" (15), like Rules and Regulations Concerning Order and Good Behaviour in State Grammar Schools. He also loves numbers: "essential and unessential statistical information, useless figures and numerical data. Exact numbers are magic" (15). Although it is never mentioned explicitly, his future is predictable: he is expected to follow his father's steps and become a successful civil servant.

Meeting Johnny disrupts this harmony. Johnny is a totally alien element in Chris's life. Many scholars have noticed similarities between Johnny and Pippi Longstocking, and Pippi is indeed mentioned as soon as Chris sees Johnny:

> Pippi Longstocking, I reckoned. Pippi Longstocking, that was it, suddenly come to life, by magic. Her hair wasn't in plaits, but the colour was right. The grin white and dazzling among a few million freckles ... (10)

But there is more than the superficial similarities; in the first place, it is Johnny's function as a chaos factor. Like Pippi, Johnny comes "from nowhere" (10), has no relatives, obeys no rules, wears unusual clothes, has some remarkable abilities—note that Pippi's horse has transformed into a bicycle. Just like Pippi, Johnny is a marginal, androgynous figure, a mixture of boy and girl.

Like Pippi, Johnny lacks a real name. Pippi's high-flown Pippilotta Delicatessa Windowshade Mackrelmint is just as much a mask as the short, impersonal Johnny. Like Pippi, Johnny has no age. Although Pippi celebrates her birthday, she does not actually get any older. Chris's first guess at Johnny's age is futile:

> How old was he then, you might well ask. Judging by his height and his weight, he looked about ten or so ... but going by the way he talked, well, he could be older than I was .... (16)

At the time of his twelfth birthday Chris feels the solemnity of the moment:

> Twelve is the magical dividing line, we all know that. I don't care what grown-ups say, but that's when your childhood comes to an end. (89)

Indeed, eleven years is the usual age for initiation in many archaic cultures. As Chris meets Johnny, he is on the verge of adulthood, when the return to childhood idyll is no longer possible. The rational Chris finds this natural: "Me, I'm only too glad to be getting older. Every year, on the fourth of March: one step nearer human dignity" (89f). Johnny on the other hand does not celebrate birthdays, because he "refuse[s] to accept age. ... I don't have an age, matterfact, said Johnny, and I never will, matterfact" (89f). At this point, Chris makes a connection to Pippi Longstocking again, and her reluctance to grow up—a clear case of authorial control when Pohl expects the reader to notice parallels to Pippi: "Pippi was a fairytale character. ... An ordinary little kid has to be pleased he can grow up till he's old enough to look after himself. Then he's grown-up as well, and there's no point to it any more" (90). At this stage, growing up has not yet become a concern for Chris.

With Johnny, not growing up gains another aspect. Chris contemplates circus performers, without making a connection to Johnny:

> These young girls were subjected to incredibly intense training from a very early age, Dad reckoned, so that their development into young women was delayed. They looked as though they were about ten years old, but in fact they could easily be twenty. (143)

Is Johnny indeed much older than he looks?

Like Pippi, who does not have any adult to tell her to go to bed, Johnny does not have to go home at regular hours. Johnny has no family bonds, he longs to have a pet (cf Pippi's horse and monkey), he enjoys food and warmth in Chris's home and can get moved to tears. This makes him different from Pippi who almost never exposes any emotions. Johnny allows Chris's mother to hug him, something that no other boy in Chris's gang would ever tolerate. Johnny can get violent, but he can also admit his fault and apologize.

There are many things about Johnny that do not make sense. He lives in what seems to be a poor repair shop, is constantly hungry, and gets beaten up, but he has the most expensive gym shoes on the market. Johnny is perfectly accomplished on his bicycle or balancing on rails, but he is not much good with a ball. He seems amazingly ignorant in several aspects. He has never seen a guinea pig. He does not recognize Red Riding Hood or Snow White, but knows everything about clowns. He has never heard grace and does not know anything about Jesus. He has never read *Donald Duck* or *Pippi Longstocking*. In fact, he can hardly read. He does not seem to attend school at all. He does not know about ration books for alcohol, which is strange, since his being beaten up at home must be put in connection with heavy drinking, at least in Chris's mind. Johnny's ignorance seems thus different from Pippi's. However, if we read the novel mythically rather than mimetically, and treat Johnny as an "alien child," it is not strange that he lacks all this knowledge. In Chris's fancies about a kidnapped circus girl he says: "She wouldn't have been to a normal school. I mean, what good would reading-riting-rithmetic be to somebody like her? She'd forget all about her normal years as an ordinary little kid" (162).

On the other hand, it turns out, to Chris's amazement, that Johnny "knew how to handle a knife and fork, and he used his serviette just about often enough" (125)—something that Pippi cannot boast of. He also seems to have a habit of visiting coffee shops. Johnny is full of contradictions which Chris fails to understand. The most remarkable thing about Johnny is that every now and then he disappears for a month or two. The "realistic" explanation we get by the end of the novel is that he is away on tour with the circus. However, if Johnny is an "alien child" he can come and go as he pleases. Blown in with East wind and blown away by West wind, like Mary Poppins. Forgetting time in his own Never-Neverland, like Peter Pan.

The notion of the "alien child," originating from E. T. A. Hoffmann's novel, has mostly been applied to fantasy. In the seemingly realistic novel, *Johnny, My Friend*, Chris, inspired by science fiction magazines, contemplates Alternative Worlds. It is never mentioned explicitly that Chris believes Johnny to be a visitor from an Alternative World, but conclusions can be drawn in several steps. Chris invents a story about little girls kidnapped into another dimension and trained to become circus performers. Since a keen reader at this point has already guessed something that Chris pretends not to, that Johnny is identical with the circus star Miss Juvenile, it is easy to continue the scenario: Johnny is one of those girls kidnapped by "little green men," trained and sold to a circus. Therefore Johnny has no age, since he has been frozen in an eternal childhood, like Peter Pan. Another possibility is that Johnny himself is one of those extraterrestials. Such interpretations can easily account for Johnny's fantastic skills, his remarkable ignorance and his lack of social network: "No dad. No mum. No name. No home" (232). This is a slightly far-fetched, but not impossible way to view Johnny. The spatial construction of the novel makes a clear distinction between the profane space, that is, Chris's world, and the sacred space, Johnny's secret world into which he disappears through a mystical, shape-changing door. Chris's profane time is concrete, chronological, measured by calendars and clocks, while Johnny exists beyond this normal time, in a mythical time of his own. Chris's solid world is well-sorted in catalog files; Johnny's marginal existence is vague and insecure.

Whoever or whatever he is, Johnny initiates a change in Chris, like a catalyst speeding up a chemical process. From now on, nothing will be the same. One of the first things Johnny teaches Chris about is colors. The rational Chris does not know much about other than basic colors, while Johnny introduces tangerine, crimson, purple, and wine-red to him. "No subtleties, no shades, no depth, no taste," Johnny comments with slight contempt (83). The metaphor is transparent: Johnny brings color into Chris's dull life. But Chris states, somewhat gloomily in retrospect, that Johnny did not want to teach: "Why couldn't Johnny teach me then, if he was such a wizard at colours and smells and taste? But Johnny wasn't interested in teaching" (83). Johnny is a guide, but not a preacher. Chris must discover all the important things by himself. Johnny also questions Chris's way of collecting and filing facts: "Pretty boring way to live, was Johnny's comment on my precious card index" (82).

Seeing Johnny in front of him, Chris realizes that most things which he has so far taken for granted are indeed a privilege. The first time Chris brings Johnny home, his mother invites Johnny to have a sandwich, to Chris's enormous amazement, since they "never used to eat at that time in our house" (46). Apparently the mother has realized that Johnny may not be getting enough food at home— something that Chris has so far never thought about. On a symbolic level, the meal confirms that "Johnny had given Mum and Dad thumbs up, and they approved of him" (45). But just as Chris does not understand a lot about Johnny, he is amazed to see tears in Johnny's eyes as he says: "God, Chris, you're a lucky blighter!" (47). This meal, interrupted by Chris's sister's appearance, may be Johnny's first experience of a family. "What a smashing flat you've got, he said, looking round at nothing more than the ordinary bits and pieces of what we call home" (53). What is ordinary for Chris must seem a paradise to Johnny. Thus the importance of home, family, and food is brought to Chris's attention.

Later Johnny discovers the fireplace, the tiled stove in the drawing room, the warmth of the family hearth. Eating sandwiches in front of the fireplace recalls "poetic scenes from the idyllic past" (84); "Johnny eventually let on he hadn't seen one of them things since he was a kid" (84). Rituals around food and warmth in Chris's home are a temporary restoration of idyll.

Johnny's role in Chris's initiation is, to begin with, to disrupt his childish faith in the stability and security of the world. However, the two most important steps into initiation are once again connected with death and sexuality. Death is pervasive in the novel. Among many statistical data which Chris collects are facts concerning road accidents. The boys in the gang entertain each other by telling stories of accidents, murders, and suicides. Johnny plays with death, balancing on the rail. Chris reads in a newspaper about a death in a fire, which one of his schoolmates is involved in; for a while he believes it is Johnny. During summer, longing for Johnny, he goes exploring a cemetery. Chris is afraid of death since he is already aware of his own mortality; however, death is still an unknown phenomenon, therefore frightening. Unlike many contemporary YA novels, but much like Katherine Paterson in *Bridge to Terabithia*, Peter Pohl is not satisfied by letting an older relative die: such death does not demand the same merciless insight about one's own death. The sacrifice must concern the dearest person in Chris's life.

As to sexuality, Chris still lives in a totally male community, both with the gang and in his privileged male school. Apart from his sister, Chris has no acquaintance of the opposite sex. His reluctance to verbalize his real feelings toward Johnny may have to do with his subconscious fear of homosexuality. Chris believes Johnny to be a boy and is therefore afraid to admit being sexually attracted, since it makes him insecure about his sexual identity. However, the story of Chris's friendship with Johnny is unmistakably a love story, with its painful longing, anguish, suspicion and bliss. It is built up successively, by very subtle means. When Johnny is about to perform his rail-balancing act, Chris is terribly scared of something happening to Johnny: "By this stage, I was so fond of Johnny he'd become part of me. He was my friend, my mate, my bosom pal, till death us do part" (62). He even decides that if anything happens to Johnny he, Chris, will not go on living. And death does finally part them, although at this early point Chris certainly does not take his own words seriously. Since Chris fails to realize that Johnny is a girl, he cannot acknowledge his feeling as love. "Johnny meant an awful lot to me, but don't ask me what" (87). During Johnny's lengthy summer absence, the longing becomes intolerable. "I missed Johnny so much, I was ill ... Oh, how I longed for Johnny! I missed him so much I was ill" (154). The phrase is repeated as if an incantation: "But I missed Johnny so much I was ill" (163); "I missed him so much I was ill" (165); "... Chris, sad, tired, and missing Johnny so much he was ill" (177). This is the closest Chris comes to expressing his emotions with words—he who at the beginning of the novel declared that words were his favorite meal. The self-assured Chris, Chris the fact collector, Catalogue Chris has met a phenomenon which he lacks words to describe.

The eroticism of Chris's feeling is emphasized in the episode when the friends are going to spend a night in a hut. On the surface, we are dealing with still another of the many adventurous episodes in children's fiction, involving an outing with a picnic. Chris's mother has prepared the food, once again demonstrating her generosity and her role of nurturer. Once again the food symbolizes affinity, and as soon as the two friends come to the hut, they "started the evening with a sandwich each" (199), thus marking that the hut is their home. It is significant that they have taken along Tizer, the drink of friendship, rather than chocolate, the beverage of the parental home.

However, there is a broader mythical significance in this scene. As we remember, an initiation rite often involves the novice entering a hut, thus symbolically being devoured by a monster, dying in order to be reborn. Inside the hut, the hero is met by a guide who will literally introduce him into the mystery of life. Often this guide is female, a priestess, and initiation includes intercourse, sometimes symbolically represented as a meal.

During the night in the hut, Chris's sexual awakening is described, he has an erection, but as he still fails to realize the obvious, that Johnny is a girl. He does not dare to verbalize his emotion, not even in retrospect. The symbolic sexual initiation is confirmed by another joint meal, including the magical drink of Tizer. Chris has passed the trial and is reborn.

Unfortunately, at the next stage Chris betrays his priestess, who is forced into the hut again and is devoured by the monster (the villain of the story is nicknamed Monster!). This is a sacrificial death: Johnny dies so that Chris can live. Thus Chris becomes initiated into the mystery of death as well. On the mimetic level of the story this is a terrible tragedy, but on the mythical level it is necessary and appropriate. There are many similarities with *Bridge to Terabithia*, but initiation to sexuality is more profound in *Johnny, My Friend*, thus the three-fold rite of passage is accomplished. Johnny the guide has fulfilled his task and can return to his Alternative World where he belongs.

Chris is left on his own. He cannot return into his childhood idyll, but must proceed. His anguish is great. For a moment, he contemplates suicide: "Pass the wheel to me, and the accelerator, I'll do the driving! Straight into the hillside over there. Thus, finis, silence" (250).

It is obvious that the complexity of psychological development described in *Johnny, My Friend* demands a sophisticated narrative technique. The complicated narrative structure of the novel, with an intricate pattern of temporal shifts, is subordinate to the main theme: the road to self-knowledge. Chris the narrator is unreliable, and his point of view is shifted against the reader's. When he begins to reiterate his year together with Johnny, it is rendered partly by his concise and reluctant replies to the police officer, partly by his thoughts and memories. There are from the very beginning clear indications in the text which divide the different text levels, although these may occasionally overlap. Chris the narrator is not identical with Chris the character; there is a year between them. Chris remarks himself that he may not remember everything exactly as it was: "It's only afterwards, when you've been through all that happened like this, that you realize how blind you were then, when it was all going on" (85).

Chris only reports a limited part of the events to the police, but in the rest of his story he may also omit, add and conceal facts, he can miscalculate his own and other people's behavior, his memory can fail. Chris the narrator as well as Chris the character are unable to judge themselves, and the discrepancy between the narrator's, the character's and the reader's point of view constitutes the very nerve of the narrative.

Chris the narrator can pretend that Chris the character does not know that Johnny is a girl; it is however impossible for the reader to decide whether this is an objective fact (the narrator states that the character did not know), a subjective memory (the narrator believes, a year later, that the character probably did not know), a self-deceit (the narrator does not realize that the character knew) or a deliberate lie (the narrator wants us to believe that the character did not know).

Chris's reluctance to accept the obvious facts (that Johnny was a girl, that he loved her, and that she is dead) and especially his reluctance to analyze his own reaction leads to the same mental block as that experienced by Jess in *Bridge to Terabithia*. However, the first-person form makes it a still greater narrative challenge.

Chris's story is a "replay" of the events, a repetition, a ritual restaging of a mythical sequence of events which leads to the novice's initiation. This repetition is necessary for Chris to realize what has actually happened: "I was just a child until a hour ago" (253). Therefore the two temporal levels merge at the end of the novel: the gap between a mythical event and its ritualistic restaging is eliminated.

Further, there is still another temporal level which may easily pass unnoticed. In one of his long italicised monologs, Chris visualizes a parallel sequence of events, a possibility which might have taken place if he had been given another chance, as happens in a computer game:

> *Let's turn the clock back, Johnny! ... We'll take the Alternative where ... you can have a home, Johnny, not just a bit of a smelly monster's den, and a name, Johnny, you can have an English mum and a Swedish dad and a French sister, and me as a brother, and regular pocket money. ...* (244)

This a typical example of "sideshadowing" (see Morson 1994, 117–172), used to give a contrasting illumination to the real event. Chris has realized that time is irreversible. His childhood time, the mythical circular time has turned into the linear time of adulthood, the time which has a beginning and an end, which goes from birth through painful growing and aging toward inevitable death.

FEASTS OF LIFE AND DEATH

Peter Pohl is the closest Swedish counterpart to the British Aidan Chambers, whose YA novels often defy the earlier taboos both in form and in contents. In *Dance on My Grave*, both death and sexual identity are central.

Another Swedish novel, *It Is All Over Between God and Myself* by Katarina Mazetti, is a story about a teenage girl who mourns her classmate's suicide. The theme itself is not new: it has been observed in Swedish juvenile fiction already in the '70s (Lindstam 1981). However, the narrative voice, genuine and engaging, without didacticism, makes this novel quite remarkable. The events are rendered through the confused mind of a young girl, much in the same manner as in *Johnny, My Friend*. It is a picture of an emotional crisis, where the sixteen-year-old narrator Linnea is most probably talking to herself, maybe to an invisible narratee (questions such as "You understand?" presupposes one). In her long monolog, memories are mixed with reflections as well as with direct address to the dead friend, again much like *Johnny, My Friend* and also *The Catcher in the Rye*, especially in the latter narrator's ruthless self-irony.

Linnea tells us about her short friendship with Pia who helped her to build up self-confidence and believe that life is worth living even though she is six feet tall with a flat chest. Paradoxically enough, it is Pia who "rejects life," as Linnea puts it. It is never said explicitly why Pia decides to commit suicide. It may be a teenage impulse, but there are hints in the text that Pia may have had an incestuous relation with her brother and is pregnant by him. Otherwise, Pia does not seem in any way different; one moment she may discuss God and afterlife, next chat away happily about boys and clothes. She plays basketball. While Linnea views herself a failure, bullied in school, betrayed by friends, misunderstood by her mother, always hopelessly in love, Pia is in her eyes brilliant, successful, tremendously popular with boys, happy and carefree. Pia becomes a kind of Pippi Longstocking for Linnea, the one who ventures to be different and still best. Two small episodes alone reveal that Pia is not as happy as she pretends. First, the two girls visit Linnea's grandmother who talks to Pia while Linnea does the dishes. As in *Johnny, My Friend*, an adult outsider knows the truth, but does not interfere. The second occasion is during an orientation competition, when Pia suddenly bursts into tears, saying: "They always give us wrong maps," a teenager's despair over the confusing messages from the adult world. Although Linnea never expresses the same envy we feel in Holden Caulfield's attitude toward his dead brother, the idea is not alien to her. Pia has chosen an easy, although tragic, way out of the anguish of adolescence, and Linnea cannot really forgive her.

Admission to the Feast by the Swedish author Gunnel Beckman goes one step further toward death than any of the novels discussed above, since it involves not a friend's death, but a young person's thoughts about her own imminent death.[3] At the time of its appearance in 1969, the novel was almost as much debated as Katherine Paterson's *Bridge to Terabithia*: at last a book for young readers about death. However, as a YA novel, it is naturally more than a book about death, and with its female protagonist it acquires an additional dimension. Indeed, we see the specific female attitude toward death when Annika, upon hearing her death sentence from a physician, thinks:

> I shall never have more than this little scrap of life ... never have time to become grownup ...
> never be anything good ... achieve anything ... do anything important ...
> never go around with a child growing inside me ... never grow old together with someone I love. ... (21)

Annika, aged nineteen, learns that she has leukemia and will probably only live for a few months. To sort out her thoughts she escapes from Stockholm to the family's country-house: once again the countryside and nature represent childhood to which Annika frantically tries to return. But nature mercilessly reminds her of the cycle of life:

> ... sun and ice should continue to spark and flare for thousands upon thousands of March evenings for ever and ever, amen.
> I hate Nature for her impudent permanence.
> Why should that stupid old bay lie there and stare for century after century—and the boulder out on the point and the oak that stands in the yard so calm and certain that new green leaves and little round acorns will appear.(7)

The season is early spring, the time of hope and rebirth, which has a deep significance in the novel. The city on the other hand is a symbol of civilization and adulthood; it is in the city that Annika receives her death sentence. The adults have betrayed Annika: her mother works somewhere in the third world, and her divorced father, with whom she reestablished relations after many years, died after just a few brief meetings.

The narrative is formed as a letter to a friend. As Annika starts writing, lonely and scared in the country-house the same day she has learned about the lethal diagnosis, she is confused and over-whelmed, and the many typos in the text reveal her state of mind. As readers, we follow Annika's self-therapy, in an narrative interplay between her memories and her reflections of the present situation, her mood changing from despair to hope to reconciliation. At one point Annika contemplates suicide. The open ending of the novel leaves it to the reader to decide what actually happens: when Annika runs out of the cottage to meet her boyfriend, she has just observed that the short cut from the bus-stop across the frozen lake may be dangerous, as the ice is too thin.

Annika's story illustrates her double identity crisis: as a young person and as a young woman. Annika is not only searching for her place in life as an individual but as a woman. She questions her mother's professional choice, resulting in her neglect of family, but Annika has chosen the same "masculine" profession, medical doctor, although in her heart of hearts she wants to write. Contemplating her relationship with her boyfriend, she realizes how suppressed she has been, how her boyfriend has formed and influenced her, and how he has acted as a substitute father. The insight provided by imminent death brings about a total reevaluation of her whole life.

The title of the novel may seem ambivalent until we come to a quoted poem by the Swedish poet Karl Vennberg: "death is only bramble/round pellucid blooms/the dark jewel/that offers admission to the feast." The "feast" does not imply the feast of life, which Annika is denied, but the feast of eternity which opens for her.

Death, often violent death, as in *Johnny, My Friend*, attempted suicide or an accomplished suicide, as in Katarina Mazetti's novel or in Irina Korschunow's highly appraised *The Things With Christoph*, has become a common motif in young adult novels. It reflects the young people's inability to reconcile with the idea of their own adulthood, and therefore their choice to remain young forever. On a mimetic level, this trend may correspond to the growing rate of teenage suicides in the world. But on a mythical level we witness the adult writers' anxiety about the younger generation, which in its turn may be a retrospective anxiety about their own life and death. Writers who choose to let their young protagonists die or commit suicide allow them to stay forever young. In a way, it is merely another way to describe Peter Pan's escape or Pippi Long-stocking's magical pills.

Anne Scott MacLeod proclaims "the end of innocence" in con-temporary children's literature, particularly with such authors as Robert Cormier. "Today's authors ... presuppose an adult society so chaotic and untrustworthy that no child could move toward it with confidence" (MacLeod 1994, 204). It seems that in YA novels, there may be only two ways to deal with growing up, death or self-denial. In Sweden, a critic has coined the notion of idyllophobia, a fear of presenting the world of childhood as idyllic. Children's and juvenile literature becomes more and more violent, not necessarily in actual depictions of violence, but in the general attitude toward the essence of childhood (cf Plotz 1988). The narrative strategies which writers use, most often the autodiegetic unreliable young narrator, amplify the tone of the novels as uncertain, insecure and chaotic. In many novels, notably Cormier's *I Am the Cheese*, we see a total disintegration of character, narrative and structure. YA novel as a narrative which goes beyond the point of no return to idyll also transgresses all conventions which are normally ascribed to chil-dren's fiction (see further Nikolajeva 1998).

NOTES

1. For a historical overview of American YA novel, see Cart 1996. There are several other studies of YA novel, mostly treating it as "issue" literature, with a thematic approach.

2. Although we as readers know that Johnny is a girl, the unreliable narrator is consistently using the pronoun "he" about his mysterious friend, which I am going to follow.

3. The novel has also been translated into English as *Nineteen Is Too Young to Die*, a much less imaginative title.

Chapter 9

Mission Complete—Mission Failed

Myths and folktales are assumed to be the very first stories in the history of humankind, closely related to rites of passage. Thus, a fairy tale becomes a travel instruction for a young person on the way toward adulthood, directions on exactly how to behave in various situations. The reason for viewing the fairy tale as a travel instruction rather than an accomplished passage lies in the situation of the listener. The addressee (in modern times most often a reader) of a fairy tale is situated outside the text; the text is based on an agreement between the sender and the addressee. Among others, Vladimir Propp maintains that the addressee of a fairy tale knows that the story is not true. This fact accounts for the recurrent final patterns of many tales, like the famous Russian: "I have been to the feast myself, drank wine and beer, but never got drunk." The assurance that the story is "true" reminds the listener of its own conventionality.

The hero's task in a folktale is totally impossible for an "ordinary" human being, it is always a symbolic or allegorical depiction. Allegories (like Dante's *Divina Commedia* or Bunyan's *Pilgrim's Progress*) are also travel instructions. But the addressee knows that you cannot die and then rise from the dead, nor be eaten by a whale and then come out again, nor descend into the realm of death, and so on. When the March sisters try to follow Bunyan's instructions for a journey, they have to "translate" the allegory into more everyday conditions. When Nora in *Agnes Cecilia* follows the instructions from the Russian fairy tale, she must adjust them to her own situation.

The modern version of a travel instruction is formula fiction in all its forms: crime novel, science fiction, horror, romance, soap opera, and so on. The addressee of these texts also knows that the story has very little to do with life. On the contrary, the text is based on detachment, especially through its exotic settings and incredible events. Many scholars have noted the similarities between fairy tales and formula fiction. As early as the 1920s Propp suggested that his model for folktale analysis could be applied to novels of chivalry and other texts with fixed narrative structures (Propp 1968, 100). Umberto Eco's structural analysis of the James Bond novels is a well-known example of such an application (Eco 1979, 144-174).

In fact, formula fiction has precisely the same narrative structure as the folktale: lack—the hero takes on an assignment—combats the villain—acquires the princess and the kingdom. The system of characters that Propp reveals in a folktale is most often present in formula fiction: dispatcher (M in James Bond novels), donor (Q), helper, and so on (see Cawelty 1976). Bond always wins a princess in passing. In children's novels, for instance in Nancy Drew books, other rewards are more usual.

As in the folktale, the hero in formula fiction is flat and static, never scared and always resolute; he knows what is right and wrong, knows what to do in any situation—once again Nancy Drew. The condition for enjoying formula novels—and the fairy tale—is that the addressees are familiar with the pattern ("travel directions") but do not have to go through initiation themselves. Identification with the hero of a fairy tale or a formula novel is minimal. Average readers know that they will never be able to match Superman or Nancy Drew, that they are not as rich and beautiful as the heroines of soap operas and they have no magic horses, swords or rings.

The symbolic meaning of food which we see in Arcadian children's books is present in travel instructions too. It has been noted that in no other children's books do the characters eat as much and with such relish as in Enid Blyton's adventure novels (Hautala 1977; Hunt 1996a). In adult formula fiction, this corresponds to excessive drinking and sexual exploits. The reader partakes in behavior which is not wholly accepted in our society, an initiation into the "other" and the forbidden.

Precisely like a fairy tale or a formula novel, the traditional, or epic, novel—to make use of Mikhail Bakhtin's notion (Bakhtin 1981)—depicts an accomplished initiation. Tom Jones and Jane Eyre, the male and the female novice, each in their own way find inner harmony after a long period of problems and trials. The interpretation of the epic novel as the portrayal of a ritual explains why so many epic adult books are read by young people, often in adaptation, for instance *Robinson Crusoe* or *Oliver Twist*. The accomplished rite becomes for young readers rather a travel instruction, since they are still at an earlier stage in their initiation than the protagonists, but unlike folktales or soap operas the novels do not depict an impossible task, and the identification is strong.

There are also a number of novels written directly for young readers, which display the Bakhtinian quality of "epic" and present an accomplished initiation. I have chosen two, with a male and a female protagonist respectively. Both are normally discussed in critical studies under the heading "Realistic Stories," "Family Stories," "Domestic Stories," although they have little in common with any of the texts I have examined, for instance, as a domestic idyll.

Hector Malot's *The Foundling* (also translated as *The Adventures of Remi*) follows a typical fairy-tale pattern very closely. Remi lives the first eight years of his life happily, if not exactly wallowing in wealth, with a loving mother, and in an idyllic, rural surrounding. He even has a little garden of his own:

> My garden was not beautiful, but I loved it and it was mine, and I always spoke of it as "my garden."
> Now the jonquils were in bud, the lilac was about to burst into flower, and the primulas would soon be out. (36)

This garden is something tangible he will miss when he loses his home.

His father is a stone-cutter and works in Paris, sending home money, until one day he has an accident, and his wife has instead to send him money for a lawsuit against his employer. To do so, she is obliged to sell her cow and live in utter poverty. When he comes home, having lost the case, Remi overhears his parents talking and learns that he is a foundling.

This is a very typical initial situation of a fairy tale, where the hero loses his identity and becomes a "nobody." The motif is found in fairy tales all over the world (and also in the Bible story of Moses) and most probably has its origin in the rite of passage where the novice was deprived of his "childhood" identity in order to be initiated into adulthood.

As in myth and fairy tale, the hero is subject to a series of trials. The first is the loss of home. Remi is sold by his foster-mother's wicked husband to an Italian entertainer, Signor Vitalis, who wanders around with three performing dogs and a monkey. Remi has nothing against this career, but he is very reluctant to leave his home and the woman whom he loves as his mother:

> The road we followed went uphill and at each turn I could see Mother Barberin's house, always getting smaller and smaller. I had walked along this road lots of times, and I knew that when we reached one bend I would be able to see it no longer. Before me was the unknown, and gone was the house where I had spent so many happy days. Perhaps I would never see it again. (38)

As it is, Remi will see his childhood home again, yet this is a definite farewell, unlike any similar scene we have seen in the texts discussed in terms of the "there-and-back" pattern. Remi will come back to repay his debt to his foster-mother, but the home is lost forever.

Vitalis is not a bad man. If anything, he has the role of the guide thorough initiation, the Wise Old Man in Jungian terminology, an indispensable figure. Vitalis teaches Remi to read, but in the first place, to understand life:

> "You are travelling through France, when most boys of your age are at school. Open you eyes and look around you and learn. If you see something you don't understand don't be afraid to ask me questions. ..." (60)

Remi's first trials are of a simple and notably material nature: sleeping in other people's barns instead of his own bed, eating stale bread for supper, being tired and cold. But he comes to like Vitalis, and he makes friends with the animals. Although he does not actually speak animal language, he often talks to them as if they understood, and they often behave "as if" they were talking back to him.[1] Of course this newly established balance must be disturbed further. Throughout the novel, Remi will be repeatedly thrown into utmost misery and then ascend again, which is also the usual pattern in fairy tales (and most probably initiation rites). Each temporary ascension anticipates his final reward, but each descent must remind him that he is not yet a fully accepted member of the community. Each descent is a symbolic death, and each recovery a resurrection. As the first step in his humiliation, Vitalis gets arrested and sentenced to two months prison. Remi is left on his own with the animals, in a sort of Robinsonnade where he is to survive without help from adults. However, as in every fairy tale, help comes exactly when needed. A rich English lady, who travels with her sick little son on a barge, asks Remi to accompany them, first for the amusement of her child, and later because she becomes sincerely fond of Remi.

In the fairy-tale character gallery, Mrs. Milligan simply has the role of a helper. In the novel, her role is immediately recognized by a keen reader, as soon as she tells Remi the story of her firstborn child, who has been stolen from her as a baby. The description of Mrs. Milligan's affection amplifies this impression: "... she often spoke to me as if I were her own child" (92). Of course, Remi is indeed her own child, but the hero has not yet passed through all the trials he is supposed to before he can be rewarded. When the two months have passed, Mrs. Milligan and Arthur, her son, want him to stay, but Vitalis won't let him. His arguments confirm once again his function as a wise guide:

> "The start in life that I am giving him is good for him, and far better than he would have with you. It is true that you would have him taught lessons, but you would develop his mind and not his character. Only the hardships of life can do that." (98)

Although Vitalis later regrets that he has not allowed Remi to stay, from the point of view of initiation he could only act that way. So the trials continue; they get lost in a snowstorm, they are attacked by wolves, and two dogs are killed. The monkey gets ill and dies. As they reach Paris, Vitalis dies from cold and starvation. These three deaths are also a necessary part of initiation. For the second time, Remi is totally exposed to his fate, and for the second time he is miraculously rescued. A kind gardener takes care of him, and he soon becomes a member of the family:

> A family! I would have a family and at last I would not be alone.
> ... Life could begin for me again. What meant most to me, more than
> the food, more than anything, was the family life I would have with
> these boys as my brothers and pretty Lise as my sister. (151)

It is worth remembering that the original title of the novel is *Sans
famille*, "Without a Family." The third major disaster comes after
Remi has stayed with his new family for two years, which go very
quickly: "Weeks, months passed, and I was very happy" (154). A
hailstorm breaks all the expensive glass frames and all flowers are
ruined. His new foster-father is arrested for debts. The four children
are taken care of by relatives, while Remi is left on his own:

> I turned away from the home where I had lived for two years and
> where I had hoped always to go on living. .... So these two years had
> been only a brief stop after all, and I must go on my way again. (162)

This time, the helper assumes the form of another street urchin,
Mattia. Together they perform as musicians, and not only earn
enough for a living, but enough to save money to buy a cow for
Mother Barberin. In between Remi visits his foster-siblings, works
in a coal mine and almost gets killed in an accident. The boys buy a
cow, are accused of stealing, and are put in prison. But everything
is straightened out by a well-wishing magistrate. They arrive at
Mother Barberin's cottage in triumph; but as I have already pointed
out, this is not a happy homecoming. As it turns out, Remi's real
parents have been looking for him, and after another series of
adventures Remi is settled in a family of thieves and drunkards in
London slums.

> I suppose I should have been overcome with happiness and have
> leapt into his arms, but I felt the reverse.
>   ...
> I went over to my mother and put my arms around her. She let me
> give her a kiss but did not return it. (214)

Here again the reader's literary competence, that is, previous knowledge of stories, prompts that this is not the real happy ending. The
plot has not been satisfactorily resolved yet, and indeed a dramatic,
although quick, complication follows, whereupon Remi is finally

established in his true identity, as Mrs. Milligan's lost son and heir to substantial riches and a fancy home. As in fairy tales, he is recognized with the help of a token (which in a fairy tale can be the princess's ring, the dragons's tongue, a lock of hair, or indeed almost anything)—the beautiful baby clothes which he was found in and which Mother Barberin has kept just for this occasion. It also appears that Remi's "princess," his little foster-sister Lise, has been adopted by Mrs. Milligan, in just another one of these many incredible fortuities on which the whole plot is dependent.

The last pages of the novel, its epilogue, present an adult narrator: "The years have passed, and I now live in my ancestors' house, Milligan Park ... with my wife, my mother, and my brother" (255). This ending, corresponding to the fairy-tale "lived happily ever after," marks that the initiation is indeed accomplished, and that the hero has successfully passed the trials and been accepted into adult-hood, including marriage and procreation: the last scene depicts the christening of his son and heir. His wife is Lise (thus the rose she gave him at an early stage in the novel acquires a strong sexual symbolism). The straight, irreversible linear development from be-ginning to end, from child to man, is nothing like the circular movement of *The Lion, the Witch and the Wardrobe,* and it also contra-dicts the definition of a children's novel which we find in the epilogue to *Tom Sawyer.*

I have already hinted at some possibilities of analyzing the novel either with Proppian, or with Jungian tools; in both cases we see a completed linear process. In Propp's model, Remi has, with the helpers' assistance, solved the difficult assignments, defeated the villain (Mr. James Milligan who has staged the whole machination for his own profit), proved his right to his true identity, and won the princess and the kingdom. In Jung's model, he has met his Shadow and his Anima, and has reached his Self in the center of his mandala, the ancestral home. He has, in other words, successfully accom-plished the process, which the characters of idyllic novels are hap-pily ignorant about, the Puer Aeternus is trying to avoid, the quest heroes enthusiastically play at, and the protagonists of YA novels accept as inevitable, but tragic.

It is tempting to call this linear development typically male; therefore I have chosen to have a brief look at a similar text with a female protagonist. *Anna All Alone* by the Swedish author Martha

Sandwall-Bergström is interesting because it came out the same year as the first *Pippi Longstocking* novel, but apparently belongs to a totally different tradition.

At the beginning, a poor girl comes from an orphanage to a peasant family who need her for housework. If this opening is reminiscent of *Anne of Green Gables*, it is the only similarity. Anna (or Gulla as she is called in Swedish) is not a tomboy and she does not have to be intimidated and civilized. In fact, she is the most perfect female stereotype imaginable: diligent, good-natured, humble and pious. Unlike Anne, she is immediately accepted by the family and the whole community. Life is hard for her. Her foster-mother and foster-siblings suffer from all possible illnesses, their grandmother dies, hunger haunts the family, but Gulla never complains and bravely manages all hardships. She also gets a powerful benefactor in the owner of the nearest manor, who sees a likeness between her and his dead daughter. If the plot summary at this stage is embarrassingly similar to *The Foundling* (and dozens of other stories), it has been my intention. Gulla is indeed the lost granddaughter of the rich proprietor, and she is recognized and established in her right with the help of the baby clothes she was once found in.

Although it takes half a dozen sequels before Gulla is happily married, her story is just as linear as Remi's. After being deprived of her true identity, she goes through trials, proves worthy of entering adult society and thus is accepted into it. The only visible dissimilarity is that Remi's trials take place primarily outdoors (male space), while Gulla's are indoors (female space). This does not change the linearity of the story, or make Gulla's initiation specifically female. Both are what we might call an Ugly Duckling story: a displaced child who turns into a splendid adult. The dubious moral of both stories is also reminiscent of *The Ugly Duckling*: you can only become a swan if you are hatched from a swan's egg.[2]

Still another novel may be recollected alongside these two: *Little Lord Fauntleroy*. If we only know it by repute and not by reading, it is easy to think that this story is very much like Remi's: a little poor orphan who eventually finds his right place and recovers the family home. But whatever trials little Cedric Errol might have had, they are all beyond the narrative, and are neglectable. True, he has lost his father, but I have already discussed a parent's death as a form of "absence," which does not introduce the protagonist to his own mortality. Cedric has his mother's undivided love (the father as a possible rival for her attention is successfully gotten rid of!), he has friends, who all adore him, and although the narrator mentions "a cheap house" that he is living in, the family has a maid and apparently does not have to go hungry. The book opens with Cedric's unexpected fortune and develops from happiness toward still greater happiness, without any serious complications, except an impostor, without whom the plot would have been incomplete. The boy is absolutely perfect in very respect from the beginning, so there is no room for improvement or development. Instead he improves and changes everything around him, working for the benefit of the poor and disseminating joy. Moreover, the little innocent child recovers Eden for his old, disagreeable grandfather, much the way Colin does for his father. Although Cedric celebrates his eighth birthday at the end of the book, thus definitely becoming a year older, he is nevertheless for ever conserved in this happy paradise, together with his mother, grandfather and friends. Unlike Remi's, Cedric's story is not an accomplished quest, but a typical domestic utopia, which, however, lacks the sophistication and the intricate imagery of *The Secret Garden*.

Little Lord Fauntleroy has been called "the best version of the Cinderella story in the modern idiom that exists" (Laski 1950, 83). It has also been discussed in the general terms of a fairy tale and as a Cinderella tale in particular (Bixler 1984). Much as the idea of the three sons, the first two being good-for-nothing, and the youngest the most handsome, kind and worthy, is a fairy-tale pattern, *Little Lord Fauntleroy*, unlike *The Foundling* or *Anna All Alone*, is definitely *not* a Cinderella plot. Cedric has in fact not done anything to deserve his sudden happiness; he has not gone through any trials nor endured any hardships, he has not had any quest nor gained any experience. His tremendous goodness alone does not qualify him to be a Cinderella. The Cinderella (or Ugly Duckling) plot moves from ashes to diamonds, from nothing to everything, from humiliation to highest reward; Cedric at most exchanges spiritual wealth for material.

The fairy-tale, completed nature of *The Foundling* and *Anna All Alone* is especially clear by comparison with a contemporary "poor orphan" story, for instance *The Great Gilly Hopkins* with its open and uncertain ending. Once again, Mikhail Bakhtin's theory of the novel helps us to see the profound difference. Epic is, in Bakhtin's terminology, a fully evolved and accomplished genre, while a novel is a genre under evolution: eclectic, changing, and open for innovations. Epic is as detached from its contemporary addressees as a fairy tale: we cannot identify with Remi. A novel is something we can relate to, identify with, feel involved in.

The modern (in Bakhtin's terminology polyphone, multivoiced) adult novel most often depicts a failed initiation when the protagonist—or still more often the reader only, since the narrator is "unreliable"—comes to the tragic conclusion that his emancipation is impossible, that he has chosen a wrong path, that the guides have betrayed him, and that he must for ever remain in the split state. The modern novel describes a never-ending quest that is doomed to fail. Therefore motifs and characters such as Faust, the Wandering Jew or Ulysses are so attractive for contemporary adult writers, and it is very easy to find literary examples (see also Watt 1996). Existential problems that torment modern protagonists do not leave any room for positive answers—after thousands of years of human civilization we still do not know why we are here. The protagonist of a modern novel interrogates his own existence, while the novel itself examines its boundaries and limits, with all the devices included in the notion of metafiction.

Contemporary YA novels and even novels for younger readers often come very close to adult fiction, both in their general pessimistic worldview and their complex narrative strategies. However, we can still distinguish a children's novel from an adult novel by its unaccomplished rite of passage and its possibility of return to circularity, if only through death.

NOTES

1. In an animated film version of the novel, the animals actually can talk.

2. This camouflaged autobiography echoes the writer's much-quoted statement: "First you must endure a lot, then you get famous." This tale has been used as evidence by some scholars who maintain that Hans Christian Andersen was in fact an illegitimate son of noble parents, perhaps the Danish king.

Chapter 10

From Idyll to Collapse

In this final chapter I will take a closer look at one of those rare works of children's fiction which span over all my major categories, taking their protagonists from a world of complete idyll through a period of quests and picnics beyond the point of no return. The work I have in mind is the Moomin suite.

The Moomin books have been often discussed in terms of idyll, for instance by Gundel Mattenklott: "In the Moomin world, there is neither death, nor sexuality. It is the price for adults not to age, and for children not to grow up" (Mattenklott 1989, 93). Mattenklott also notices the autonomy of the Moomin world, maintaining that Tove Jansson has re-created a childhood paradise. Apparently, the critic fails to see the dynamic character of the suite, instead treating the novels as a static corpus of identical texts. Unlike Mattenklott and most other scholars, who tend to treat each Moomin novel individually (Jones 1984; Westin 1988), I view them as an inseparable whole in which its ultimate meaning is only revealed through assembling the meaning of its components.

I will therefore consider the Moomin novels as one text, arranging them in an order that makes sense according to my approach, not the order they were written and published. I start with the most idyllic novel, *Finn Family Moomintroll,* and the one where idyll is slightly disturbed but soon restored, *Moominsummer Madness.* I proceed with the most explicit quest novel, *Comet in Moominland,* presenting a clear "there-and-back" pattern. Also *Moominland Midwinter* is a typical time-out, which for the first time confronts the protagonist with death, but nevertheless brings him back to idyll.

Moominpappa at Sea is a breakthrough into linearity, where idyll is for ever left behind, and *Moominvalley in November* depicts the total disintegration of childhood paradise.[1]

Unlike previous critical works, I treat most characters as parts of a collective protagonist, with Moomintroll as a nucleus, complemented by other characters, in the first place Sniff. Sniff is the worst side of Moomintroll's personality: grumpy, cowardly, greed, and selfish. Snufkin represents the most independent and mature part of Moomintroll, the part which, unlike Moomintroll himself, is already prepared to leave home.

The characters not considered parts of the collective protagonist are those apprehended as "adults," like Pappa and Mamma. Pappa's role in the early novels is remarkably peripheral: he makes decisions, prepares punch for parties, and is constantly writing his memoirs. He can mend things and make witty comments. But otherwise Pappa does not emerge as a significant figure in Moomintroll's life until *Moominpappa at Sea*. Moominmamma is all the more important, and it is her oppressive protection Moomintroll must overcome. In the early novels, Mamma is the source of security, warmth, and food, her constant attribute, a handbag, being a clear transformation of Cornucopia.

Muskrat, a parody on an old, grumpy philosopher, and undoubtledly an adult, has in *Comet* mostly the function of a "dispatcher" (Propp), who by telling the hero about the problems sets him on his task. In *Finn Family* he is peripheral and then disappears. Too-ticky, the enigmatic figure in *Midwinter*, is another adult with a special role in the text.

Hemulens are the most ambivalent race in the world of Moomins. In *Exploits,* a female Hemulen, who runs the orphanage where pappa lives as a child, represents all the worst sides of adults. The jailer Hemulen in *Madness* is portrayed as both stupid and insensitive. His relative, the little kind-hearted female Hemulen, is said to be a failure, "from a Hemulic point of view" (128). The butterfly-collecting Hemulen in *Comet* is definitely an adult and has the function of a helper, rescuing Moomintroll, Sniff and Snufkin from a precipice. His cousin, the stamp-collecting Hemulen, is a more complicated person. He may seem just as much a bore, but he has some very attractive features. This Hemulen is definitely not an adult, and he participates in the "children's" adventures as their equal.

Snork Maiden, although included in the group of "children," is obviously not a part of the collective protagonist, since her role is that of a "princess" (in Propp's meaning). She makes Moomintroll aware of his identity as a male, supposedly brave and protective. Snork Maiden is the second female in Moomintroll's life, after his mother, and although he is quite infatuated, Mamma is as yet more important for him. Moreover, male friendship is likewise more important: "Snufkin was his best friend. Of course, he also liked the Snork Maiden a lot, but still it can never be quite the same with a girl" (*Madness* 17).

It is amazing how easily Tove Jansson gets rid of her characters. Sniff, so important in the early novels, is not even mentioned in *Madness* and later works. Snork, introduced together with his sister, is absent from further novels, and Snork Maiden, Moomintroll's preadolescent love and transitional object, vanishes completely after a short appearance in the end of *Midwinter*. The notion of a collective protagonist easily accounts for this peculiarity. A secondary character, which is a part of the collective protagonist, is present only as long as it is necessary for the protagonist's development. When Sniff disappears, Moomintroll has won over the greedy and cowardly part of himself. Snork Maiden, Moomintroll's temporary Anima, is replaced by other, more complicated symbols.

IN THE ENCHANTED PLACE

The setting of the Moomin novels is extremely important:

> It was a wonderful valley, full of happy little animals and flowering trees, and there was a clear narrow river that came down from the mountain, looped around Moominhouse and disappeared in the direction of another valley, where no doubt other little animals wondered where it came from. (*Comet* 9)

The house they live in has been built by Moominpappa, exactly as he has imagined it in *Exploits*.[2] The house is round. The formal explanation is that it has to remind Moomins of the round tile stoves where their ancestors used to live. The symbolic implication of a round house is very strong: it is deliberately created as a model of the world. "It was a world that was very private, and self-contained, and to which nothing could be added" (*Sea* 8).

The house has no keys, and everybody is always welcome. When the family comes to live in the valley, there are four of them: the parents, the son and their foster-child Sniff. As the story unfolds, new characters are constantly added, as in a cumulative tale:

> Moomintroll's mother and father always welcomed all their friends in the same quiet way, just adding another bed and putting another leaf in the dining-room table. And so Moominhouse was rather full—a place where everyone did what they liked and seldom worried about tomorrow. (*Family* 16)

When Thingummy and Bob come to the valley, and Mamma has not even seen them properly, she immediately asks Pappa to put up two more beds, and as it turns out that the newcomers talk a funny language, she is rather upset: "How shall I know what they want for pudding on their birthday, or how many pillows they like to have" (*Family* 116).

The community is completely happy and lives in harmony. They have no enemies, and they do not have to think about their daily bread, it takes care of itself. The family's general view of life can be gathered from their attitude to food:

> In Moominhouse they had pancakes for luncheon—big yellow pancakes with raspberry jam. There was porridge from the day before as well, but as nobody wanted it they decided to save it for the next morning. (*Family* 52)

Food, like everything else, is a source of joy. Material things, on the other hand, are of no importance. When a storm is blowing and Pappa asks whether anybody has taken in the hammock, and nobody has, he says: "Good. ... it was a horrid colour" (*Madness* 25). When Pappa breaks a dish, Mamma hurries to say: "It's really a good thing it's broken—it was so ugly" (*Comet* 31). When Mamma wakes up in the end of *Midwinter* to discover that her winter guests have taken away half of her possessions, besides having eaten a year's supply of jam, she is only relieved, because property has no value for the Moomins. Moomintroll has dropped Mamma's golden bracelet into a pond because it makes the water gleam so beautifully, and Mamma says: "We'll always keep our bangles in brown pond water in the future. They're much more beautiful that way" (*Madness* 14). This is a perfect illustration of a happy and harmonious child's attitude to life.

Finn Family Moomintroll begins with a prologue, describing the first day of winter when the Moomins are going to sleep. The intrusive narrator comments: "All Moomintrolls go to sleep about November. This is a good idea, too, if you don't like the cold and the long winter darkness" (11). Winter is the time of a ritual, mythical "nonbeing" for the Moomins, and it is taken care of in just a few sentences. The novel proper starts with spring, a new cycle of life. Moomintroll awakens from his sleep—just the way a little child awakens after a night's sleep and finds joy and delight in the fact that the world is just as he left it the evening before.

The things that can interrupt the idyll are of a harmless nature, so that they add suspense to the everyday, but can scarcely disturb order. In this novel, the cause of adventure is magic. But it is benevolent magic, initiating an almost endless string of enjoyable adventures. Typically for this early novel, the omniscient narrator tells the readers in advance that the hat belongs to the Hobgoblin, so anything can be expected. The nature of magic in *Finn Family* is much like that in Edith Nesbit's books: unpredictable, but not dangerous; it makes fun of you and is over by sunset.

The adults do not prevent the children from having fun: Mamma is too busy cooking, and Pappa writing his memoirs. As in all idyllic narratives, the adults are comfortably removed as obstacles, while they are always there for the child as a source of security (Mamma recognizes Moomintroll even though he is transformed), comfort—and food. The adults may, however, take part in the adventures, for instance by joining in a picnic, always a happy improvisation: "Stop eating now, children—we'll take the food with us" (53). Mamma's packing for the picnic is reminiscent of many similar enumerations:

> She collected blankets, saucepans, birch-bark, a coffee-pot, masses of food, suntan-oil, matches, and everything you can eat out of, on or with. She packed it all with an umbrella, warm clothes, tummy-ache medicine, an egg-whisk, cushion, a mosquito-net, bathing-drawers and a table cloth in her bag. (54)

Mamma is careful about taking all sources of domestic security with her. Her handbag, like a circus conjuror's, contains all this easily, and much more.

The nice, harmless sea excursion anticipates the final break-out in *Moominpappa at Sea*, creating a sharp contrast to it. Although the adventurers experience a thunderstorm and the Hattifatteners' nightly attack, it is all fun and no danger. They have enough food in Mamma's bag to last for ever. The island is nice, idyllic, and full of wonderful surprises. It has everything a paradise island should have. It is a miniature replica of the Moominvalley: a sandy beach, a fine harbor, forests, green glades, and magnificent flowers. There is a great difference between playing Robinson and being indeed stranded in the harsh, unwelcome setting they will find in the later novel.

The only real disturbance of idyll is the appearance of the Groke, a reminder of dark, incomprehensible things, which so far are remote and nothing to bother about. "She was not particularly big and didn't look dangerous either, but you felt that she was terribly evil and would wait for ever" (120). This sounds like a description of Death. The trial of the Groke—an intertexual link on the trial in *Alice in Wonderland* [3]—is a sort of defense against fear, turning it into a farce. "It was the last time she was seen in the Valley of the Moomins" (127), says the narrator, sharing the child's perspective and pretending not to know that the ultimate encounter with the Groke is inevitable. The end of novel completes the temporal cycle: "It is autumn in Moomin Valley, for how else can spring come back again?" (155)

In *Moominsummer Madness* the valley is suddenly threatened, not by an enemy, but by natural forces: a volcano eruption followed by a huge flood. As usual, the family takes it easy. When the ground floor of the house is flooded they simply move upstairs. Moomintroll dives into the kitchen to get breakfast. The family thinks it is exciting and helpful to view their own life from a new angle: "It felt very refreshing to see one's kitchen like that" (28). This is the first anticipation of a more profound change of perspective when the family is forced to find refuge in something that is marvelously described by using the device of estrangement:

> It was quite clearly a kind of house. Two golden faces were painted on its roof; one was crying and the other one laughing at the Moomins. Beneath the grinning faces gaped a kind of large rounded cave filled with darkness and cobwebs. Obviously the great wave had carried away one of the walls of the house. On either side of the yawning gap drooped velvet curtains. ... (39)

The new home does not affect the family's life radically. It is not the child going on adventures on his own yet, but once again the whole family experiencing something new and exciting. The implication of the theater in this novel is discovering that things are not always what they seem to be:

> All things around them were false. Their pretty colours were a sham, and everything he touched was made of paper or wool or plaster. The golden crowns weren't nice and heavy, and the flowers were paper flowers. The fiddle had no strings and the boxes no bottoms, and the books couldn't even be opened. (46)

In this novel, the family is separated. Moomintroll and Snork Maiden sleep in a tree, while the theater floats away without them. For Moomintroll, it means a chance to show his manliness and protect Snork Maiden. But first he remembers the picnic basket that Mamma had given them for breakfast: "All of a sudden Moomintroll had a feeling that the situation wasn't so very perilous" (72). Food provides the most secure link to home. Moominmamma is confident that her son will find his way back again. Little My, who has fallen off the floating theater, is rescued by Snufkin on his way to the valley. Thus the separation also brings about a reunion, which, as in all Moomin stories, is turned into a big celebration. "It was as if nothing had ever happened and as if no danger could ever threaten them again" (160). The picnic is harmless and comfortable, and the order restored almost before it was genuinely disturbed.

QUEST FOR SELF-KNOWLEDGE

In *Comet in Moominland*, the first real journey is undertaken, and the author builds it around lucid symbols and metaphors. At the beginning of the story, Sniff discovers a path in the woods. "I shall have to tell Moomintroll about this, and we can explore it together,

because it would be a bit risky for me to go alone" (10). The two
figures are interchangeable parts of the Self. Sniff is too scared to
swim in the sea, but Moomintroll dives into it to fish for pearls—a
very suitable Jungian symbol. Sniff on the other hand finds a cave,
another transparent symbol.

When the two friends learn about the comet, Sniff is earnestly
scared, while Moomintroll is curious and decides to go on a expedition to find out more. Significantly, he does not tell Sniff where
they are going and why: the curious part of the mind is trying to
subdue the frightened part. Snufkin who joins them on their quest
is in this book more of a guide (= adult) than in any other. Also
Snufkin's artistic nature is revealed here: on hearing that the earth
will explode if a comet hit it, Snufkin says: "It would be awful if the
earth exploded. It's so beautiful," while Sniff's reaction is: "And
what about us?" (58). Here we see clearly a poet's and a selfish
child's attitude. Sniff is consistently portrayed as selfish and self-
centered in this book. When they find garnets in a cave, Snufkin says
they are beautiful, while Sniff thinks about all the things he can buy.
He is also punished for his greed. On learning that there is too little
left of Snufkin's magical sun-oil to save them all, Sniff asks whether
there is enough to save only him. When the adventures become too
scary he wants to go home.

Viewing the journey as the character's exploration of his inner
world, Moomintroll is learning to get rid of his most childish and
solipsistic qualities. His trust in his mother is still unlimited: "If only
we can get home to mamma before it [the comet] comes nothing can
happen. She will know what to do" (93). The encounter with Snork
Maiden is decisive for this novel (see also my interpretation in
Nikolajeva 1996, 105ff). He rescues her in a most heroic fashion, and
she rescues him later, in a feminine way, by intuition. On the
journey, Snork Maiden takes over mamma's role in preparing food.
One of the lessons Moomintroll learns is the importance of home:
"You must go on a long journey before you can really discover how
wonderful home is" (114). But there is another important gained
insight since Moomintroll is no longer afraid: "it must be because
we've sort of got to know the comet" (155). The child has learned to
control his fear. Maybe this is the reason why Sniff, the frightened
part of the Self, disappears in the later novels.

It is worth mentioning that they find refuge in a cave, a female symbol: that is they go back into Mamma's womb to survive the catastrophe. After this temporary regression everything is once again as it used to be.

MEETING WITH DEATH

Moominland Midwinter is still a circular, "domestic" story, without any big adventures. But "… something happened that had never happened before, not since the first Moomin took to his hibernating den. Moomintroll awoke and found that he couldn't go back to sleep again" (13). The circular pattern of the Moomin time with its routines and winter hibernation is disturbed. "All the clocks had stopped ages ago …" (13), discovers Moomintroll and makes an attempt to recover time: "I'll wind all the clocks," he thought. "Perhaps that makes the spring come a tiny bit earlier" (26). But the very meaning of measurable, chronological time is gone: "All the clocks were running again. Moomintroll felt less lonely after he had wound them up. As time was lost anyway, he set them at different hours" (39).

His first sensation is hunger—a need for security:

> He went out in the kitchen. It … looked dismally tidy and empty. The larder was just as desolate. He found nothing there, except a bottle of loganberry syrup that had fermented, and a half packet of dusty biscuits. (16)

Moomintroll's usual secure universe is there no more. He finds himself in a "strange and dangerous world" (18).

Nordic winter is indeed a desolate world, cold and dark. In December, the sun does not rise for days. For a southerner—or a Moomin—it may easily seem a realm of death: "It's dead. All the world has died while I slept. This world belongs to somebody else whom I don't know. Perhaps to the Groke. It isn't made for Moomins" (19). From the world of eternal summer, Moomintroll is introduced to the opposite. Everything that used to be in motion is still, there is no greenery, no light, no warmth. He feels lonely because this world is new and unfamiliar. Everything is mysterious, and this frightens him much more than the comet. Still worse, he must cope with it alone, since Mamma will not wake up.

The Great Cold is represented in this novel as a female, a traditional Scandinavian image (cf Andersen's Snow Queen): "... very beautiful. ... But if you look her in the face you'll be frozen to ice." (50) Cold is identical with death, and when the squirrel is frozen to death, Moomintroll gets very upset, because it is the first time he meets death.

> "When one's dead, then one's dead," said Too-ticky kindly. "This squirrel will become earth all in his time. And still later on there'll grow trees from him, with new squirrels skipping about in them. Do you think that's so very sad?" (57)

Too-ticky is Moomintroll's substitute parent in this novel, and she has the same role in explaining death and the cycle of life to the frustrated child as does Tuck in *Tuck Everlasting*.

As in the previous books, the secondary characters, except Too-ticky, are parts of the collective protagonist of which Moomintroll is the center. They all demonstrate different ways of dealing with winter: little My who has fun toboganning on Mamma's silver tray, the melancholy dog Sorry-oo, or Salome the Little Creep. Hemulen's part is especially important. He ignores the deathly meaning of winter, enjoys it and makes the most of it. Moomintroll wonders "slightly troubled, why he couldn't find the Hemulen a jolly person. Although he has been longing and longing for somebody who wouldn't be secretive and distant but cheery and tangible, exactly like the Hemulen" (100). Hemulen cannot be Moomintroll's guide through the mysteries of winter, because he does not take them seriously and neglects dangers. As Hemulen himself puts it, cold weather "puts a stop to all unnecessary thoughts and fancies" (100).

But for Moomintroll, winter becomes the source of deep contemplation. "Now I've got everything," Moomintroll said to himself. "I've got the whole year. Winter too. I'm the first Moomin to have lived through an entire year" (138). This is not really true, because it is as yet a "time-out," a game. Spring is coming back, and summer idyll will soon be restored. Still, Moomintroll will never feel secure again: "Now came spring, but not at all as he had imagined its coming. He had thought that it would deliver him from a strange and hostile world, but now it was simply a continuation of his new experience. ..." (140). Moomintroll becomes aware that life and death (as summer and winter) are impossible without each other. He enjoys the long spring and does not want the family to wake up. Still he certainly enjoys Mamma's usual reaction: "Everything's going to be all right" (152). She immediately starts busying herself with her customary chores, and Moomintroll feels secure again. As to Snork Maiden, Moomintroll wonders "whether he would ever be able to tell her about his winter so that she'd understand it" (162). Apparently he has outgrown her. Indeed, as I have pointed out earlier, she disappears from later novels.

The special role of Too-ticky is accentuated by the narrative structure, where she is, in a subtle manner, presented as a possible narrative voice. When Moomintroll hurries to rescue Little My, Too-ticky comments: "It's always like this in their adventures. To save and be saved. I wish somebody would write a story sometimes about the people who warm up the heroes afterwards" (147). This metafictive statement suggests that Too-ticky belongs outside the story. If the "story" is the reenacting of a rite of passage, Too-ticky is the guide who belongs both within and outside it. In the rescue scene, she is watching Moomintroll without interfering, until she is forced to, when things go really badly—exactly the role of the guide.

BREAKING AWAY

As the title suggests, Moominpappa is the central character of *Moominpappa at Sea*. Why does the author suddenly feel compelled to put forward Pappa, who has so far been kept relatively in the shade? The novel begins:

> One afternoon at the end of August, Moominpappa was walking about in the garden feeling at a loss. He had no idea what to do with himself, because it seemed everything there was to be done had already been done or was being done by somebody else. (7)

We may decide that Pappa is the protagonist and find confirmation both throughout the text and in the end, which also features Pappa all alone. However, I insist that Moomintroll is the kernel of the collective protagonist of the whole suite, and if the focus is shifted onto a peripheral part of this collective protagonist, there must be a very good reason. In the previous novel, Moomintroll discovered the delights and horrors of winter all on his own, without the supervision of his mother. Her substitute Too-ticky is an androgynous figure, a father as well as a mother. In *Moominpappa at Sea*, it is time for Moomintroll to liberate himself wholly from his mother and start identifying with his father, that is, to find a gender identity. In Lacanian psychology, this passage is described as a traumatic process, implying a transition from chaos into order and adjusting to social rules. In plain words, it is time for the little troll to grow up.

The novel can be analyzed in Jungian terms, as Pappa's individuation, and in feminist terms, as Mamma's creative liberation. In both cases, Moomintroll is completely ignored. However, I continue to view Moomintroll as a protagonist. The events of this book are, for my purpose, best described in Lacanian terms, as a passage from maternal to paternal stage in the child's development. Subsequently, it means that the father's role must be amplified, since he will from now on be the model for his child, while the mother's dominance diminishes, and she must accept her new secondary role and adjust to it. Pappa must take on his responsibilities as a father and stop being just another spoiled child to Moominmamma. Mamma must learn to fill the emptiness that the grown-up child has left in her life. She does so by becoming a creative artist.

Since there are three parallel psychological processes within this novel, its narrative pattern differs from the previous texts. The three characters are focalized internally, one at a time (polyfocalization), which is something other than the traditional omniscient narrator. The final picture is asembled by the reader from the three consciousnesses, in a puzzle-like method (a puzzle is featured in the novel as one of its many powerful images), while the intrusive narrator of the early novels has completely withdrawn. The post-structural notion of intersubjectivity (absence of a single, fixed subject), as well as that of Bakhtin's dialogics, is manifest in this text.

The fourth character, Little My, the family's adopted daughter, is a brave, determined, and independent creature, "the one member of the family who seemed to manage all right by herself" (35). My's role in the story is that of a clown, a commentator; she always has a punchline to every situation. She is never focalized and does not participate in the psychological process, other than by showing an example of free will and strong mind. As Moomintroll remarks with envy: "She does exactly what she feels like doing, and no one opposes her. She just does it" (70).

As the novels opens, Pappa is worried about forest fires, whereupon the family says: "He *always* talks about forest fires in August" (8; my emphasis). The family is used to not taking Pappa seriously, and they manage elegantly without him; while he is worried about fires, they extinguish one. But the marker "always" suggests the iterative. Pappa is longing to break the circle, to do something singulative, since he has realized that it is time for him to be a model of masculinity for his son. "I'd love to be sailing. Sailing right out to sea, as far as I can go ..." (9). This represents a longing to go over from the circular female/child pattern to linear male/adult one.

In the Moominvalley, there is a blue crystal ball, "the centre of the garden, of the valley, and of the whole world" (12). Pappa is going to shift the center of the world, and he will soon say explicitly: "... my lighthouse will be the centre of the world" (28). The crystal ball, a dark and mysterious mirror, will be replaced first by a storm lantern and finally by the lighthouse. If anything, it is also a shift in the author's evaluation of her writing (cf the treatment of mirror and lamp in Abrams 1953).

Long before Pappa says anything about his plans, Mamma guesses about them, looking at the map of the archipelago, at a little island "in the middle of nowhere":

> "That's where we're going to live and lead a wonderful life, full of troubles ...—That's pappa's island. Pappa is going to look after us there. We're going to move there and live there all our lives, and start everything afresh, right from the beginning." (18)

Mamma verbalizes Pappa's dreams, because, playwright and memoir-writer as he is, he seems unable to express them himself. Pappa has never been to the island. By building his model lighthouse he is creating a fantasy universe, much as the way he built his imaginary house in his youth. But this time, it seems as if he is going from play to reality (I will leave the discussion of the lighthouse as a phallic symbol to a more trained Freudian).

Remarkably, no one questions Pappa's decision. Moreover, they feel that "... the lighthouse was calling to *them. They* knew that they must go to the island, and go soon" (23; my emphasis). The collective protagonist submits to the will of its temporarily strongest part. They travel by night, which is contrary to reason, but an important symbol: "One makes a trip by day, but by night one sets out on a journey" (25). This is a crucial moment in the whole Moomin suite. They are leaving their Arcadia to start a new life, when nothing forces them—except the urge to grow up.

As usual, Mamma packs everything, but they all know that the situation is anything but usual: "Now the proper thing to do was that they should begin an entirely new life, and that Moominpappa should provide everything they needed, look after them and protect them. Life must have been too easy for them up till now" (25). The children are leaving the nursery. Real life begins.

At first, Pappa is enjoying his new role and feels very confident. "Pappa was steering the boat ... he was guiding them safely across the vast ocean through the silent, blue night" (28). When they fail to see the lighthouse, Pappa is not worried: "You can depend on it that the lighthouse is working all right. There are some things one can be absolutely sure of: sea currents, the seasons, the rising of the sun, for example. And that lighthouses always work, too" (31). Pappa has so far retained the child's belief in stability.

Disappointments come one after another. Not only is the lighthouse not working, it is also locked, and the grand entré, which Pappa has envisioned for his family, fails. The island is barren, cold and unwelcoming. There is no soil for Mamma's garden. There is no path and no jetty for the boat. Moomintroll alone retains his firm belief in Mamma's powers: "They would be eating soon, and Moominmamma would make a fire between some stones and lay the meal out on the steps of the lighthouse. Then somehow or other things would be all right" (44). He cannot imagine that Mamma has resigned all her power to Pappa.

Unfortunately, Pappa fails to light the lamp. He then tries to occupy himself with something else: "It was a very satisfying feeling putting a net out. It was a man's job, something one did for the whole family" (76). There is only seaweed when he takes in the nets; it takes Mamma and Moomintroll two days to clean them, and Pappa makes no further attempts. Instead, he has great visions: "I want to build big things, strong things, I want so terribly much ... But I don't know ... It's so very difficult being a father!" (95f). This is the only sentence in the book where Pappa acknowledges his responsibility. But he is still extremely childish. He makes a belt for mamma out of broken green glass and rice. Little My's comment is: "Well, that's good-bye to rice pudding!" (99). Although Mamma hurries to say: "We can eat gruel just as well," a terrible thought crosses Pappa's mind. "Dearest, if I had to choose between a jewel and rice pudding," Moominmamma began, but Moominpappa interrupted her saying, "How much of the food is eaten?" (99). This is the first time hunger haunts Moominfamily. They are no longer in the benevolent Moominvalley where food appeared all by itself. In this new world, food has to be provided. Typically, it is not Moomintroll, but Pappa who comes to this insight. His for once sensible reaction is to take his fishing rod and go fishing: "He had only one very determined thought in his head: getting food for the family" (103). This is a totally new experience for the Moomins.

> "He's not playing at it—he's serious," Moominmamma thought. "I've put salt fish in all the jars and containers we possess, and still he goes on fishing. Of course it's grand to have so much food, but somehow it was jollier when we didn't have so much." (104)

Meanwhile, Moominmamma, deprived of all activities (she is not even allowed to carry baskets from the boat to the lighthouse), is completely paralyzed. We may wonder why she suddenly tolerates Pappa's follies; but we must read the text symbolically, expecting no reasonable behavior. Mamma knows that the journey is a part of her son's initiation: "Everything was as it should be. In time she would probably get used to being looked after, perhaps she would come to like it" (34). From the very first moment, as they come to the island, she is completely resigned to her new fate:

> Of all strange things, that was the strangest, the way Moomin-mamma could sleep in this new place without unpacking, without making their beds and without giving them a sweet before they went to sleep. She had even left her handbag behind her on the sand. It was a little bit frightening in a way, but all the same cheering; it meant that all this was a real change, and not just an adventure. (35)

Not used to idleness, Mamma tries to set up a garden and has wonderful visions of it:

Mamma felt calm and happy. She dreamed of carrots, radishes and potatoes, and of how they grew fat and round in the warm soil. She could see green leaves appearing in strong, heavy clusters. She saw them waving in the wind against the blue sea, heavy with tomatoes, peas and beans for the family to eat. She knew that nothing of this would come true until the following summer, but it didn't matter. She had something to dream about. And deep down inside she dreamed most of all of having an apple tree. (57)

Mamma's dreams are futile, since the first rainstorm destroys her garden, and even the rose she has taken from Moominvalley dies of cold and rain. Mamma's normal household duties do not make her happy any more: "There was no need for her to do much cleaning. … Preparing meals was easy, too, provided one did it in the most light-hearted way possible. And so the days came to seem long in quite the wrong way" (116). Trying to invent something meaningful to do, Mamma begins painting the walls. She paints Moominvalley and enters her own painting, like Wu Lao-Tsu, to the family's surprise and despair:

"You mustn't frighten us like that. … You must remember that we're used to your being here when we come home in the evening."
"That's just it," Moominmamma sighed. "But one needs a change sometimes. We take everything too much for granted, including each other." (155f)

Typically, it is Pappa who needs her to be there for him. But apparently Mamma has become free, from her confined role as Mother, comforter, and everybody's first aid.

Moomintroll's trials begin already before they leave Moominvalley, when the Groke appears from the darkness. The Groke is the most mysterious figure of the Moomin suite, so cold that the earth she treads on gets frozen. Her origins are never explained, but her role in the narrative is obvious, especially with some Jungian symbolism. The Groke is Moominmamma's dark side, which it is now time for Moomintroll to acknowledge and accept. In the illustrations, the Groke can indeed be identified as Mamma's dark reflection, a Shadow. No wonder Mamma seems to know all about the Groke: "… she isn't dangerous. You know she isn't, even though she may be frightful. … we're afraid of the Groke because she's just cold all over. All because she doesn't like anybody. But she's never done any harm" (17).

If Moomintroll in the early novel felt only aversion for the Groke—he was not ready yet to investigate his attitude toward his mother—now he is curious and feels some sort of empathy:

> Moomintroll imagined he was the Groke. He shuffled along slowly, all hunched up, through a pile of dead leaves. He stood still, waiting while he spread the mist round him. He sighed and stared longingly toward the window. He was the loneliest creature in the whole world. (20)

In a short passage at the beginning of the novel, the Groke is focalized as she prepares to follow the family to the island: "... she was never in a hurry. Time for her was endless and passed very slowly. Time for her contained nothing, except the occasional lamps, which were lit as autumn approached" (27). This focalization confirms the interpretation of the Groke as Mamma's dark side. The usual, cheerful and obliging Mamma accepts her husband's foolish venture. The lonely, unhappy, oppressed Mamma is left behind and feels miserable.

When Moomintroll wonders why the Groke has become the way she is, Mamma explains:

> "It was probably because nobody did anything at all. Nobody bothered about her, I mean. I don't suppose she remembers anyway, and I don't suppose she goes around thinking about it either. She's like the rain or the darkness, or a stone you have to walk around if you want to get past. ... No one talks to her, or about her either, otherwise she gets bigger and starts to chase one. And you mustn't feel sorry for her. You seem to imagine that she longs for everything that's alight, but all she really wants to do is to sit on it so that it'll go out and never burn again." (29)

This passage is worth a closer look. "Nobody bothered" about the Groke, just as nobody has ever bothered about Mamma. She was there for everybody, but nobody cared about her feelings, or her birthdays, or her need of pillows. "She does not remember or goes around thinking about it"—of course Mamma is not consciously resentful, and nobody talks to her about her dark feelings, otherwise it will cast too large a shadow on their happy existence. Finally, the Groke's wish to extinguish light must be Mamma's suppressed aggression—everything she would really like to do to her selfish husband and her infantile son if societal rules permitted her. At the same time she tells her son not to feel sorry for her; she seems to be trying to convey that it is all right for a Mamma to have a dark side.

Well on the island, Moomintroll finds a tiny silver horseshoe on the beach. As he is used to giving everything beautiful he finds to his mother, so he does again. But he is fascinated by the idea of sea horses, and, overcoming his fear of darkness, goes out at night to meet them. The sea horses, beautiful females with long manes, directly associated by Moomintroll with Snork Maiden's fringe, are unmistakable sexual symbols. Moomintroll's awakening sexuality in this novel is apparent. For the first time he has secrets from his mother. He is forced to ask her to give him back the silver horseshoe, without being able to explain why. The female sexual power—amplified by the full moon—is for the first time stronger than links to mother, and the Groke's dark shadow is present all along. In his pretense-games before he goes to sleep, Moomintroll now rescues the sea horse, not Mamma. This is no longer the childish infatuation with Snork Maiden.

> Something had happened to him. He had become quite a different troll, with quite different thoughts. He liked being all by himself. It was much more exciting to play games in his imagination, to have thoughts about himself and the sea-horses, of the moonlight, and the Groke's shadow was always in his thoughts, too. (115)

Moomintroll moves into his own "house." This is not an adventure anymore, like sleeping in the cave with Sniff, this is a breakout. As Mamma says: "That's all right. You can take your sleeping-bag with you as usual." "Mamma," said Moomintroll, and his throat felt very dry, "this isn't 'as usual.'" (133). He feels that the parents do not understand him any more—a typical teenager problem. It seems as if Mamma understands about the sea horse though. She also understands that she cannot do anything about it. She is no longer an equal rival. She had no problems overshadowing the little coquettish Snork Maiden, but she is no match for the sea horse, the incarnation of sexuality. Mamma is asexual by definition, and so was Snork

Maiden. But now the protagonist is finally initiated into the deepest mystery of life.

DISINTEGRATION

Moominvalley in November is the only Moomin novel where the family is absent. At the beginning, Snufkin packs his tent and prepares to go south—seemingly, everything is as usual. However, usually Snufkin goes away merely to come back soon: winter is the nonexistent time in the Moomin universe. In November, the flow of actual time, chronos, is accentuated:

> The garden was quite empty. The clothes-line has been taken in and the woodpile had gone. There was no hammock and no garden furniture. There was none of the charming disorder that generally surrounds a house in summer, no rake, to bucket, no left-behind hat, no saucer for the cat's milk, none of the other homely things that lie around *waiting for the next day* and make the house look welcoming and lived in. (12; my emphasis)

The emphasized phrase suggests that there is no "next day" in the mythic time, that time has opened into a linear, singulative mode. Snufkin does not realize this, he is still thinking in the iterative, "it has always been like this":

> Snufkin walked on, lit his pipe and thought: they're waking up in Moominvalley. Moominpappa is winding up the clock and tapping the barometer. Moominmamma is lighting the stove. Moomintroll goes out on the veranda and sees that my camping-site is deserted. He looks in the letter-box down at the bridge and it's empty, too. I forgot my good-bye letter, I didn't have time. But all the letters I write are the same: I'll be back in April, keep well. I am going away but I'll be back in the spring, look after yourself. He knows anyway.
> And Snufkin forgot all about Moomintroll as easily as that. (14ff)

The passage is iterative but for one sentence, "I forgot my good-bye letter." Snufkin does not pay much attention to this, but this breach of the iterative is only the first, slight indication of the great time disruption which this last Moomin novel brings about. So far, Snufkin performs a ritual act, something he has been doing year after year after year of the mythical Moominvalley time, without any changes or effects. Snufkin does not know that the family is not in the house, Pappa is not winding up the clock, Mamma is not lighting the stove, and there is no Moomintroll to discover the empty spot on the camping site. The circular flow of time has been irreversibly disturbed.

Since Moomintroll, the centerpiece of the collective character, is absent, we must look for a substitute. My only explanation why Tove Jansson chooses to spare Moomintroll the final passage into linearity is her consideration for the reader—and probably for herself. Just as we do not have to share the ultimate trauma of Christopher Robin and instead are given a milder version of the toys' emotions, so does Tove Jansson remove our primary identification object (and her own projection) to subdue the pain.

The collective character in this novel consist of six parts, with a reason each to seek Moominvalley. As in *The Wind in the Willows*, this centripetal movement is necessary to counterbalance Moomintroll's centrifugal one. To the substitute figures, Moominvalley is still the center of the world. Snufkin, the only familiar part of Moomintroll's Self, has to go back to Moominvalley because he has lost five bars of music there; he is, in other words, going through a creative crisis.

The next character in the gallery is Fillyjonk. Fillyjonks are described in earlier novels and short stories as pedantic, boring, and misanthropic. They are often treated by critics as representing adults, but this particular Fillyjonk is no more grown-up than Toad or Mole. Her living all alone does not make her adult either. Like Snufkin, Fillyjonk suddenly finds herself in a crisis, although of a more tangible nature, and probably more female. She finds that she cannot do any cleaning, something that may be best interpreted in Julia Kristeva's terms of abjection. She is nauseated and feels inexplicably scared. It also seems that she "sees" herself for the first time: "Her eyes looked different: fancy having eyes to see with, she thought, and how *does* one see ...?" (28; author's emphasis). She realizes that she has too many possessions:

> Such an awful lot of coffee cups. Far too many serving dishes and roasting dishes, and stacks of plates, hundreds of things to eat from

and eat on, and only one fillyjonk. And who would have them all
when she died?

I'm not going to die at all, whispered Fillyjonk, and shut the
cupboard door with a bang. (28)

Fillyjonk decides to become a new person:

> I shall never save old dusters again, I shall never save anything
> again, I shall be extravagant, I shall stop cleaning up, I do too much
> of it anyway, I'm pernickety. ... I shall be something quite different
> but not a fillyjonk, ... This is what Fillyjonk thought, imploringly but
> hopelessly, because a fillyjonk can never, of course, be anything but a
> fillyjonk. (27)

Also Hemulen has an identity crisis: he "woke up slowly and
recognized himself and wished he had been someone he didn't
know" (32). Hemulen is reminiscent of Toad: a big spoiled child. He
wants to do something and to become something, but, unlike Toad,
he lacks energy, saying as people usually do, that he lacks time. He
owns a boat, but he has never sailed with it. "He tried to find
something pleasant to think about that would drive away this
morning melancholy, he tried and tried and gradually a friendly and
distant memory of summer came to him. The Hemulen remembered
Moominvalley" (34). Maybe he is after all an adult remembering his
childhood. He longs for a carefree life when someone else will take
charge: "... there was no hurry to do anything. Morning coffee was
waiting on the veranda, everything would arrange itself and go of
its own accord" (35).

The next creature lacks identity altogether: "One dark autumn
morning he woke up and had forgotten what his name was. It's a
little sad when you forget other people's names but it's lovely to be
able to completely forget your own" (47). It means that you have lost
your own identity and can become whatever you wish. So after
trying on several names and identities, he decides to be Grandpa-
Grumble. With this identity, he feels that he wants to visit the valley
"where he had once been a very long time ago. It was just possible
that he had only heard about the valley, or perhaps he had read
about it, but it made no difference really" (48). If Grandpa-Grumble
is an adult, he is trying to return to his childhood. However,
Grandpa does not recognize his own reflection in a mirror (110), a

stage Lacanian psychology identifies as early infancy. Formally the oldest of them, Grandpa is actually the baby of the group. Notably, the others humor him in his delusion.

Mymble is the only one content with herself: "it's nice being a mymble. I feel absolutely splendid from top to toe" (57). She comes to the valley because she "had got an urge to see her little sister, Little My ..." (57). Mymble's role in the story is not quite clear, probably to counterbalance Fillyjonk as another female. She is everything that Fillyjonk is not: confident, joyful, feminine; her chief attribute is her long and beautiful hair, and she likes to dance.

Last, but most important is Toft, the primary substitute for Moomintroll. Toft is a small, inconspicuous creature, totally lacking identity. As an archetypal orphan, Toft is an opposite to Moomintroll. Lonely and scared in his uncomfortable abode in Hemulen's boat, Toft has created a vision of paradise for himself: "It was all about the Happy Family. He told it until he went to sleep, and the following evening he would go on from where he had left off, or start all over again from the beginning" (19). Toft has never been to Moominvalley, so his vivid descriptions are pure imagination. The following passage has often been treated as metafiction, an artist creating his imaginary universe. I prefer to view it as a lonely child's dream of "felicitous space":

> Toft generally began by describing the happy Moominvalley. He went slowly down the slopes where the dark pines and the pale birch-trees grew. It became warmer. He tried to describe to himself what it felt like when the valley opened into a wild green garden lit by sunshine, with green leaves waving in the summer breeze, the green grass all round him with patches of sunlight in it, and the sound of bees, and everything smelling so nice, and he walked on slowly until he heard the sound of the river.
>
> It was important not to change a single detail: once he had placed a summer-house by the river, but it has been a mistake. (19)

The description, the very act of storytelling is iterative: "He had done this hundreds of times ..." (21). The object of Toft's desire is Moominmamma. As he proceeds with his imaginary walk through the valley, approaches the house and pauses outside, he expects Mamma to come out, but she never does, because by that time Toft usually goes to sleep. Toft has never met Moominmamma, she is his abstract idea of a mother, "round in the way that mamas should be round" (21). As autumn goes on, Toft notices that he has difficulties entering the valley in his imagination, there is a mist preventing him. He decides to go to the Moominhouse in reality.

Thus the six-fold character, an amalgam of child and adult, a character outside time, finds its way to the lost Arcadia. The narrative pattern is different from early Moomin novels, but more like *Moominpappa at Sea*: each character is focalized one at a time, often internally—the device I have called polyfocalization. The intrusive narrator is almost gone.

Hemulen is the first to arrive in Moominvalley:

> He walked straight into the garden and stopped, with a puzzled look on his face. Something wasn't right. Everything was the same but somehow not the same. A withered leaf floated down and landed on his nose.
> How silly, the Hemulen exclaimed. It's not summer at all. It's autumn! In some way or another he had always thought of Moominvalley in summer. (37)

Here is another illustration of Moominvalley as a memory of childhood with its eternal summer. Notably, only the hysterical Fillyjonk is terrified by the absence of the family, while the others accept it. Hemulen chops wood, lights the stove and makes coffee, overtaking both Pappa's and Mamma's roles. He winds up the clock and taps the barometer. The tasks are new and strange, but they give him a sense of importance. The kitchen becomes once again the center of the house. Very soon, however, they discover that something essential is lacking:

> "Have you had dinner?" Snufkin asked.
> "We can't," the Hemulen answered. "We can't agree about who's going to do the washing-up. ... Fillyjonk and Mymble ought to keep house for us all, the womenfolk should do these things, eh?" (65)

Hemulen is used to organizing things, and he is trying to organize and plan, to the others' irritation. But he feels uncomfortable himself: "I won't organize a thing! I want to live in a tent and be independent!" (66) This is a child's discovery that things do not take care of themselves. Food becomes an important element in the child's investigation of the mechanisms of the world:

> All the time, right from the beginning, Fillyjonk had thought that she would be the one to prepare the food. She loved arranging small jars and bags on the shelves, she thought it was fun to work out new way of doing up left-overs in puddings and rissoles so that nobody could recognize them. She loved doing the cooking as economically as possible, and knowing that not a single drop of semolina had been wasted. (67)

With such an attitude, Fillyjonk has no good prospects to replace the generous and spontaneous Moominmamma. Besides, Fillyjonk does not wish to be ordered about and cook and wash up merely because it is what womenfolk do. The mere thought of food makes her dizzy, just like the thought of cleaning (= abjection). But when Grandpa at long last manages to catch a fish, Fillyjonk volunteers to cook it.

> The Fillyjonk's fish was ready at exactly two o'clock. It was concealed in a huge, steaming light-brown pudding. The whole kitchen smelt convincingly and comfortingly of food. The kitchen had really become a kitchen, a safe room where one could take charge of things. The heart of the mysteries of the house and a source of confidence. (98)

Although she is so proud of herself, Fillyjonk's cooking is a disaster simply because she is a fillyjonk. She tries to act as a mother toward Toft, but fails. She is trying hard to play Moominmamma's role, but it does not work. She must learn to be herself and eventually gets some confidence. Before leaving Moominhouse she cleans it up thoroughly—returning to her natural self.

The characters have their own quest each, pointing towards a possibility for the real protagonist, Moomintroll. They also try very hard to be friends—a complex character coming to terms with himself. There are minor and major conflicts between them, but they learn to compromise and reconcile. They all have their Shadows, their dark fears, their monsters in cupboards. This novel, more than any other Moomin book, invites Freudian-Lacanian interpretations, with its imagery of closets, cold rooms, and mirrors.

There are many indications that the characters are going through a ritual, restaging something that has already taken place:

> "There's one thing that's funny", said the Hemulen. "Sometimes I feel that everything we say and do and everything that happens has happened once before, eh? ... Everything is the same."
> "And why should it be different?" Mymble asked. "A hemulen is always a hemulen and the same things happen to him all the time ...."
> "Will you always be the same?" Fillyjonk asked her out of curiousity.
> "I certainly hope so!" Mymble answered. (153f)

The solutions the characters find to their problems are based on the firm belief that everything will always be the same. Mymble has no difficulties believing in eternity. Snufkin finds his melody and is prepared to go back to the circular flow of time. He goes off, catching up on the weeks he has lost. To correct his earlier blunder, he writes a letter to Moomintroll and puts it in the letter-box, as he has always done. The circle is complete. In his own, personal mythic time, he will return in spring to find Moomintroll waiting impatiently for him on the bridge.

Grandpa-Grumble is for ever stuck at his premirror stage. He goes into hibernation, to wake up, as all the Moomins have always done, to the joys and delights of spring, skipping the cold and dark and long winter: "Of course, when you hibernate you're much younger when you wake up ..." (161).

Hemulen has been trying hard to make everybody happy, but feels a failure. He goes sailing only to find it horrible. He has fulfilled his dream and found that it did not suit him: "And now I know I don't have to sail. Funny, isn't it? I've just realised I don't ever need to sail again" (168). He can never become another Momminpappa, just as Fillijonk cannot become Moominmamma. But at least he is able to admit this openly. He is also ready to go home.

Toft's confidence, impersonated in his imaginary friend, a prehistorical sea-creature Nummulite of whom he has read in a book, is growing every day. Toft becomes less shy. He ventures to speak and express his opinion, and gets angry at times. He feels a new person, and it scares him. The Creature created by his imagination soon gets out of control and grows into a huge monster, worse than the Groke has ever been. Although Toft seems able to manage the monster at times, there is no guarantee that the victory is definite. Unlike Moomintroll and the Groke, Toft is both afraid of the monster and aggressive toward it.

> What's wrong is that I'm too small …. I don't want friends who are kind without really liking me and I don't want anybody who is kind just so as not to be unpleasant. And I don't want anybody who is scared. I want somebody who is never scared and who really likes me. I want a mamma! (128f)

So here is where the long quest has taken our hero—back to mamma! Doesn't it remind us of the Mouse child?

Toft gets terribly upset when Mymble tells him that Pappa and Mamma could get angry sometimes: "Moominmamma was never like that! She was the same all the time" … Mymble was lying. She didn't know anything about Moominmamma. She didn't know that it was impossible for a mamma to behave badly" (132). Toft holds fast to his image of Mamma, and, much like Moomintroll in the early novels, believes that she will always get everything right. "Every time he thought about Moominmamma he got a headache. She had grown so perfect and gentle and consoling that it was unbearable …" (172).

Our interpetation of the protagonist's development is dependent on our identification. How does Tove Jansson manipulate the reader to exclude everyone but Toft as identification objects? He is not focalized more than the other figures. Perhaps the less attractive nature of the other characters makes us choose Toft. It is not easy to identify with Snufkin, even when we share his perceptional point of view, because he is a mysterious and aloof person, and we are never allowed to enter his mind. Snufkin is a teenager, already half-way into adulthood, which for a young child implies that he is definitely the Other. Fillyjonk with her fastidious manners and lack of generosity does not invite empathy, and neither does the narcissistic Grandpa-Grumble. Hemulen is too bossy, and the image of hemulens from the previous books prevents us from identifying with him. Finally, Mymble is described too superficially and has too many stereotypical female traits.

This leaves Toft, and it is not a coincidence that Toft is the last one left when the rest have gone home. We must then see his choice as

Moomintroll's. He sees—or thinks he sees—"a tiny but steady light
… shining in the crystal ball. The family had hung the storm-lantern
at the top of the mast and they were on their way home to hibernate
for the winter" (171). The crystal ball is the only magical object left
in the enchanted world of Moomins, "the focal point of the whole
valley and it always mirrored those who lived there" (44). Throughout the book, Toft has been looking into the crystal ball hoping to
see the family returning. Now his dreams are coming true.

Since the family's return is actually never described (although the
chapter is entitled "Coming Home"), the ending is open, and we
cannot be sure whether it is a fact or Toft's wishful thinking. If they
do return home from the lighthouse island to hibernate and wake
up in spring, and Moominmamma puts on the coffee and asks Toft
what kind of pudding he wants for his birthday—then the mythical,
circular time is restored and the happy childhood secured. At least,
this is how we can, if we wish, interpret the very last paragraph of
the novel, when Toft sees the boat far away from a high mountain
and knows that he has "plenty of time to go down through the forest
and along the beach to the jetty, and be just in time to catch the line
and tie up the boat" (175). He will anchor himself firmly in the
neverending childhood.

It is, however, doubtful. This is the last Moomin novel, and the
family has left Moominvalley for ever. In his heart of hearts, Toft
knows this: "The whole of Moominvalley had somehow become
unreal, the house, the garden and the river were nothing but a play
of shadows on a screen and Toft no longer knew what was real and
what was only his imagination" (172). "His description of the valley
and the Happy Family faded and slipped away, Moominmamma
glided away and became remote, an impersonal picture, he didn't
even know what she looked like" (174).

Toft, Moomintroll's substitute, has come to the insight that his
beautiful dreams will never come true, because childhood is over
and it is time to go further. We will meet the Moomins again, in the
adult world of Tove Jansson's later novels, where they pretend to
be humans, but where we recognize them, the grow-up Moomins,
the eternal Bohemian teenager Snufkin, the melancholy Fillyjonk
and the busybody, childish Hemulen. I just wonder what happened
to Snork Maiden.

NOTES

1. I do not include *Exploits of Moominpappa* in my "text" because it is a background story which in a way merely doubles Moomintroll's quest in *Comet in Moominland. The Little Trolls and the Big Flood,* not available in English, is the prelude to the suite, and *Tales from Moominvalley* is a set of independent short stories.

2. In the early version of *Exploits,* from which the English translation has been made, Moominpappa actually builds his house and calls Hodgkins to admire it. In a later, reworked version, Pappa only dreams of building a house, and when he invites Hodgkins to inspect his work, he sees nothing but some sketches in the sand.

3. It may be of interest to know that Tove Jansson has illustrated *Alice.*

Except Ye Be Converted, and Become As Little Children …

Children's fiction is written—with very few exceptions—by adult writers for young readers. Consequently the notion of childhood and the ideas about growing, procreation and death which we meet in children's fiction reflect adults' views, which may or may not correspond to the real status of children and childhood in any given society. The central concept is that childhood is something irretrievably lost for adults, and this lost Arcadia can only be restored in fiction. With this premise, children's fiction is not, as it is commonly defined, literature addressed to children, but a sort of storytelling therapy for frustrated adults. The central theme in children's fiction, as I have demonstrated throughout my study, is the irreversibility of time and the high price any individual who defies it must pay. In adult fiction, *The Picture of Dorian Gray* takes up the same theme. I have tried to connect the idea of lost childhood and the dream of eternal youth to archaic thought and contemporary humanity's lost ties with the archaic past. It is my aspiration that the essence of children's fiction appears in a new light against this background. The difference between my three major categories of texts—prelapsarian, carnivalesque, and postlapsarian—involves all levels of narrative. The secluded, autonomous, rural setting is replaced by an open and predominantly urban one. Collective protagonists are exchanged for individual. Omniscient, didactic narrators are replaced by unreliable ones. Circular time opens into linearity, and the singulative, rather than iterative frequency prevails. Awareness of linearity and, as a consequence, of death becomes a central theme. Harmony gives way to chaos. The social, moral, political, and sexual innocence of the child is interrogated.

As I am well aware, my study is ahistorical, which means that I do not take into account the changing values during the last 150 years, the period from which most of my texts come. However, this aspect cannot be totally ignored. Kimberley Reynolds demonstrates the radical difference between British children's fiction in the 1890s—utopian—and in the 1990s—aimed at growing up (Reynolds 1994). Humphrey Carpenter maintains in his study that the Golden Age of children's literature is over with World War I (Carpenter 1985, 210), by which he probably means the waning dominance of Arcadian-type books. But it would be essentially wrong to assume that the era of utopian domestic or animal stories is definitely over; they are still written and published and are too numerous to name. As I have tried to show, Arcadia is a generic rather than historical category. It may be true that we find more pure Arcadian texts in "classic" (which in an Anglo-Saxon context means Victorian-Edwardian) children's fiction, and that mid-20th-century British literature displays more examples of carnival, for instance in *The Hobbit* and the Narnia Chronicles. However, as I have shown, the bulk of Soviet children's fiction is basically utopian. A tendency to depict childhood as Arcadia has to do with the role which children's literature plays in a society, as well as the view of childhood as such. As long as children's literature is chiefly the implement for adult manipulation of young readers, children's novels will try to conserve children in the state of innocence and thus present childhood as a neverending paradise.

Carpenter points out the differences between British and American children's fiction, emphasizing the American wish to be conserved versus the contemporary British children's writers encouraging children to grow up. He sees this as one of the problems for British books to be adequately appraised in North America. Several American scholars maintain that the ideals of domestic Utopia were rediscovered in the United States after World War II: "Several decades of economic deprivation and war had denied Americans the pleasures of domesticity, and they were determined ... to invest in the private Utopia of family life" (Strickland 1985, 157). Lois Kuznets shows how the sense of pastoral is evoked in contemporary realistic fiction with urban settings (Kuznets 1983). For several post-war decades American children's fiction was exceptionally idyllic, and not until the emergence of writers such as

Katherine Paterson or Patricia MacLachlan did contemporary American children's fiction depart from its Arcadia.

Astrid Lindgren, writing after World War II, looks back at the time of her own childhood in a Noisy Village-like rural Sweden with a strong sense of nostalgia. I have in another context shown the principal difference between Swedish and Canadian national mentality as illustrated by Pippi Longstocking and Jacob Two-Two: Jacob wants to grow up and become strong, Pippi is strong and does not want to grow up (see Nikolajeva 1997b). However, Astrid Lindgren's later novels show a totally different attitude to maturity, either because of the changing societal values or because of her personal evolution.

Among the many critics who interrogate the essence of children's literature, Jacqueline Rose has observed that "writing for children can contribute to prolonging or preserving—not only for the child but also for us—values which are constantly on the verge of collapse. The child, therefore, is innocent and can restore that innocence to us" (Rose 1984, 44). I would, however, immediately add: the child Rose is speaking about is our—adult—image of the child, a myth of a child. Rose's statement echoes Fred Inglis: "The best children's books reawaken our innocence" (Inglis 1981, 8). Kimberley Reynolds speaks of childhood as adult fantasy (Reynolds 1994, 17–27). The mythical, imaginary child of children's fiction "restores" the adult to a more natural state. Is this the true purpose of children's fiction?

Anita Moss concludes her examination of two pastoral novels by remarking that an honest children's writer knows that he is not creating the world as it is, but "expresses the wish that human beings may someday attain the fullness of experience and yet retain the innocent sense of newness which assures them that they are at the beginning of a great new adventure" (Moss 1982, 140). To me this sounds like a wish to have one's cake and eat it too.

Perry Nodelman states in an essay entitled "Progressive Utopia, or How to Grow Up Without Growing Up" that while the assumption that children think, see, and feel differently helps us adults to assess children, it creates problems, in that it separates us from our past selves and makes children into strangers. Childhood becomes "agonizingly enticing *to us*" and "forces *us* into a fruitless nostalgia" (Nodelman 1980, 153; my emphasis). Nodelman maintains, however, that in the so-called novels of Progressive Utopia, we can experience childhood again: "It is the secret desire of grownups to be children again that makes these novels appealing to them.... a central concern of children's literature, no matter where or when it was written—how to grow up, as one inevitably must, without losing the virtues and delights of childhood" (Nodelman 1980, 154).

While Nodelman speaks of Progressive Utopia, I cannot but call it, on the contrary, regressive or even conservative. A child who does not grow up is conserved in his or her childhood, while a grown-up who goes back to the innocence of childhood is undoubtedly regressing, mentally and morally. If children's fiction has as its main function the fulfillment of adults' secret desires, why do we, as scholars, hypocritically call it "children's fiction"? On the other hand, if children's fiction is indeed intended for children, mustn't we, as mediators, acknowledge it as a powerful socialization tool used to make children believe that they are happier than adults? Aren't we then lying to them instead of to each other?

Fortunately children's fiction is not as homogeneous as some scholars wish to see it. Besides reading children's fiction as a displacement of myth, we see clearly that the different categories of children's fiction have different purposes. Utopian fiction introduces us to the sacred, which is probably most explicitly shown in *The Secret Garden*:

> "Sometimes since I've been in the garden I've looked up through the trees at the sky and I have had a strange feeling of being happy, as if something were pushing and drawing in my chest and making me breathe fast. Magic is always pushing and drawing and making things out of nothing. ... The Magic in the garden has made me stand up and now I'm going to be a man." (194)

Carnivalesque texts, taking children out of Arcadia, but insuring a sense of security by bringing them back, allow an introduction to death, which inevitably follows the insight about the linearity of time. A sincere writer may even choose to paint the picture of aging in a positive light:

> The quiet transition from autumn to winter is not a bad time at all. It's a time for protecting and securing things and for making sure you've got in as many supplies as you can. It's nice to gather together

everything you possess as close to you as possible, to store up your
warmth and your thoughts and burrow yourself into a deep hole
inside, a core of safety where you can defend what is important and
precious and your very own. Then the cold and the storms and the
darkness can do their worst. (*Moominvalley in November* 13f)

Finally the texts which take the character beyond the point of no
return, agonizing as it may be, introduce them and the young
readers to the inevitable Fall, a definite departure from innocence
and entrance into adulthood, which includes sexuality and procreation as indispensable constituents. The three stages of initiation, as
depicted by Mircea Eliade, are tentatively achieved in the three main
types of children's fiction. When the initiation is complete, we are
dealing with adult literature.

The fact that so many children's texts are treated differently by
different scholars (animals—toys, fantasy—humor, family story—
pastoral) reveals their vague generic status. Moreover, most texts
that I have discussed as purely idyllic or purely carnivalesque, that
is, either preserving children in a state of innocence or bringing them
successfully back to it, are treated in critical studies unproblemati-
cally as "children's fiction," while all texts showing a deviation from
these patterns or interrogating them are immediately labeled as "in
actual fact not books for children": *Peter Pan, Winnie-the-Pooh, The
Little Prince, The Mouse and His Child* or *Johnny, My Friend.* In the
Moomin suite, the early, idyllic novels are, according to education-
alists, "suitable for children," while *Moominpappa at Sea* and
Moominvalley in November are "in actual fact" books for adults. The
relatively new coinage "young adult fiction" is an attempt to cir-
cumvent the problem of audience concerning texts which depict
collapse. Among many genre transgressions of the past ten years,
the crossing of boundaries between what is normally considered
children's and adult fiction is remarkable. A well-known example
is Jostein Gaarder's *Sophie's World,* a mediocre, speculative, and
extremely didactic children's novel which has conquered the international book market as an adult book, apparently filling some
secret nostalgic need.

As always when speaking of children's fiction we are dealing
with a double set of codes. Unlike adult fiction, in children's fiction
we have double narratees and double implied readers. An adult

writer evoking an adult reader's nostalgia is merely one aspect. Hopefully, the child reader is targeted as well, although in a different manner. With my approach, the difference between children's and adult fiction does not concern subjects, style ("readability") and the like, but the stage of initiation described in the text. The fact that children's novels seldom involve topics like sexuality, parenthood, or adultery does not depend on the subjects as such being unsuitable or tabooed, but exclusively on the problems not being relevant at the stage depicted. For young adult novels, on the contrary, sexual awakening is often the central motif. While sexual identity is irrelevant in idyllic fiction, it is all the more dominant at the stage of collapse.

Further, we can also explain why so many writers all around the world choose to write for children, although children's literature has lower status and brings less income. Like the archaic returning god, a child exists out of linear time. Child protagonists have their potential intact, they have not yet taken the decisive step, which means that in children's fiction there is still the possibility of hope for the future which modern adult literature has so often lost. Christopher Robin experiences the same existential crisis as Stephen Dedalus. However, Christopher Robin is still mouldable, he can change, he has not yet failed in his quest for identity like most contemporary novel heroes. This must give a children's writer an inner freedom of expression, which is denied to the writer of a modern existential novel. For me, this is a more attractive idea than adult writers indulging in their nostalgia at the expense of young readers.

My view of children's fiction in the present study erases three important boundaries which have always existed in traditional literary criticism. First, it eradicates the difference between the implicit addressees, which are two very heterogeneous groups general referred to as children and adults. Second, it ignores the principal division of literature into realistic and nonrealistic modes, which at least within children's literature research is still the predominant view on genres. Finally, it disregards the distinction between "high" and "low" genres, quality literature and formula fiction. The apparent convergence of genres and transgression of boundaries in contemporary literature make all these divisions both superfluous and imprecise. In the first place the question of "realism," meaning "a direct reflection of reality," becomes totally irrelevant. Art goes back to its symbolic, ritual significance, which it possessed in archaic thought.

Bibliography

PRIMARY SOURCES

Only the first title in a series is mentioned, unless individual books are treated separately. Original titles of non-English language books are given in parentheses. The English titles in quotation marks are approximate translations for books not published in English.

Adams, Richard. *Watership Down*. Harmondsworth: Penguin, 1973.

Ainsworth, Ruth. *Rufty Tufty, the Golliwog*. London: Heineman, 1952.

Alcott, Louisa May. *Little Women* (1868). Harmondsworth: Penguin, 1988.

Alexander, Lloyd. *The Book of Three*. New York: Holt, 1964. The first of the five chronicles of Prydain.

_____. *Westmark*. New York: Dutton, 1981. The first book in the Westmark trilogy.

_____. *The Illyrian Adventure*. New York: Dutton, 1986. The first book in the Vesper series.

_____. *The Arcadians*. New York: Dutton, 1995.

Andersen, Hans Christian. *The Complete Fairy Tales and Stories*. Trans. Erik Christian Haugaard. New York: Doubleday, 1974.

Babbitt, Natalie. *Tuck Everlasting*. New York: Farrar, Straus & Giroux, 1975.

Barrie, James M. *Peter Pan and Wendy* (1911). London: Hodder & Stoughton, 1951.

_____. *Peter Pan in Kensington Gardens* (1906). London: Weatherwane Books, 1975.

Baum, L. Frank. *The Wonderful Wizard of Oz*. New York: Random House, 1968.

Bawden, Nina. *Carrie's War*. Philadelphia: Lippincott, 1973.

Beckman, Gunnel: *Admission to the Feast*. Trans. Joan Tate. New York: Holt, 1971 (*Tillträde till festen* 1969; also translated as *Nineteen Is Too Young to Die*. London: Macmillan, 1971).

Beresford, Elizabeth. *The Wombles*. London: Benn, 1968. The first title in the Wombles series.

Berg, Leila. *The Adventures of Chunky*. London: Oxford UP, 1950.

Bianco, Margery. *The Velveteen Rabbit*. London: Heinemann, 1922.

Blyton, Enid. *Five on a Treasure Island*. London: Hodder & Stoughton, 1942. The first book in the Famous Five series.

Bond, Michael. *A Bear Called Paddington*. London: Collins, 1958. The first title in the Paddington series.

_____. *Here Comes Thursday*. London: Harrap, 1966.

Boston, Lucy M. *The Children of Green Knowe*. London: Faber, 1954. The first book in the Green Knowe suite.

Brisley, Joyce. *Milly-Molly-Mandy Stories*. London: Harrap, 1928.

Brooks, Terry. *The Sword of Shannara*. New York: Random House, 1977. The first of Shannara novels.

Bruce, Dorita Fairley. *Dimsie Goes to School*. Oxford: Oxford UP, 1920.

de Brunhoff, Jean. *The Story of Babar, The Little Elephant*. Trans. Merle Haas. New York: Random House, 1933 (Babar 1931). The first of many picture books about Babar.

Burnett, Frances Hodgson. *Little Lord Fauntleroy* (1886). New York: Dutton, 1962.

_____. *The Secret Garden* (1911). London: Heinemann, 1968.

Burnford, Sheila. *The Incredible Journey*. Boston: Little, Brown, 1960.

Carroll, Lewis. *Alice's Adventures in Wonderland* (1865). In *The Penguin Complete Lewis Carroll*. Harmonsworth: Penguin, 1982.

Chambers, Aidan. *Dance on My Grave*. London: Bodley Head, 1982.

Christopher, John. *The Prince in Waiting*. New York: Macmillan, 1970.

Clare, Helen. *Five Dolls in a House*. London: Bodley Head, 1953.

Cleary, Beverly. *Ramona the Pest*. New York: Morrow, 1968. The first book in the series about Ramona.

Collodi, Carlo. *The Adventures of Pinocchio*. Trans. Ann Lawson Lucas. Oxford: OUP, 1996. (*Le avventure di Pinocchio* 1881).

Coolidge, Susan. *What Katy Did*. Boston: Little Brown, 1872.

_____. *What Katy Did at School*. Boston: Roberts, 1874.

Cooper, Susan. *Over Sea, Under Stone*. London: Cape, 1965. The first book in *The Dark Is Rising* suite.

Cooper, Susan. *Seaward*. London: Bodley Head, 1973.

Cormier, Robert. *I Am the Cheese*. New York: Panteon, 1977.

Crompton, Richmal. *Just William*. London: Newness, 1922. The first in a series of more than forty books about William.

Dahl, Roald. *Charlie and the Chocolate Factory*. New York: Knopf, 1964.

Defoe, Daniel. *Robinson Crusoe* (1719). New York: Norton, 1975.

Dodge, Mary Mapes. *Hans Brinker, or The Silver Skates* (1865). New York: Scribner, 1958.

Ende, Michael. *The Neverending Story*. Trans. Ralph Manheim. New York: Doubleday, 1983. (*Die unendliche Geschichte* 1979).

Farmer, Nancy. *The Ear, the Eye and the Arm*. New York: Orchard, 1994.
Farmer, Penelope. *Charlotte Sometimes*. London: Chatto & Windus, 1969.
Fitzhugh, Louise. *Harriet the Spy*. New York: Harper, 1964.
_____. *The Long Secret*. New York: Dell, 1965.

Gaarder, Jostein. *Sophie's World*. Trans. Paulette Moller. New York: Farrar, Straus & Giroux, 1994. (*Sofies verden* 1991).
Garfield, Leon. *Smith*. London: Constable, 1967.
Garner, Alan. *Elidor*. London: Collins, 1965.
_____. *The Owl Service*. London: Collins, 1967.
_____. *Red Shift*. London: Collins, 1973.
George, Jean Craighead, *Julie of the Wolves*. New York: Harper, 1972.
Godden, Rumer. *The Dolls House*. London: Macmillan, 1947.
Grahame, Kenneth. *The Golden Age* (1895). New York: Garland, 1976.
_____. *The Wind in the Willows* (1908) London: Methuen, 1970.
Gripe, Maria. *Agnes Cecilia*. Trans. Rika Lesser. New York: Harper, 1990. (*Agnes Cecilia—en sällsam historia* 1981).
_____. *Skuggan över stenbänken*. Stockholm: Bonnier, 1982. ("Shadow Over the Stone Bench").

Haugen, Tormod. *Slottet det hvite*. Oslo: Gyldendal, 1980. ("The White Castle").
_____. *Dagen som forsvant*. Oslo: Gyldendal, 1983. ("The Day that Disappeared").
_____. *Vinterstedet*. Oslo: Gyldendal, 1984 ("Winter Place").
_____. *Skriket fra jungelen*. Oslo: Gyldendal, 1989 ("A Cry from the Jungle").
_____. *Øglene kommer*. Oslo: Gyldendal, 1991 ("The Lizards Are Coming").
Held, Kurt. *Die Rote Zora*. Aarau: Sauerländer, 1941
Hoban, Russell. *The Mouse and His Child*. New York: Harper, 1967.
Hoffmann, E. T. A. *The Nutcracker*. Adapted by Janet Schulman. New York: Dutton, 1979. (*Nussknacker und Mausekönig* 1816).
Hughes, Thomas. *Tom Brown's Schooldays* (1856). Harmondsworth: Penguin, 1971.

Janosch [pseud. for Horst Eckert]. *The Trip to Panama*. Trans. Anthea Bell. London, Andersen Press, 1978. (*Oh, wie schön ist Panama* 1978). The first of many Little Tiger and Little Bear books.

Jansson, Tove. *Småtrollen och den stora översvämningen*. Stockholm: Hassel-
gren, 1945. ("The Little Trolls and the Big Flood").
_____. *Moominsummer Madness*. Trans. Elisabeth Portch. New York:
Walck, 1961. (*Farlig midsommar* 1954).
_____. *Moominland Midvinter*. Trans. Thomas Warburton. New York:
Walck, 1962. (*Trollvinter* 1957).
_____. *Tales from Moominvalley*. Trans. Thomas Warburton. New
York: Walck, 1964. (*Det osynliga barnet* 1962).
_____. *Finn Family Moomintroll*. Trans. Elizabeth Portch. New York:
Walck, 1965. (*Trollkarlens hatt* 1949).
_____. *Exploits of Moominpappa*. Trans. Elisabeth Portch. New York:
Walck, 1966. (*Muminpappans bravader* 1950).
_____. *Moominpappa at Sea*. Trans. Kingsley Hart. New York: Walck,
1967. (*Pappan och havet* 1965).
_____. *A Comet in Moominland*. Trans. Elisabeth Portch. New York:
Walck, 1968. (*Kometjakten* 1946).
_____. *Moominvalley in November*. Trans. K. Hart. New York: Walck,
1971. (*Sent i november* 1970).
Jones, Diana Wynne. *Fire and Hemlock*. London: Methuen, 1985.
_____. *Howl's Moving Castle*. London: Methuen, 1986.
Juster, Norton. *The Phantom Tollbooth*. New York: Knopf, 1961.

Kästner, Erich. *The Flying Classroom*. Trans. Cyrus Brooks. London: Cape,
1934 (*Das fliegende Klassenzimmer* 1933).
_____. *Lottie and Lisa*. Trans. Cyrus Brooks. Boston: Little, Brown,
1951. (*Das doppelte Lottchen* 1949).
_____. *The Animals' Conference*. Trans. Zita de Schauensee. New York:
D. McKay, 1955. (*Die Konferenz der Tiere* 1949).
_____. *The 35th of May*. Trans. Cyrus Brooks. New York: Watts, 1961.
(*Der 35. Mai* 1931).
Keene, Carolyn (pseud). *The Secret of the Old Clock*. New York: Grosset &
Dunlap, 1930. The first book in the Nancy Drew series.
Kingsley, Charles. *The Water Babies* (1863). Oxford: Oxford UP, 1948.
Kipling, Rudyard. *Stalky & Co* (1899). London: Macmillan, 1951.
_____. *The Jungle Book* (1894). London: Macmillan, 1950.
Konigsburg, Elaine. *From the Mixed-Up Files of Mrs. Basil E. Frankweiler*. New
York: Atheneum, 1967.
Korczak, Janusz. *King Matt the First*. Trans. Richard Lourie. Introduction
Bruno Bettelheim. New York: Farrar, Straus and Giroux, 1986. (*Krol
Macius Pierwszy* 1923).
Korschunow, Irina. *Die Sache mit Christoph*. Zürich: Benzinger, 1978.
Kullman, Harry. *The Battle Horse*. Trans. George Blecher & Lone Thygesen-
Blecher. Scarsdale, NY: Bradbury, 1981 (*Stridshästen* 1977).

Lada, Josif. *Purrkin the Talking Cat.* Trans. Renata Symonds. London: Harrap, 1966. (*O Mikesovi* 1934).

Lagerlöf, Selma. *The Wonderful Adventures of Nils.* Trans. Velma Swanston Howard. Vol I-II. Minneapolis: Skandisk, 1991. (*Nils Holgerssons underbara resa genom Sverige* 1906-07).

Lawrence, Louise. *The Disinherited.* London: Random House, 1994.

Le Guin, Ursula. *A Wizard of Earthsea.* New York: Parnassus, 1968. The first book in the Earthsea suite.

_____. *Tehanu.* New York: Atheneum, 1990.

Lewis, C. S. *The Lion, the Witch and the Wardrobe.* New York: Macmillan, 1950.

_____. *The Silver Chair.* New York: Macmillan, 1953.

_____. *The Magician's Nephew.* New York: Macmillan, 1955.

_____. *The Last Battle.* New York: Macmillan, 1956.

Lindgren, Astrid. *Pippi Longstocking.* Trans. Florence Lamborn. New York: Viking, 1950. (*Pippi Langstrump* 1945).

_____. *Pippi Goes on Board.* Trans. Florence Lamborn. New York: Viking, 1957. (*Pippi Langstrump gar ombord* 1946).

_____. *Pippi in the South Seas.* Trans. Florence Lamborn. New York: Viking, 1959. (*Pippi Langstrump i Söderhavet* 1948).

_____. *Mio, My Son.* Trans. Marianne Turner. New York: Viking, 1956. (*Mio, min Mio* 1954).

Lindgren, Astrid. *The Children of Noisy Village.* Trans. Florence Lamborn. New York: Viking, 1962. (*Alla vi barn i Bullerbyn* 1947; also as *The Six Bullerby Children.* Trans. Evelyn Ramsden. London: Methuen, 1963).

_____. *Emil's Pranks.* Trans. Michael Heron. Chicago: Folett, 1971. (*Emil i Lönneberga* 1963).

_____. *The Brothers Lionheart.* Trans. Joan Tate. New York: Viking, 1975. (*Bröderna Lejonhjärta* 1973).

_____. *Ronia, the Robber's Daughter.* Trans. Patricia Crampton. New York: Viking, 1983. (*Ronja Rövardotter* 1981).

Linklater, Eric. *The Wind on the Moon.* London: Macmillan, 1948.

Lofting, Hugh. *The Story of Dr. Dolittle.* London: Cape, 1922. The first of Dr Dolittle stories.

Lowry, Lois. *The Giver.* New York: Doubleday, 1993.

Lunn, Janet. *The Root Cellar.* Toronto: Lester and Orpen, 1980.

MacDonald, George. *At the Back of the North Wind* (1871). New York: Macmillan, 1964.

_____. *The Princess and the Goblin* (1872). Harmondsworth: Penguin, 1964.

_____. *The Princess and Curdie* (1883). Harmondsworth: Penguin, 1966.

Magorian, Michelle. *Back Home.* New York: Harper, 1984.

Malot, Hector. *The Foundling*. Trans. (abridged) Douglas Munro. Edinburgh: Canongate, 1984. (*Sans famille* 1878; also translated as *The Adventures of Remi*).

Mazetti, Katarina. *Det är slut mellan Gud och mig*. Stockholm: Alfabeta, 1995. ("It Is All Over Between God and Myself").

McCloskey, Robert. *Homer Price*. New York: Viking, 1943.

McNeill, Janet. *My Friend Specs McCann*. London: Faber, 1955.

Milne, A. A. *Winnie-the-Pooh* (1926). London: Methuen, 1965.

_____. *The House At Pooh Corner* (1928). London: Methuen, 1965.

Montgomery, L. M. *Anne of Green Gables* (1908). Harmondsworth: Penguin, 1964.

Moon, Elizabeth. *Sheepfarmer's Daughter*. New York: Baen, 1988. The first novel in the Paksenarrion series.

Nesbit, Edith. *The Story of the Treasure Seekers* (1899). Harmondsworth: Penguin, 1958.

_____. *Five Children and It* (1901). Harmondsworth: Penguin, 1959.

_____. *The Story of the Amulet* (1906). Harmondsworth: Penguin, 1959.

_____. *The Railway Children* (1906). Harmondsworth: Penguin, 1958.

_____. *The House of Arden* (1908). Harmondsworth: Penguin, 1986.

_____. *Harding's Luck* (1910). London: Benn, 1949.

Norton, Mary. *The Borrowers*. New York: Harcourt, Brace & World, 1952.

Nöstlinger, Christine. *Konrad*. Trans. Anthea Bell. New York: Avon, 1982. (*Konrad oder das Kind aus der Konservenbüchse* 1975).

Oldham, June. *Foundling*. London: Hodder, 1995.

Orwell, George. *Animal Farm*. Harmondsworth: Penguin, 1951.

_____. *1984*. (1948). Harmondsworth: Penguin, 1989.

Park, Ruth. *Playing Beatie Bow*. Sydney: Thomas Nelson, 1980

Paterson, Katherine. *Bridge to Terabithia*. New York: Crowell, 1977.

_____. *The Great Gilly Hopkins*. New York: Crowell, 1978.

_____. *Park's Quest*. New York: Dutton, 1988.

Paton Walsh, Jill. *Fireweed*. London: Macmillan, 1969.

Paulsen, Gary. *The Island*. New York: Dell, 1988.

Pausewang, Gudrun. *Fall-out*. Trans. Patricia Crampton. London: Viking, 1994. (*Die Wolke* 1987).

Pearce, Philippa. *Tom's Midnight Garden* (1958). Harmondsworth, Penguin, 1976.

_____. *A Dog So Small*. London: Constable, 1962.

Pierce, Meredith Ann. *The Darkangel*. New York: Atlantic, 1982.

Pohl, Peter. *Johnny, My Friend*. Trans. Laurie Thompson. London: Turton & Chambers, 1991. (*Janne min vän* 1985).

Potter, Beatice. *The Tale of Peter Rabbit*. London: Warne, 1902.

Pratchett, Terry. *Truckers*. New York: Doubleday, 1989.

Preussler, Ottfried. *The Little Witch*. Trans. Anthea Bell. New York: Abelard-Schuman, 1961.. (*Die kleine Hexe* 1957).

_____. *The Little Ghost*. Trans. Anthea Bell. New York: Abelard-Schuman, 1967 (*Das kleine Gespenst* 1968).

Prøysen, Alf. *Little Old Mrs. Pepperpot and Other Stories*. Trans. Marianne Helwig. New York: Astor-Honor, 1960. (*Kjerringa som ble sa lita som ei teskje* 1957). The first of many books about Mrs. Pepperpot.

Pullman, Philip. *Northern Lights*. London: Scholastic, 1995. (published in the United States as *The Golden Compass*).

_____. *The Subtle Knife*. London: Scholastic, 1997.

Ransome, Arthur. *Swallows and Amazons*. London: Cape, 1930.

Raud, Eno. *Three Jolly Fellows*. Vol 1-4. Trans. Evi Mannermaa. Tallinn: Perioodika, 1982-85 (*Naksitrallid* 1972-82).

Reuterswärd, Maud. *A Way from Home*. Trans. Joan Tate. London: Turton & Chambers, 1990. (*Flickan och dockskapet* 1979).

Richler, Mordecai. *Jacob Two-Two Meets the Hooded Fang*. New York: Knopf, 1975.

Rodari, Gianni. *The Befana's Toy Shop*. Trans. Patric Craig. London: Benn, 1970. (*La freccia azzura*).

Saint-Exupéry, Antoine de. *The Little Prince*. Trans. Katherine Woods. Harmonsworth: Penguin, 1962. (*Le petit prince* 1943).

Salinger, Jerome D. *The Catcher in the Rye*. Boston: Little, Brown, 1951.

Sandwall-Bergstm, Martha. *Anna All Alone*. Trans. Joan Tate. London: Blackie, 1972. (*Kulla-Gulla* 1945).

Scott, Hugh. *Why Weeps the Brogan?* London: Walker Books, 1989.

Sendak, Maurice. *Where the Wild Things Are*. New York: Harper, 1963.

Seton, Ernest Thompson. *Wild Animals I Have Known* (1899). New York: Grosset & Dunlap, 1966.

Sewell, Anna. *Black Beauty* (1877). London: Dent, 1948.

Sleigh, Barbara. *Jessamy*. Indianapolis: Bobbs Merrill, 1967.

Smith, Dodie. *The Hundred and One Dalmatians*. New York: Viking, 1957.

Spyri, Johanna. *Heidi*. Harmondsworth: Penguin, 1971.(*Heidi* 1881).

Stark, Ulf. *Dåfinkar och dönickar*. Stockholm: Bonnier 1984. ("The Nuts and the No-Goods").

Stevenson, Robert Louis. *Treasure Island* (1883). New York: Doubleday, 1954.

Streatfeild, Noel. *Ballet Shoes* (1936). Harmondsworth: Penguin, 1949.

Sutcliff, Rosemary. *The Eagle of the Ninth*. London: Oxford UP, 1954.

Swift, Jonathan: *Gulliver's Travels into Several Remote Nations of the World* (1726). New York: Dent, 1978.

Tetzner, Lisa. *Die Kinder auf der Insel.* Aarau: Sauerländer, 1944.
Tolkien, J. R. R. *The Hobbit.* London: Allen & Unwin, 1937.
Travers, Pamela. *Mary Poppins* (1934). London: Collins, 1971.
Twain, Mark. *The Adventures of Tom Sawyer* (1876). Harmondsworth, Penguin, 1985.
_____. *The Adventures of Huckleberry Finn* (1884). Harmondsworth, Penguin, 1966.

Uttley, Alison. *A Traveller in Time* (1939). Harmondsworth: Penguin, 1977.

Vestly, Anne-Cath. *Eight Children and a Truck.* Trans. Patricia Crampton. London: Methuen, 1973. (*Åtte sma, to store og en lastebil* 1957).
Voigt, Cynthia. *Homecoming.* New York: Atheneum, 1981.

Wahl, Mats. *Anna-Carolinas krig.* Stockholm: BonniersJunior, 1986. ("Anna-Carolina's War").
Waugh, Sylvia. *The Mennyms.* London: Random House, 1993. The first book about the Mennyms.
Wernström, Sven. *De hemligas ö.* Stockholm: Gebers, 1966. ("The Secret Island").
Westall, Robert. *The Kingdom by the Sea.* New York: Farrar, 1991.
White, E. B. *Stuart Little.* New York: Harper & Row, 1945.
_____. *Charlotte's Web.* New York: Harper & Row, 1952.
Wilder, Laura Ingalls. *Little House in the Big Woods* (1932). New York: Harper & Row, 1953.
Williams, Ursula Moray. *Adventures of a Little Wooden Horse.* London: Harrap, 1938.
Williamson, Henry. *Tarka the Otter* (1927). Harmondsworth: Penguin, 1937.

SECONDARY SOURCES

The bibliography includes all sources quoted in the study, as well as several others which have formed the general line of my thought.

Aarne, Antti. *The Types of the Folktale.* Trans. and enlarged by Stith Thompson. Helsinki: FF Communications, 1961.
Abrams, M. H. *The Mirror and the Lamp: Romantic Theory and Critical Tradition.* OUP, 1953.
Aers, Lesley. "The Treatment of Time in Four Children's Books." *Children's Literature in Education* 2 (1970): 69–81.

Åhmansson, Gabriella. *A Life and its Mirrors. A Feminist Reading of L. M. Montgomery's Fiction.* Uppsala: Acta Universitatis Upsaliensis, 1991.

_____. "Mayflowers Grow in Sweden Too: L. M. Montgomery, Astrid Lindgren and the Swedish Literary Consciousness." In Rubio, Mary, Ed. *Harvesting Thistles: The Textual Garden of L. M. Montgomery.* Guelph: Canadian Children's Press, 1994: 14–22.

Aippersbach, Kim. "Tuck Everlasting and the Tree at the Center of the World." *Children's Literature in Education* 21 (1990) 2: 83–97.

Allison, Alida. "Living the Non-Mechanical Life: Russell Hoban's Metaphorical Wind-Up Toys." *Children's Literature in Education* 22 (1991) 3: 189–194.

Anderson, William, and Patrick Groff. *A New Look at Children's Literature.* Belmont, CA: Wadsworth, 1972.

Apel, Friedmar. *Die Zaubergärten der Phantasie. Zur Theorie und Geschichte der Kunstmärchens.* Heidelberg: Carl Winter Universitätsverlag, 1978.

Arbuthnot, May Hill, and Zena Sutherland. *Children and Books.* 4th ed. Glenview, IL: Scott, Foresman, 1972.

Ariès, Philippe. *Centuries of Childhood: A Social History of Family Life.* New York: Vintage Random House, 1962.

_____. *Western Attitude Toward Death.* Baltimore: Johns Hopkins UP, 1974.

Attebery, Brian. *The Fantasy Tradition in American Literature. From Irwing to Le Guin.* Bloomington: Indiana UP, 1980.

Auerbach, Nina. *Communities of Women: An Idea in Fiction.* Cambridge, MA: Harvard UP, 1978.

Avery, Gillian. *Nineteenth Century Children: Heroes and Heroines in English Children's Stories 1780–1900.* London: Hodder & Stoughton, 1965.

_____. *Childhood's Pattern. A Study of the Heroes and Heroines of Children's Fiction 1770–1950.* London: Hodder & Stoughton, 1975.

_____. "Home and Familly: English and American Ideals in the Nineteenth Century." In Butts, Dennis, Ed. *Stories and Society. Children's Literature in its Social Context.* London: Macmillan, 1992: 37–49.

_____. *Behold the Child. American Children and Their Books 1621-1922.* Baltimore: Johns Hopkins UP, 1994.

Bache-Wiig, Harald. "Østens och Vestens drage. Om brytningen mellom utopi och dystopi i *Øglene kommer.*" In Losløkk, Ola, and Bjarne Øygarden, Eds. *Tormod Haugen - en artikkelsamling.* Oslo: Gyldendal, 1995: 201–224.

Bachelard, Gaston. *The Poetics of Space.* New York: Orion, 1964.

Bak, Krzysztof. "Die Zeitmodalitäten im Märchen von der Insel der Glückseligkeit." In Heindricks, Ursula, Ed. *Die Zeit im Märchen.* Kassel: Röth, 1989: 62–67.

Bakhtin, Michail. *Rabelais and His World.* Cambridge, MA: MIT Press, 1968.
_____. *The Dialogic Imagination.* Austin: U of Texas P, 1981.
_____. *Problems of Dostoyevsky's Poetics.* Minneapolis: U of Minnesota P, 1984.
Bal, Mieke. *Narratology. Introduction to the Theory of Narrative.* 2nd ed. Toronto: U of Toronto , 1997.
Banerjee, Jacqueline. *Through the Northern Gate. Childhood and Growing Up in British Fiction 1719–1901.* New York: Peter Lang, 1996. (Studies in Nineteenth-Century British Literature, vol. 6).
Barlby, Finn, Ed. *Det flyende spejl. Analyser av H.C. Andersens "Den lille Havfrue."* Copenhagen: Dråben, 1995.
Bator, Robert, Ed. *Signposts to Criticism of Children's Literature.* Chicago: American Library Association, 1988.
Baumgärtner, Alfred C., and Karl E. Maier, Eds. *Mythen, Märchen und moderne Zeit. Beiträge zur Kinder- und Jugendliteratur.* Würzburg: Königshauser & Neuman, 1987.
Beckett, Sandra, Ed. *Reflections of Change. Children's Literature Since 1945.* Westport, CT: Greenwood, 1997.
Bergsten, Staffan. *Mary Poppins and Myth.* Stockholm: Almqvist & Wiksell International, 1978. (Studies published by the Swedish Institute for Children's Books no. 8).
Bergstrand, Ulla, and Maria Nikolajeva. "Läckergommarnas kungarike. Matens roll i barnlitteraturen." *Barnboken* (1996) 2: 14–20.
Bettelheim, Bruno. *The Uses of Enchantment: The Meaning and Importance of Fairy Tales.* New York: Knopf, 1976.
Birkhäuser-Oeri, Sibylle. *The Mother. Archetypal Image in Fairy Tales.* Toronto: Inner City Books, 1988.
Bixler, Phyllis. "Tradition and the Talent of Frances Hodgson Burnett. *Little Lord Fauntleroy, A Little Princess,* and *The Secret Garden.*" In Butler, Francelia, and Richard Rotert, Eds. *Reflections on Literature for Children.* Hamden, CT: Library Professional Publications, 1984: 201–214.
_____. *The Secret Garden. Nature's Magic.* New York: Twayne, 1996.
Blake, Kathleen. "The Sea-Dream. *Peter Pan* and *Treasure Island.*" In Butler Francelia, and Richard Rotert, Eds. *Reflections on Literature for Children.* Hamden, CT: Library Professional Publications, 1984: 215–228.
Bloomingdale, Judith. "Alice as Anima. The Image of the Woman in Carroll's Classic." In Phillips, Robert, Ed. *Aspects of Alice.* New York: Vanguard Press, 1971: 378–390.
Blount, Margaret J. *Animal Land. The Creatures of Children's Fiction.* New York: Morrow, 1974.
Breen, Else. *Slik skrev de. Verdi og virkelighet i barnebøker 1968–1983.* Oslo: Aschehoug, 1988.

Bowers, Joan. "The Fantasy World of Russell Hoban." *Children's Literature* 8 (1980): 80–96.

Butler, Francelia, and Richard Rotert, Eds. *Reflections on Literature for Children.* Hamden, CT: Library Professional Publications, 1984.

Butler, Francelia. "Death in Children's Literature." In Butler, Francelia, and Richard Rotert, Eds. *Reflections on Literature for Children.* Hamden, CT: Library Professional Publications, 1984 (a): 72–90.

Butts, Dennis, Ed. *Stories and Society. Children's Literature in its Social Context.* London: Macmillan, 1992.

_____. "The Adventure Story." In Butts, Dennis, Ed. *Stories and Society. Children's Literature in its Social Context.* London: Macmillan, 1992: 65–83.

Byrnes, Alice. *The Child. An Archetypal Symbol in Literature for Children and Adults.* New York: Peter Lang, 1995.

Cadogan, Mary, and Patricia Craig. *You're a Brick, Angela! The Girls' Story 1839–1985.* London: Gollancz, 1986.

Cameron, Eleanor. *The Green and Burning Tree. On the Writing and Enjoyment of Children's Books.* Boston: Little, Brown, 1969.

_____. "The Pleasures and Problems of Time Fantasy." In her *The Seed and the Vision. On the Writing and Appreciation of Children's Books.* New York: Dutton, 1993: 167–204.

Campbell, Joseph. *The Hero with a Thousand Faces.* New York: Pantheon, 1949.

Camton, Glauco. "Pinocchio and Problems of Children's Literature." *Children's Literature* 2 (1973): 50–60.

Carpenter, Humphrey. *Secret Gardens. The Golden Age of Children's Literature.* London: Unwin Hyman, 1985.

Cart, Michael. *From Romance to Realism. 50 Years of Growth and Change in Young Adult Literature.* New York: HarperCollins, 1996.

Cawelty, John G. *Adventure, Mystery and Romance: Formula Stories as Art and Popular Culture.* Chicago: U of Chicago P, 1976.

Chambers, Aidan. "All of a Tremble to See His Danger." *Signal* 51 (1986): 193–212.

Chaston, Joel D. "The Other Deaths in Bridge to Terabithia." *Children's Literature Association Quarterly* 16 (1991-92) 4: 238–241.

Chatman, Seymour. *Story and Discourse. Narrative Structure in Fiction and Film.* Ithaca, NY: Cornell UP, 1978.

_____. *Coming to Terms.* Ithaca, NY: Cornell UP, 1990.

Clark, Beverly Lyon. "A Portrait of the Artist as a Little Woman." *Children's Literature* 17 (1989): 81–97.

Clark, Katerina. *The Soviet Novel. History as Ritual.* Chicago: U of Chicago P, 1981.

Clausen, Christopher. "Home and Away in Children's Fiction." *Children's Literature* 10 (1982): 141–152.

Connolly, Paula. *Winnie-the-Pooh and The House at Pooh Corner. Recovering Arcadia.* New York: Twayne, 1995. (Twayne's Masterworks Studies no. 156).

Cooper, J. C. *Fairy Tales. Allegories of Inner Life.* Wellingborough: The Aquarian Press, 1983.

Cott, Jonathan. *Pipers at the Gate of Dawn: The Wisdom of Children's Literature.* New York: Random House, 1983.

Coveney, Peter. "Introduction." In Twain, Mark. *The Adventures of Huckleberry Finn.* Harmondsworth: Penguin, 1966: 9–41.

_____. *The Image of Childhood. The Individual and Society: A Study of the Theme in English Literature.* Harmondsworth: Penguin, 1967.

Crews, Frederick C. *The Pooh Perplex.* London: Robin Clark, 1979.

Crouch, Marcus. *Treasure Seekers and Borrowers. Children's Books in Britain 1900–1960.* London: Library Association, 1962.

_____. *The Nesbit Tradition. The Children's Novel 1945–1970.* London: Benn, 1972.

Curtius, Ernst Robert. *Europäische Literatur und lateinische Mittelalter.* 2 Aufg. Bern: A. Franke, 1954.

DeLuca, Geraldine. "'A Condition of Complete Simplicity': The Toy as Child in *The Mouse and His Child.*" *Children's Literature in Education* 19 (1988) 4: 211–221.

Dierks, Margarete et al., Eds. *Kinderwelten. Kinder und Kindheit in der neueren Literatur.* Festschrift für Klaus Doderer. Weinheim: Beltz, 1985.

Doderer, Klaus, Ed. *Ästhetik der Kinderliteratur. Plädoyers für ein poetisches Bewusstsein.* Weinheim: Beltz, 1981.

_____. *Literarische Jugendkultur. Kulturelle und gesellschaftliche Aspekte der Kinder und Jugendliteratur in Deutschland.* Weinheim: Juventa, 1992 (Jugendliteratur - Theori und Praxis).

Dusinberre, Juliet. *Alice to the Lighthouse. Children's Books and Radical Experiments in Art.* London: Macmillan, 1987.

Duve, Arne. *Symbolikken i H. C. Andersens eventyr.* Oslo: Psychopress, 1967.

Eco, Umberto. *The Role of the Reader.* Bloomington: Indiana UP, 1979.

Edström, Vivi. "Fangenskapsymboler i ungdomsboken." In Edström, Vivi & Kristin Hallberg, Eds. *Ungdomsboken. Värderingar och mönster.* Stockholm: Liber, 1984: 69–96.

_____. *Astrid Lindgren - vildtoring och lägereld.* Stockholm: Rabén & Sjögren, 1992. (Studies published by the Swedish Institute for Children's

Books no 43) - With a summary in English: *Astrid Lindgren - Campfire Rebel.*

_____. *Astrid Lindgren och sagans makt.* Stockholm: Rabén & Sjögren, 1997. (Studies published by the Swedish Institute for Children's Books no 62). With a summary in English: *Astrid Lindgren and Fairy-Tale Power.*

Edwards, Bruce L., Ed. *The Taste of the Pineapple. Essays on C. S. Lewis as Reader, Critic, and Imaginative Writer.* Bowling Green, OH: Bowling Green State University Popular Press, 1988.

Egan, Michael. "The Neverland of Id: Barrie, Peter Pan and Freud." *Children's Literature* 10 (1982): 37–55.

Egoff, Sheila et al., Eds. *Only Connect. Readings on Children's Literature.* 2nd ed. Toronto: OUP, 1980.

_____. *Worlds Within. Children's Fantasy from the Middle Ages to Today.* Chicago: American Library Association, 1988.

Eliade, Mircea. *The Myth of the Eternal Return.* London: Routledge & Kegan Paul, 1955.

_____. *The Sacred and the Profane.* New York: Harper & Row, 1961a.

_____. *Birth and Rebirth. The Religious Meanings of Initiation in Human Culture.* London: Harvill, 1961b.

_____. *Myth and Reality.* New York: Harper & Row, 1963.

_____. *Rites and Symbols of Initiation: The Mysteries of Birth and Rebirth.* New York: Harper & Row, 1965.

Eliot, Alexander. *The Global Myths. Exploring Primitive, Pagan, Sacred and Scientific Mythologies.* New York: Continuum, 1993.

Empson, William. *Some Versions of Pastoral. A Study of the Pastoral Form in Literature.* London: Chatto & Windus, 1968 (orig. 1935).

Estes, Angela M., and Kathleen M. Lant. "Dismembering the Text: The Horror of Louisa May Alcott's *Little Women.*" *Children's Literature* 17 (1989): 98–123.

Estés, Clarissa Pinkola. *Women Who Run With the Wolves. Myths and Stories of the Wild Woman Archetype.* New York: Ballantine, 1997.

Evans, Gwyneth. "The Girl in the Garden: Variations in a Feminine Pastoral." *Children's Literature Association Quarterly* 19 (1984) 1: 20–24.

Ewers, Hans-Heino. "Kinder, die nicht erwachsen werden. Die Geniusgestalt des ewiges Kindes bei Goethe, E.T.A. Hoffmann, J.M. Barrie, Ende und Nöstlinger." In Dierks, Margarete et al., Eds. *Kinderwelten. Kinder und Kindheit in der neueren Literatur. Festschrift für Klaus Doderer.* Weinheim: Beltz, 1985: 42–70.

_____ et al, Eds. *Kinderlitteratur und Moderne.* Weinheim: Juventa, 1990.

Eyre, Frank. *British Children's Books in the Twentieth Century.* London: Longman, 1971.

Felman, Shoshana. *Writing and Madness*. Ithaca, NY: Cornell UP, 1985.

Fisher, Margery. *Intent Upon Reading. A Critical Appraisal of Modern Fiction for Children*. Leicester: Brockhampton, 1964.

_____. *The Bright Face of Danger. An Exploration of the Adventure Story*. London: Hodder & Stoughton, 1986.

Foster, Shirley, and Judy Simons. *What Katy Read. Feminist Re-readings of "Classic" Stories for Girls*. London: Macmillan, 1995.

Francis, Elizabeth. "Feminist Versions of Pastoral." *Children's Literature Association Quarterly* 7 (1982) 4: 7–9.

Franz, Marie-Louise von. "The Process of Individuation." In Jung, C. G., Ed. *Man and His Symbols*. London: Aldus, 1964: 160–229.

_____. Interpretation of Fairy Tales. Zürich: Spring, 1970.

_____. *Problems of the Feminine in Fairytales*. Zürich: Spring, 1972.

_____. *Shadow and Evil in Fairy Tales*. Zürich: Spring, 1974.

_____. *Puer Aeternus. A Psychological Study of the Adult Struggle with the Paradise of Childhood*. 2nd ed. Santa Monica, CA: Sigo, 1981.

Frazer, James G. *Folklore in the Old Testament*. London: Macmillan, 1919.

_____. *Man, God and Immortality*. London: Macmillan, 1927.

_____. *Myths of the Origins of Fire*. London: Macmillan, 1930.

_____. *The New Golden Bough*. New York: New American Library, 1959.

French, Warren. *J. D. Salinger, Revisited*. Boston: Twayne, 1988.

Frommlet, Wolfgang. "Science fiction und soziale Utopie im Kinder- und Jugendliteratur." In Oberfeld, Charlotte et al., Eds. *Zwischen Utopie und Heiler Welt. Zur Realismusdebatte in Kinder-und Jugendmedien*. Frankfurt: Haag Herchen, 1978. (Studien zur Kinder-und Jugendmedienforschung), 63–75.

Frye, Northrop. *Anatomy of Criticism. Four Essays*. Princeton, NJ: Princeton UP, 1957.

_____. *Fables of Identity. Studies in Poetic Mythology*. New York: Harcourt, Brace & World, 1963.

Gaarder, Bonnie. "The Inner family of *The Wind in the Willows*." *Children's Literature* 22 (1994): 43–57.

Gagnon, Laurence. "Webs of Concern. *The Little Prince* and *Charlotte's Web*." In Butler, Francelia, and Richard Rotert, Eds. *Reflections on Literature for Children*. Hamden, CT: Library Professional Publications, 1984: 66–71.

Genette, Gérard. *Narrative Discourse. An Essay in Method*. Ithaca, NY: Cornell UP, 1980.

Gilbert, Sandra M., and Susan Gubar. *The Madwoman in the Attic. The Woman Writer and the Nineteenth Century Literary Imagination*. New Haven, CT: Yale UP, 1977.

Gilbert, Sandra. "Costumes of the Mind: Transvestism in Modern Literature." *Critical Inquiery* 7 (1980): 391–417.

Gilead, Sarah. "The Undoing of Idyll in *The Wind in the Willows*." *Children's Literature* 16 (1988): 145–158.

Gillin, Richard. "Romantic Echoes in the Willows." *Children's Literature* 16 (1988): 169–174.

Goddard, Cliff. *Pitjantjatjara/Yankunytjatjara to English Dictionary*. 2nd ed. Alice Springs, Australia: Institute for Aboriginal Development, 1992.

Golden, Joanne M. *The Narrative Symbol in Childhood Literature. Exploration in the Construction of Text*. Berlin: Mouton, 1990.

Gould, Eric. *Mythical Intentions in Modern Literature*. Princeton, NJ: Princeton UP, 1981.

Green, Roger Lancelyn. *Tellers of Tales. British Authors of Children's Books from 1800 to 1964*. London: Ward, 1965.

Greimas, Algirdas Julien. *Sémantique structurale: recherche de méthode*. Paris: Larousse, 1966.

Grenz, Dagmar. "Literature for Young People and the Novel of Adolescence." In Nikolajeva, Maria, Ed. *Aspects and Issues in the History of Children's Literature*. Westport, CT: Greenwood, 1995: 173–182.

Griswold, Jerry. *The Classic American Children's Story. Novels of the Golden Age*. New York: Penguin, 1996a.

_____. "Desexualizing Tom Sawyer: What Really Happens in the Cave." *Para*doxa* 2 (1996) 3–4: 486–489b.

Grînbech, Bo. *Hans Christian Andersen*. New York: Twayne, 1980.

Harrison, Barbara, and Gregory Maguire, Eds. *Innocence and Experience. Essays and Conversations on Children's Literature*. New York: Lothrop, Lee & Shepard, 1987.

Hatfield, Len. "From Master to Brother: Shifting the Balance of Authority in Ursula K. Le Guin's *Farthest Shore* and *Tehanu*." *Children's Literature* 21 (1993): 43–65.

Hautala, Kattrina. "Kosten i några Blytonböcker." *Barn och kultur* (1977) 5: 119–120.

Havecker, Cyril. *Understanding Aboriginal Culture*. Sydney: Cosmos, 1987.

Haviland, Erwin Miller. "In Memoriam: Allie Caulfield." In Bloom, Harold, Ed. *Holden Caulfield*. New York: Chelsea, 1990: 132–143.

Hawking, Stephen. *A Brief History of Time. From Big Bang to Black Holes*. New York: Bantam, 1988.

Haymonds, Alison. "Pony Books." In Hunt, Peter, Ed. *International Companion Encyclopedia of Children's Literature*. London: Routledge, 1996: 360–367.

Heindricks, Ursula, Ed. *Die Zeit im Märchen*. Kassel: Röth, 1989.

Heisig, Fr. James. "Pinocchio: Archetype of the Motherless Child." *Children's Literature* 3 (1974): 23–35; also in Butler, Francelia, and Richard Rotert, Eds. *Reflections on Literature for Children*. Hamden, CT: Library Professional Publications, 1984: 155–170.

Heller, Mikhail, and Aleksandr Nekrich. *Utopia in Power. The History of the Soviet Union from 1917 to the Present*. New York: Summit Books, 1986.

Henderson, Joseph L. "Ancient Myths and Modern Man." In Jung, C. G., Ed. *Man and His Symbols*. London: Aldus, 1964: 106–157.

Higgins, James E. *The Little Prince. A Reverie of Substance*. New York: Twayne, 1996. (Twayne's Masterwork Studies no. 150).

Hoffeld, Laura. "Pippi Longstocking: The Comedy of the Natural Girl." *The Lion and the Unicorn* 1 (1977) 1: 47–53.

Hollander, Anne. "Reflections on *Little Women*." *Children's Literature* 9 (1981): 28–39. Also in Butler Francelia, and Richard Rotert, Eds. *Reflections on Literature for Children*. Hamden, CT: Library Professional Publications, 1984: 191–200.

Hollindale, Peter. *Choosing Books for Children*. London: Paul Elek, 1974.

_____. *Signs of Childness in Children's Books*. Stroud: Thimble Press, 1997.

Hume, Kathryn. *Fantasy and Mimesis. Responses to Reality in Western Literature*. New York: Methuen, 1984.

Hunt, Caroline C. "Dwarf, Small World, Shrinking Child: Three Versions of Miniature." *Children's Literature* 23 (1995): 115–136.

Hunt, Peter. "Arthur Ransome's *Swallows and Amazons*: Escape to a Lost Paradise." In Nodelman, Perry, Ed. *Touchstones: Reflections of the Best in Children's Literature*. West Lafayette, IN: Children's Literature Association, 1985, vol 1: 221–231.

_____. "Dialogue and Dialectic: Language and Class in *The Wind in the Willows*." *Children's Literature* 16 (1988): 159–168.

_____. *Criticism, Theory and Children's Literature*. London: Blackwell, 1991.

_____. "*Winnie-the-Pooh* and Domestic Fantasy." In Butts, Dennis, Ed. *Stories and Society. Children's Literature in its Social Context*. London: Macmillan, 1992: 112–124.

_____. *An Introduction to Children's Literature*. Oxford: Oxford UP, 1994a.

_____. *The Wind in the Willows: A Fragmented Arcadia*. New York: Twayne, 1994b.

_____, Ed. *Children's Literature. An Illustrated History*. Oxford: Oxford UP, 1995.

_____, "Coldtonguecoldham. ..." *Journal of the Fantastic in the Art* 7 (1996a) 1: 5–22.

_____, Ed. *International Companion Encyclopedia of Children's Literature.* London: Routledge, 1996b.

Huse, Nancy. "Katherine Paterson's Ultimate Realism." *Children's Literature Association Quarterly* 9 (1984) 3: 99–101.

Hutcheon, Linda. *A Poetics of Postmodernism. History, Theory, Fiction.* New York: Routledge, 1988.

Inglis, Fred. *The Promise of Happiness. The Value and Meaning in Children's Fiction.* Cambridge: Cambridge UP, 1981.

Jackson, Rosemary. *Fantasy: The Literature of Subversion.* New York: Methuen, 1981.

Jan, Isabelle. *On Children's Literature.* London: Allen Lane, 1973.

Jones, Raymond E. "Philippa Pearce's *Tom's Midnight Garden:* Finding and Losing Eden." In Nodelman, Perry, Ed. *Touchstones: Reflections of the Best in Children's Literature.* West Lafayette, IN: Children's Literature Association, 1985, vol 1: 212–221.

Jones, W. Glyn. *Tove Jansson.* Boston: Twayne, 1984.

Jung, C. G., Ed. *Man and His Symbols.* London: Aldus, 1964.

Kaminski, Winfred. *Jugendliteratur und Revolte: Jugendprotest und seine Spiegelbild in det Literatur für junge Leser.* Frankfurt am Main: dipa, 1982.

_____. "Das Innenbild der Aussenwelt. Annotationen zu den Kindergestalten im Werk Michael Ende." In Dierks, Margarete et al, Eds. *Kinderwelten. Kinder und Kindheit in der neueren Literatur. Festschrift für Klaus Doderer.* Weinheim: Beltz, 1985: 71–85.

_____. *Einfürung in der Kinder- und Jugendliteratur: literarische Phantasie under gesellschaftliche Wirklichkeit.* Weinheim: Juventa, 1987.

Katz, Wendy R. "Some Uses of Food in Children's Literature." *Children's Literature in Education* 11 (1980) 4: 192–199.

Kelley-Lainé, Kathleen. *Peter Pan. The Story of Lost Childhood.* Shaftesbury Great Britain: Element, 1997.

Kett, Josheph. *Rites of Passage: Adolescence in America: 1790 to the Present.* New York: Basic Books, 1977.

Keyser, Elizabeth Lennox. "'The Most Beautiful Things in All the World'? Families in *Little Women.*" In Butts, Dennis, Ed. *Stories and Society. Children's Literature in its Social Context.* London: Macmillan, 1992: 50–64.

Krips, Valerie. "Mistaken Identity: Russell Hoban's *The Mouse and His Child.*" *Children's Literature* 21 (1993): 92–100.

Kristeva, Julia. "The Adolescent Novel." In her *Abjection, Melancholia and Love.* London: Routledge, 1990: 8–23.

Kuhn, Reinhard. *Corruption in Paradise. The Child in Western Literature.* Hanover, NH: Brown UP, 1982.

Kumar, Krishan. *Utopia and Anti-Utopia in Modern Times.* London: Blackwell, 1987.

Kuznets, Lois. "Toad Hall Revisited." *Children's Literature* 7 (1978): 115–128.

_____. "The Fresh-Air Kids, or Some Contemporary Versions of Pastoral." *Children's Literature* 11 (1983): 156–168.

_____. *Kenneth Grahame.* Boston: Hall, 1987.

_____. "Kenneth Grahame and Father Nature, or Wither Blows The Wind in the Willows?" *Children's Literature* 16 (1988): 175–181.

_____. *When Toys Come Alive. Narratives of Animation, Metamorphosis and Development.* New Haven, CT: Yale UP, 1994.

Lacan, Jacques. *Ecrits: A Selection.* New York: Norton, 1977.

Landsberg, Michele. *The World of Children's Books. A Guide of Choosing the Best.* London: Simon & Schuster, 1988.

Laski, Marghanita. *Mrs. Ewing, Mrs. Molesworth and Mrs. Hodgson Burnett.* London: Barker, 1950.

Lawson Lucas, Ann. "Introduction." In Collodi, Carlo. *The Adventures of Pinocchio.* Trans. Ann Lawson Lucas. Oxford: Oxford UP, 1996: vii–xvi.

Le Guin, Ursula. *The Language of the Night. Essays on Fantasy and Science Fiction.* New York: Berkley Books, 1979.

Lehnert, Gertrud. *Maskeraden und Metamorphosen. Als Männer verkleidete Frauen in der Literatur.* Würzburg: Köningshausen & Neumann, 1994.

Lesnik-Oberstein, Karín. *Children's Literature. Criticism and the Fictional Child.* Oxford: Clarendon, 1994.

Lévi-Strauss, Claude. *The Raw and the Cooked. Introduction to a Science of Mythology.* Chicago: U of Chicago P, 1983

Lewis, C. S. "On Three Ways of Writing for Children." In Egoff, Sheila, Ed. *Only Connect.* Toronto: Oxford UP, 1980: 207–220.

Lindstam, Birgitta. *Självmordet som problemlösning.* Stockholm: Centre for the Study of Childhood Culture, 1981.

_____. "Hästboken som kärleksroman." *Barn och kultur* (1982) 1: 16–20.

Lochhead, Marion. *The Renaissance of Wonder in Children's Literature.* Edinburgh, Canongate, 1977.

Löfgren, Eva M. *Schoolmates of the Long-Ago. Motifs and Archetypes in Dorita Fairlie Bruce's Boarding School Stories.* Stockholm: Symposion, 1993.

Lukens, Rebecca J. *A Critical Handbook of Children's Literature,* 4th ed. New York: HarperCollins, 1990.

Lundell, Torborg. *Fairy Tale Mothers.* New York: Peter Lang, 1990.

Lundqvist, Ulla. *Århundradets barn. Fenomenet Pippi Långstrump och dess förutsättningar.* Stockholm: Rabén & Sjögren, 1979. With a summary in English: *The Child of the Century.*

_____. *Tradition och förnyelse. Svensk ungdomsbok från sextiotal till nittiotal.* Stockholm: Rabén & Sjögren, 1994. (Studies published by the Swedish Institute for Children's Books no. 51). With a summary in English: *Traditional Patterns and New Ones. Swedish Books for Young Adults from the Sixties to the Nineties.*

Lurie, Alison. "Back to Pooh Corner." *Children's Literature* 2 (1973): 11–17; also in Butler, Francelia, and Richard Rotert, Eds. *Reflections on Literature for Children.* Hamden, CT: Library Professional Publications, 1984: 32–38.

Lurie, Alison. *Don't Tell the Grownups. Subversive Children's Literature.* Boston: Little, Brown, 1990.

Lynch-Brown, Carol, and Carl M. Tomlinson. *Essentials of Children's Literature.* Boston: Allyn and Bacon, 1993.

Lynn, Joanne. "Threadbare Utopia: Hoban's Modern Pastoral." *Children's Literature Association Quarterly* 11 (1986) 1: 19–24.

Lypp, Maria. "Kindheit als Thema des Kinderbuchs. Die Metapher des kindlichen König bei Janusz Korczak." *Wirkendes Wort* (1986) 3: 210–219.

MacDonald, Ruth K. "Louisa May Alcott's *Little Women:* Who is Still Reading Miss Alcott and Why." In Nodelman, Perry, Ed. *Touchstones: Reflections of the Best in Children's Literature.* West Lafayette, IN: Children's Literature Association, 1985, vol. 1: 13–20.

MacLeod, Anne Scott. "An End to Innocence: The Transformation of Childhood in Twentieth-Century Children's Literature." In Smith, Joseph H, and William Kerrigan, Eds. *Opening Texts: Psychoanalysis and the Culture of the Child.* Baltimore: Johns Hopkins UP, 1985: 100–117.

_____. *American Childhood. Essays on Children's Literature of the Nineteenth and Twentieth Century.* Athens, GA: U of Georgia P, 1994.

Manlove, C. N. *Modern Fantasy. Five Studies.* Cambridge: Cambridge UP, 1975.

_____. *The Chronicles of Narnia. The Patterning of a Fantastic World.* New York: Twayne, 1993.

Marshall, Cynthia. "Bodies and Pleasures in *The Wind in the Willows.*" *Children's Literature* 22 (1994): 58–69.

Mattenklott, Gundel. *Zauberkreide. Kinderliteratur seit 1945.* Stuttgart: Metzler, 1989.

de Mause, Lloyd, Ed. *The History of Childhood.* New York: Harper & Row, 1974.

McGillis, Roderick. "Fantasy as Adventure: Nineteenth Century Children's Fiction." *Children's Literature Association Quarterly* 8 (1983) 3: 18–22.

_____. "Utopian Hopes: Criticism Beyond Itself." *Children's Literature Association Quarterly* 9 (1984-85) 4: 184–186.

_____, Ed. *For the Childlike. George MacDonald's Fantasies for Children.* Metuchen, NJ: Scarecrow, 1992.

_____. *The Nimble Reader. Literary Theory and Children's Literature.* New York: Twayne, 1996.

Meek, Margaret et al., Eds. *The Cool Web. The Patterns of Children's Reading.* London: Bodley Head, 1977.

Meek, Margaret. "Speaking of Shifters." *Signal* 54 (1984): 152–167.

_____. "The Limits of Delight." *Books for Keeps* (1991) 68:24–25.

Meigs, Cornelia. *Louisa M. Alcott and the American Family Story.* London: Bodley Head, 1970.

Mendelson, Michael. "*The Wind in the Willows* and the Plotting of Contrast." *Children's Literature* 16 (1988): 127–144.

Metcalf, Eva-Maria. "The Invisible Child in the Works of Tormod Haugen." *Barnboken* (1992) 1: 15–23.

_____. *Astrid Lindgren.* New York: Twayne, 1995a (Twayne's World Authors Series no 851).

_____. "Leap of Faith in Astrid Lindgren's Brothers Lionheart." *Children's Literature* 23 (1995b): 165–178.

Meyer Spacks, Patricia. *The Adolescent Idea: Myths of Youth and the Adult Imagination.* New York: Basic Books, 1981.

Mitrokhina, Xenia. "The Land of Oz in the Land of the Soviets." *Children's Literature Association Quarterly* 21 (1996-97) 4: 183–188.

Moebius, William. "*L'enfant terrible* Comes of Age." In Cantor, Norman F., Ed. *Notebooks in Cultural Analysis* vol 2. Durham, NC: Duke UP, 1985: 32–50.

Molson, Francis. "Mark Twain's *The Adventures of Tom Sawyer:* More Than a Warm Up." In Nodelman, Perry, Ed. *Touchstones: Reflections of the Best in Children's Literature.* West Lafayette, IN: *Children's Literature Association,* 1985, vol. 1: 262–269.

Morrissey, Thomas J., and Richard Wunderlich. "Death and Rebirth in *Pinocchio.*" *Children's Literature* 11 (1983): 64–75.

Morson, Gary Saul. *Narrative and Freedom. The Shadows of Time.* New Haven, CT: Yale UP, 1994.

Morton, Miriam. *A Harvest of Russian Children's Literature.* Edited, with Introduction and Commentary, by Miriam Morton. Berkeley: U of California P, 1967.

Moss, Anita. "The Spear and the Piccolo: Heroic and Pastoral Dimensions of William Steig's *Dominic* and *Abel's Island.*" *Children's Literature* 10 (1982): 124–140.

Mueller Nienstadt, Irma. *Die Mumins für Erwachsene. Bilder zur Selbstwerdung.* Düsseldorf: Walter, 1994.

Murray, Heather: "Frances Hodgeson Burnett's *The Secret Garden:* The Organ(ic)ized World." Nodelman, Perry, Ed. *Touchstones: Reflections of the Best in Children's Literature.* West Lafayette, IN: Children's Literature Association, 1985, vol. 1: 30–43.

Nelson, Claudia. "The Beast Within. *Winnie-the-Pooh* Reassessed." *Children's Literature in Education* 21 (1990) 1:17–22.
_____. *Boys Will Be Girls. The Feminine Ethic and British Children's Fiction, 1857-1917.* New Brunswick, NJ: Rutgers UP, 1991.
Nières, Isabelle. "La nouriture comme fiction." *La revue des livres pour enfants* (1987) 114: 60–64.
Nikolajeva, Maria. *The Magic Code. The Use of Magical Patterns in Fantasy for Children.* Stockholm: Almqvist & Wiksell International, 1988. (Studies published by the Swedish Institute for Children's Books no. 31).
_____. "A Typological Approach to the Study of The Root Cellar." *Canadian Children's Literature* 63 (1991): 53–60.
_____. "Fantasy: The Evolution of a Pattern." In Bunbury, Rhonda, Ed. *Fantasy and Feminism in Children's Books.* Geelong, Australia: Deakin UP, 1993: 1–39.
_____. "Stages of Transformation: Folklore Elements in Children's Novels." *Canadian Children's Literature* 73 (1994): 48–54.
_____. "Literature as a Rite of Passage: A New Look at Genres." *Compara(i)son* 2 (1995): 117–129.
_____. *Children's Literature Comes of Age. Towards a New Aesthetics.* New York: Garland, 1996.
_____. "The Child as Self-Deceiver: Narrative Strategies in Katherine Paterson's and Patricia MachLachlan's Novels." *Papers* 7 (1997a) 1: 5–15.
_____. "Two National Heroes: Jacob Two-Two and Pippi Longstocking." *Canadian Children's Literature* 86 (1997b): 7–16.
_____. "Exit Children's Literature?" *The Lion and the Unicorn* 22 (1998) 2: 221–236.
Nilsen, Alleen Pace, and Kenneth L. Donelson. *Literature for Today's Young Aduts.* 4th ed. New York: Harper, 1993.
Nodelman, Perry. "Progressive Utopia, or How to Grow Up without Growing Up." In Ord, Priscilla A., Ed. *Proceedings of the 6th Annual Conference of ChLA.* Villanova, PA: Villanova UP, 1980, 146–154.
_____, Ed. *Touchstones: Reflections of the Best in Children's Literature.* Vol 1-3. West Lafayette, IN: Children's Literature Association, 1985a–87.
_____. "Interpretation and the Apparent Sameness of Children's Literature." *Studies in the Literary Imagination* 18 (1985b) 2: 5–20.
_____. *The Pleasures of Children's Literature.* New York: Longman, 1992, 2nd ed. 1996.
_____. "Reinventing the Past: Gender in Ursula K. Le Guin's *Tehanu* and the Earthsea Trilogy." *Children's Literature* 23 (1995): 179–201.

288   Bibliography

O'Dell, Felicity Ann. *Socialization Through Literature. The Soviet Example.* Cambridge: Cambridge UP, 1978.

Ongini, Vincio, Ed. *Una fame da leggere. Il cibo nella letteratura per l'infanzia.* Firenze: Unicoop, 1994.

Pape, Walter. *Das literarische Kinderbuch.* Berlin: de Gruyter, 1981.

———. "Happy Endings in a World of Misery: A Literary Convention between Social Constraints and Utopia in Children's and Adult Literature." *Poetics Today* 13 (1992) 1: 179–196.

Paterson, Katherine. *A Sense of Wonder. On Reading and Writing Books for Children.* New York: Penguin, 1995.

Pattison, Robert. *The Child Figure in English Literature.* Athens: U of Georgia P, 1978.

Paul, Lissa. "Enigma Variations. What Feminist Criticism Knows about Children's Literature." In Hunt, Peter, Ed. *Children's Literature. The Development of Criticism.* London: Rutledge & Kegan Paul, 1990: 148–166.

Perrot, Jean. "Pan and Puer Aeternus: Aestheticism and the Spirit of the Age." *Poetics Today* 13 (1992) 1: 155–167.

Philip, Neil. "'Tom's Midnight Garden' and the Vision of Eden." *Signal* 37 (1982): 21–25.

———. "Kenneth Grahame's *The Wind in the Willows:* A Companionable Vitality." In Nodelman, Perry, Ed. *Touchstones: Reflections of the Best in Children's Literature.* West Lafayette, IN: Children's Literature Association, 1985, vol. 1: 96–105.

Piaget, Jean. *The Child's Conception of Time.* London: Rutledge & Kegan Paul, 1969.

Pinsent, Pat. "Paradise Restored: The Significance of Coincidence in Some Children's Books." *Children's Literature in Education* 20 (1989) 2: 103–110.

Plotz, Judith. "The Disappearance of Childhood." *Children's Literature in Education* 19 (1988) 2: 67–79.

———. "Literary Ways of Killing a Child: The 19th Century Practice." In Nikolajeva, Maria, Ed. *Aspects and Issues in the History of Children's Literature.* Westport, CT: Greenwood, 1995: 1–24.

Poss, Geraldine. "An Epic in Arcadia: The Pastoral World of *The Wind in the Willows.*" *Children's Literature* 4 (1975): 80–90; also in Butler, Francelia, and Richard Rotert, Eds. *Reflections on Literature for Children.* Hamden, CT: Library Professional Publications, 1984: 237–246.

Prickett, Stephen. *Victorian Fantasy.* Hassocks: Harvester Press, 1979.

Propp, Vladimir. *Morphology of the Folktale.* Austin: U of Texas P, 1968.

———. *Theory and History of Folklore.* Manchester: Manchester UP, 1984.

Purkiss, Diana. *The Witch in History. Early Modern and Twentieth-Century Representations.* London: Routledge, 1996.

Quigly, Isabel. *The Heirs of Tom Brown: The English School Story*. London: Chatto & Windus, 1982.

Rabkin, Eric S. *The Fantastic in Literature*. Princeton, NJ: Princeton UP, 1976.
Rahn, Suzanne. "The Boy and the Wild Geese: Selma Lagerlöf's Nils." In her *Rediscoveries in Children's Literature*. New York: Garland, 1995: 39–50.
Rayner, Mary. "Some Thoughts on Animals in Children's Books." *Signal* 28 (1979):81–87.
Reeder, Kik. "Pippi Longstocking - a Feminist or Anti-feminist Work?" In Stinton, Judith, Ed. *Racism and Sexism in Children's Literature*. London: Writers and Readers, 1979: 112–117.
Rees, David. *The Marble in the Water. Essays on Contemporary Writers of Fiction for Children and Young Adults*. Boston: The Horn Book, 1980.
Reynolds, Kimberley. *Girls Only? Gender and Popular Children's Fiction in Britain 1880–1910*. Hemel Hempstead: Harvester, 1990.
_____. *Children's Literature in the 1890s and the 1990s*. Plymouth: Northcote House, 1994.
Richards, Jefferey. "The School Story." In Butts, Dennis, Ed. *Stories and Society. Children's Literature in its Social Context*. London: Macmillan, 1992: 1–21.
Richter, Dieter. "Nachwort." In his *Das Land, wo man nicht stirbt. Märchen vom Leben und vom Tod*. Frankfurt: Fischer, 1982, 134–143.
Ricoeur, Paul. *Time and Narrative*. Chicago: U of Chicago P, 1984.
Rimmon-Kenan, Shlomith. *Narrative Fiction. Contemporary Poetics*. London: Routledge, 1983.
Röhrich, Lutz. "Der Tod in Sage und Märchen." In *Leben und Tod in den Religionen. Symbol under Wirklichkeit*. Darmstadt: Wissenschaftliche Buchgesellschaft, 1980: 165–183.
Rönnerstrand, Torsten. "Barn- och ungdomslitteraturen ur jungianskt perspektiv." In Nikolajeva, Maria, Ed. *Modern litteraturteori och metod i barnlitteraturforskningen*. Stockholm: Center for the study of childhood culture, 1992: 75–112. With a summary in English: *Children's and Youth Literature in a Jungian Perspective*.
Rose, Jacqueline. *The Case of Peter Pan, or The Impossibility of Children's Fiction*. London: Macmillan, 1984.
Rubio, Mary. "*Anne of Green Gables:* the Architect of Adolescence." In Nodelman, Perry, Ed. *Touchstones: Reflections of the Best in Children's Literature*. West Lafayette, IN: Children's Literature Association, 1985, vol. 1: 173–187.
Russ, Joanna. *To Write Like a Woman. Essays in Feminism and Science Fiction*. Bloomington: Indiana University Press, 1995.
Russell, David L. "Pinocchio and the Child-Hero Quest." *Children's Literature in Education* 20 (1989) 4: 203–213.

Rustin, Margaret, and Michael. *Narratives of Love and Loss. Studies in Modern Children's Fiction.* London: Verso, 1987.

Sale, Roger. *Fairy Tales and After.* Cambridge: Cambridge U P, 1978.

Saltman, Judith. *Modern Canadian Children's Books.* Toronto: Oxford UP, 1987.

Sammonds, Martha C. *A Guide Through Narnia.* London: Hodder & Stoughton, 1979.

_____. *"A Better Country."* The Worlds of Religious Fantasy and Science Fiction. New York: Greenwood, 1988.

Schakel, Peter J. *Reading with the Heart: The Way Into Narnia.* Grand Rapids, MI: William B. Eerdman, 1979.

Schwarcz, Joseph. "Machine Animism in Modern Children's Literature." In Fenwick, Sara, Ed. *A Critical Approach to Children's Literature.* Chicago: U of Chicago P, 1967: 78–95.

Scott, Carole. "Between Me and the World: Clothes as Mediator between Self and Society in the Works of Beatrix Potter." *The Lion and the Unicorn* 16 (1992) 2: 192–198.

_____. "Clothed in Nature or Nature Clothed: Dress as Metaphor in the Illustrations of Beatrix Potter and C. M. Barker." *Children's Literature* 22 (1994): 70–89.

_____. "A Century of Dislocated Time: Time Travel, Magic and the Search for Self." *Papers* 6 (1996a) 2:14–20.

_____. "Magical Dress: Clothing and Transformation in Folk Tales." *Children's Literature Association Quarterly* 21 (1996b-1997) 4:151–157b.

Showalter, Elaine. "Little Women: The American Female Myth." In her *Sister's Choice. Tradition and Change in American Women's Wriring.* Oxford: Clarendon, 1991: 42–64.

Sigman, Joseph. "The Diamond in the Ashes. A Jungian Reading of the "Princess" Books." In McGillis, Rod, Ed. *For the Childlike. George MacDonald's Fantasies for Children.* Metuchen, NJ: Scarecrow, 1992: 183–194.

Smedman, M. Sarah. "Springs of Hope: Recovery of Primordeal Time in 'Mythic' Novels for Young Readers." *Children's Literature* 16 (1988): 91–107.

_____. "When Literary Works Meet: Allusion in the Novels of Katherine Paterson." *International Conference of the Children's Literature Association* 16 (1989): 59–66.

Smith, Joseph H., and William Kerrigan, Eds. *Opening Texts: Psychoanalysis and the Culture of the Child.* Baltimore: Johns Hopkins UP, 1985.

Smith, Karen Patricia. *The Fabulous Realm. A Literary-Historical Approach to British Fantasy, 1780–1990.* Metuchen, NJ: Scarecrow, 1993.

Stanger, Carol A. "Winnie the Pooh Through a Feminist Lens." *The Lion and the Unicorn* 11 (1987) 2: 34–50.

Stephens, John. *Language and Ideology in Children's Fiction*. London: Long-
man, 1992.
_____. "Gender, Genre and Children's Literature." *Signal* 79 (1996):
17–30.
Stewig, John Warren. *Children and Literature*. Boston: Houghton Mifflin,
1980.
Stott, Jon C. "Jean George's Arctic Pastoral. A Reading of *Julie of the Wolves*."
Children's Literature 3 (1974): 131–139.
_____. "From Here to Eternity: Aspects of Pastoral in the Green
Knowe Series." *Children's Literature* 11 (1983): 145–155.
_____. "Alexander's Chronicles of Prydain: The Nature of Begin-
ning." In Nodelman, Perry, Ed. *Touchstones: Reflections of the Best in
Children's Literature*. West Lafayette, IN: Children's Literature Associa-
tion, 1985, vol. 1: 21–29.
Strickland, Charles. *Victorian Domesticity. Families in the Life and Art of Louisa
May Alcott*. Tuscaloosa, Alabama: U of Alabama P, 1985.
Styles, Morag, Eve Bearne, and Victor Watson, Eds. *After Alice. Exploring
Children's Literature*. London: Cassell, 1992.
Swinfen, Ann. *In Defence of Fantasy. A Study of the Genre in English and
American Literature since 1945*. London: Rutledge & Kegan Paul, 1984.

Tatar, Maria. *Off With Their Heads! Fairy Tales and the Culture of Childhood*.
Princeton, NJ: Princeton UP, 1992.
Tebbutt, Susan. *Gudrun Pausewang in Context. Socially Critical 'Jugendlitera-
tur', Gudrun Pausewang and the Search for Utopia*. Frankfurt: Peter Lang,
1994.
Thompson, Susan. "Images of Adolescence." *Signal* 34 (1981): 37–59; 35
(1981): 111–125.
Todorov, Tzvetan. *The Fantastic: A Structural Approach to a Literary Genre*.
Cleveland, OH: Case Western Reserve University Press, 1973.
_____. *The Poetics of Prose*. Ithaca, NY: Cornell UP, 1977.
Toijer-Nilsson, Ying. *Fantasins underland. Myt och idé i den fantastiska berät-
telsen*. Stockholm: EFS-förlag, 1981. With a summary in English: *The
Wonderland of Fantasy. Myth and Ideology in Fantasy Literature*.
_____. "Tormod Haugen." In *De skriver för barn och ungdom*. Lund:
Bibliotekstjänst, 1991: 169–178.
Tolkien, J. R. R. "On Fairy Stories." In his *Tree and Leaf*. London: Allen &
Unwin, 1968: 11–70.
Townsend, John Rowe. *A Sense of Story. Essays on Contemporary Writers for
Children*. London: Longman, 1971.
_____. *Written for Children. An Outline of English-Language Children's
Literature*. 2nd ed. Harmondsworth: Kestrel, 1974.

_____. "Slippery Time." In *Travellers in Time: Past, Present and to Come.* Cambridge, MA: Green Bay, 1990: 83–94.

Travellers in Time: Past, Present and to Come. Cambridge, MA: Green Bay, 1990.

Trites, Roberta Selinger. *Waking Sleeping Beauty. Feminist Voices in Children's Novels.* Iowa City: University of Iowa Press, 1997.

Tucker, Nicholas. *The Child and the Book. A Psychological and Literary Exploration.* Cambridge: Cambridge UP, 1981.

_____. "Fly Away, Peter?" *Signal* 37 (1982): 43–49.

Tuman, Myron C. "*Pride and Prejudice:* An Adolescent Fairy Tale." *Children's Literature in Education* 11 (1980) 3:129–132.

Veglahn, Nancy. "Images of Evil: Male and Female Monsters in Heroic Fantasy." *Children's Literature* 15 (1987): 106–119.

Vonessen, Franz. "Der richtige Augenblick. Über den Kairos im Märchen." In Heindricks, Ursula, Ed. *Die Zeit in Märchen.* Kassel: Röth, 1989, 35–52.

Waddey, Lucy E. "Home in Children's Fiction: Three Patterns." *Children's Literature Association Quarterly* 8 (1983) 1: 13–15.

Walker, J. M. "*The Lion, the Witch and the Wardrobe* as Rite of Passage." *Children's Literature in Education* 16 (1985): 177–188.

Wall, Barbara. *The Narrator's Voice. The Dilemma of Children's Fiction.* London: Macmillan, 1991.

Warner, Marina. *From the Beast to the Blonde. On Fairy Tales and Their Tellers.* New York: Farrar, Straus & Giroux, 1994.

Watkins, Tony. "Making a Break for the Real England: The River-Bankers Revisited." *Children's Literature Association Quarterly* 9 (1984) 1: 34–35.

_____. "Reconstructing the Homeland: Loss and Hope in the English Landscape." In Nikolajeva, Maria, Ed. *Aspects and Issues in the History of Children's Literature.* Westport, CT: Greenwood, 1995: 165–172.

Watt, Ian. *Myths of Modern Individualism. Faust, Don Quixote, Don Juan, Robinson Crusoe.* Cambridge: Cambridge UP, 1996.

Waugh, Patricia. *Metafiction. The Theory and Practice of Self-Conscious Fiction.* London: Methuen, 1984.

Westin, Boel. *Familjen i dalen. Tove Janssons muminvärld.* Stockholm: Bonnier, 1988. With a summary in English: *The Family in the Valley. The Moomin World of Tove Jansson.*

Whitrow, Gerald James. *The Natural Philosophy of Time.* Oxford: Oxford UP, 1980.

Wilkie, Christine. "Digging Up The Secret Garden: Noble Innocents or Little Savages?" *Children's Literature in Education* 1997:28 (2), 73–83.

Williams, Raymond. *The Country and the City.* London: The Hoggarth Press, 1993.

Wilson, Anita. "Milne's *Pooh* Books: The Benevolent Forest." In Nodelman, Perry, Ed. *Touchstones: Reflections of the Best in Children's Literature*. West Lafayette, IN: Children's Literature Association, 1985, vol. 1: 163–172.

Wilson, Anne. "Magical Thought in Story." *Signal* 36 (1981): 138–151.

_____. *Magical Throught in Creative Writing*. Stroud: Thimble Press, 1982.

Wolf, Virginia L. "Paradise Lost? The Displacement of Myth in Children's Novels." *Studies in the Literary Imagination* 18 (1985) 2: 47–64.

Wullschläger, Jackie. *Inventing Wonderland. The Lives and Fantasies of Lewis Carroll, Edward Lear, J.M. Barrie, Kenneth Grahame and A. A. Milne*. London: Methuen, 1995.

Wunderlich, Richard, and Thomas J. Morrissey. "Carlo Collodi's *The Adventures of Pinocchio:* A Classic Book of Choices." In Nodelman, Perry, Ed. *Touchstones: Reflections of the Best in Children's Literature*. West Lafayette, IN: Children's Literature Association, 1985, vol 1: 53–64.

Zipes, Jack. *Fairy Tales and the Art of Subversion*. New York: Wildman, 1983.

_____. *Fairy Tale as Myth, Myth as Fairy Tale*. Lexington: UP of Kentucky, 1994.

_____. *Creative Storytelling*. New York: Routledge, 1995.

Index of Titles

General Index

Coveney, Peter 141
Crews, Frederick 93
Cumulative narrative 97, 234

Dahl, Roald 55–56
Dante 221
Death 6–7, 12–14, 21–22, 27–31, 41,
    66, 71, 89–90, 104, 107, 109, 113,
    122–123, 128, 131–132, 140, 150,
    152, 159–161, 165, 172–173, 177,
    184, 187–192, 197–199, 207, 212–
    219, 231, 236, 239–241, 259, 262
Displacement of myth 2, 8, 191, 262
Domestic story 41–59, 151
Dragunsky, Victor 68
Dusinberre, Juliet 23
Dystopia 6, 167–174

Eco, Umberto 222
Egan, Michael 87, 92
Eliade, Mircea 5–6, 10–11, 14, 263
Empson, William 20
Ende, Michael 112
Estrangement 193, 236
Ewers, Hans-Heino 112

Fairy tales 6, 13–15, 129, 137, 182,
    185–186, 192, 202, 221, 223–227,
    229–230
Fantasy 1, 3, 8, 48–50, 53–54, 61, 133–
    134, 143, 145, 148–149, 181–183,
    187, 210
Farmer, Nancy 168–169
Felicitous space 19, 252
Filter, narrative 81, 197–198, 201
Fisher, Margery 50, 53
Focalization, focalizer 39, 97, 116,
    136, 158, 193–194, 197, 242, 247,
    253
Folktales 12–16, 53, 109, 137, 206,
    221–223
Food vii, 11–16, 26, 43, 55-59, 94,
    98–103, 115–117, 128–131, 184–

186, 192–196, 213, 222, 234, 245,
254
Formula fiction 48, 222
Forsås-Scott, Helena vii
Franz, Marie-Louise von 2, 120–121,
123
Fredlund, Charlotte 40
Freudian model 87–88, 92, 106, 188,
243, 254
Frye, Northrop 2, 3, 10, 145, 187, 191
Function model 2

Gaidar, Arkady 69
Garner, Alan viii, 135, 164
Genette, Gérard 9
Gender 37, 42, 71–72, 96, 153, 190,
242
Genres 1–2, 8, 145, 263–264
Gilbert, Sandra M. 149
Grahame, Kenneth 19–28, 31–34, 37
Greimas, Algirdas Julien 2, 115
Gripe, Maria 150, 159–165, 172
Griswold, Jerry 140

Haugen, Tormod 169–173
Hedén, Birger vii
Held, Kurt 61
Higgins, James 120
Historical novel 143, 145
Hoban, Russell 174–181
Hoffmann, E. T. A. 146, 210
Hollander, Anne 27, 36
Horse and pony stories 53
Hunt, Peter viii, 3, 10, 19, 23, 37, 94,
96–98, 100, 145
Hutcheon, Linda 8
Huxley, Aldous 167

Ideology 1, 50
Idyll, idyllic 1, 24, 28, 42–43, 47–49,
52–54, 64, 75, 94, 98, 100, 107, 118,
125, 128, 131, 138–139, 151, 174,
177, 191, 197, 206–207, 212, 219,

About the Author

Maria Nikolajeva is an Associate Professor at the Departments of Comparative Literature, Stockholm University (Sweden) and Åbo Academy University (Finland), where she teaches children's literature and literary theory. She is the author and editor of several books on children's literature, among them *Children's Literature Comes of Age: Toward the New Aesthetic* (1996), a ChLA Honor Book. She has also published a large number of articles in professional journals and essay collections. Her academic honors include a Fulbright Grant at the University of Massachusetts, Amherst, a research fellowship at the International Youth Library, Munich, and Donner Visiting Chair at Åbo Academy University. She was the President of the International Research Society for Children's Literature in 1993-97. At present she co-leads the interdisciplinary research project "Children's Literature: Pure and Applied" at Åbo Academy.